My Flint Hills

Other Books by Jim Hoy

The Cattle Guard: Its History and Lore

Cowboys and Kansas: Stories from the Tallgrass Prairie

Vaqueros, Cowboys, and Buckaroos
(with Jerald Underwood and Lawrence Clayton)

Prairie Poetry: Cowboy Verse of Kansas (ed.)

Flint Hills Cowboys: Tales from the Tallgrass Prairie

Cowboy's Lament: A Life on the Open Range (ed.)

Plains Folk: A Commonplace of the Great Plains (with Tom Isern)

Plains Folk II: The Romance of the Landscape (with Tom Isern)

Riding Point: A Centennial History of the Kansas Livestock Association

A Window on Flint Hills Folklife: The Mardin Ranch Diaries, 1862–1863

My Flint Hills

Observations and Reminiscences from America's Last Tallgrass Prairie

Jim Hoy

University Press of Kansas

Published by the University Press of Kansas (Lawrence, Kansas 66045), which was organized by the Kansas Board of Regents and is operated and funded by Emporia State University, Fort Hays State University, Kansas State University, Pittsburg State University, the University of Kansas, and Wichita State University.

Library of Congress Cataloging-in-Publication Data
Names: Hoy, James F., author.
Title: My Flint Hills : observations and reminiscences from America's last tallgrass prairie / Jim Hoy.
Other titles: Observations and reminiscences from America's last tallgrass prairie
Description: Lawrence, KS : University Press of Kansas, [2020] | Includes index.
Identifiers: LCCN 2020008281
ISBN 9780700629930 (cloth)
ISBN 9780700629947 (epub)
Subjects: LCSH: Ranchers—Flint Hills (Kan. and Okla.)—Biography. | Flint Hills (Kan. and Okla.)—Rural conditions—Anecdotes. | Ranch life—Flint Hills (Kan. and Okla.)—Anecdotes. | Ranching—Flint Hills (Kan. and Okla.) | Flint Hills (Kan. and Okla.)—History. | Flint Hills (Kan. and Okla.)—Biography.
Classification: LCC F687.F55 H693 2020 | DDC 978.1/88—dc23
LC record available at https://lccn.loc.gov/2020008281.

British Library Cataloguing-in-Publication Data is available.

Printed in the United States of America

10 9 8 7 6 5 4 3 2 1

The paper used in this publication is acid free and meets the minimum requirements of the American National Standard for Permanence of Paper for Printed Library Materials Z39.48-1992.

Cathy Hoy, 1944–2019. (Photo by Gwen Obermeyer)

On July 21, 2019, Cathy, my loving wife of fifty-four years, died from the complications of pancreatic cancer. She loved the Flint Hills, to ride in them, to drive through them, to see paintings and photographs of them. In 2015 we shared the honor of being named Friend of the Flint Hills by the Flint Hills Discovery Center Foundation. She was a true champion of this last tallgrass prairie, my best critic, and my best editor. It is with great joy and with great sadness that I dedicate this book to her memory.

Contents

Some Ranches

On the Road

Life Around Cassoday

Nature

Legends and Tales

Scatterings

Riding Back: Conclusion

Passed very ruff flint hills. My feet blistered and very sore.
I stood on a hill and in one view below me saw buffalo, elk, deer,
cabrie [pronghorn antelope] *and panthers.*

From Zebulon Pike's journal, September 12, 1806,
recorded after crossing somewhere between present-day Bazaar
and Cedar Point in Chase County, Kansas. Pike's is the earliest
known record of anyone calling this area the Flint Hills.

Preface and Acknowledgments

This book results from my lifelong residence in (except for four years of graduate school at Columbia, Missouri) and from my deep love of the Flint Hills. As the subtitle indicates, the book covers a variety of topics. Some pieces are informative essays, some more contemplative, some autobiographical. Some date back a quarter of a century or so, while others were written expressly for this book. Many had their origins in the "Plains Folk" newspaper columns that Tom Isern and I have alternated writing weekly since 1983. All of the essays represent various interests that have appealed to me over many years of experience in the pasture and in academe (both teaching and researching). Many derive from my interest in the cattle culture of the Flint Hills, many others from personal experience growing up on a small stock ranch near Cassoday, and still others from topics that have caught my interest along the way.

This is not meant to be a scholarly work, although many of the essays are based on research. It is, however, meant to be informative and entertaining. I have in many instances tried to convey a conversational or colloquial tone, as if telling a story or talking to a friend. Thus the reader will notice some repetition of information in various places, and a scrupulous reader may occasionally detect some grammatical or usage infelicities that are intentional. I take responsibility, however, for any unintentional infelicities or errors that have escaped proofreading and remain in the printed text.

I would like to thank my daughter, Farrell Hoy Jenab, for her editing, my Emporia State University colleague Mel Storm for his advice on usage, my friends Mark Feiden, Dave Kendall, and Gary Sneed for help with photographs, and Bethany Mowry, Kelly Chrisman Jacques, Karl Janssen, and Joyce Harrison of the University Press of Kansas for their encouragement of this project. All photos in this book, unless otherwise noted, are from my collection.

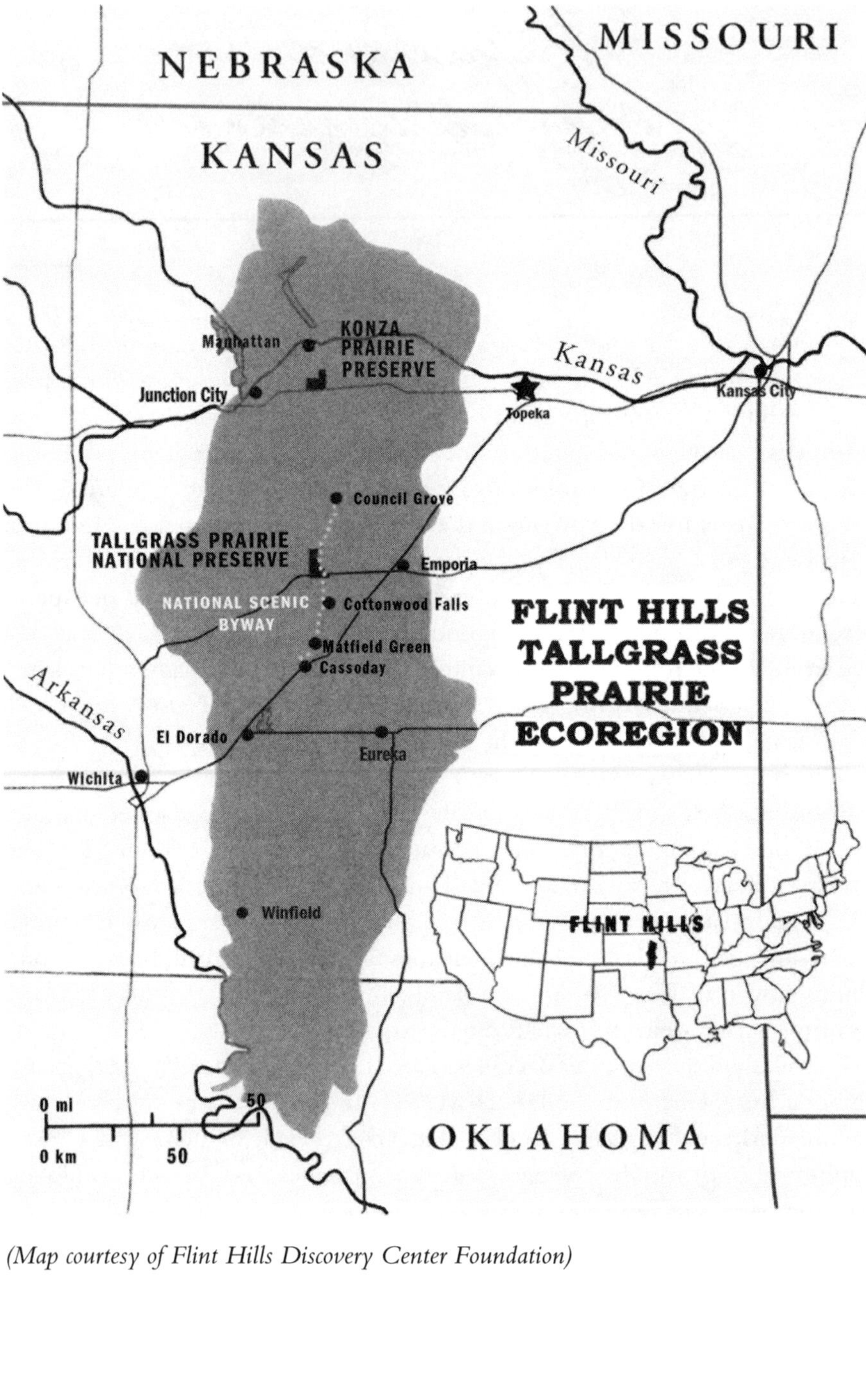

(Map courtesy of Flint Hills Discovery Center Foundation)

My Flint Hills

RIDING OUT: INTRODUCTION

Like No Other Place on Earth

Beginning near the Nebraska border, the Flint Hills of Kansas extend south into Osage County, Oklahoma, where they are called the Osage Hills. Not only is this area, sometimes referred to as the Bluestem Grazing Region, renowned throughout cattle country for its ability to pack pounds onto stocker cattle, it is also the last surviving remnant of a tallgrass prairie that once ranged from Canada to Texas, from western Indiana to central Kansas. Less than 5 percent of the original 170 million acres of this native prairie survives, and almost all of that is in the Flint Hills.

In addition to flint, the two other major types of rock found in abundance here are shale and limestone. There was even an attempt earlier on to call them the Limestone Hills or the Bluestem-Limestone Hills. Thankfully neither name caught on, for Flint Hills is a much more colorful appellation than either of those. Technically, the flint is of a type called chert, but again Flint Hills sounds better than Chert Hills. Because a tallgrass prairie requires good rainfall, which is also a prerequisite for crop agriculture, the rest of America's tallgrass prairie can now be seen in the rich farmland of Illinois and Iowa, where eons upon eons of the passing seasons have turned that grass into the deep, rich soil that farmers love. But the grass that grows there today is corn or milo.

It was the limestone and flint that rest on the surface of the Flint Hills, or lie just a few inches below it, that saved this area from the plow. It is said that an Osage tribesman, coming across a pioneer family with a plow strapped to the side of their covered wagon, told the young farmer, "You will have a hard time putting that iron thing into the ground here."

Dozens of different grasses can be found in the Flint Hills, but the four major species are big bluestem, little bluestem, Indian grass, and switchgrass. During late spring and continuing through mid- to late summer, these grasses, whose roots can extend fifteen or more feet into the ground, take energy from

Ridgeline limestone boulders. (Photo by Mark Feiden)

the sun and transform it into protein in the leaves. Not only that, but limestone is a soluble rock, and those long roots growing down around and through that stone carry the mineral to their leaves in the form of calcium. Young steers grazing on Flint Hills bluestem are thus taking in both protein and calcium. Calcium makes their bones grow, and the bigger the skeletal structure, the more meat can be hung on it.

This combination of protein and calcium explains why young cattle turned into Flint Hills pastures in the spring can gain from two and a half up to four pounds of weight per day eating nothing but grass. The grass. Grass is key to successful ranching in the Flint Hills. A good rancher raises grass, not cattle. A ten-thousand-acre Flint Hills ranch can handle as many cattle as a hundred-thousand-acre ranch in New Mexico or a million acres in the high desert of Nevada. My son, Josh, cowboyed on an 83,000-acre ranch near Pueblo, Colorado, that ran 2,700 head of cattle. A friend of his buckarooed on a million-acre Nevada ranch that ran 2,700 head of cattle. In 1996, when Josh and his cousin, Warren Kruse, started the Flying W Ranch in the Flint Hills with ten thousand acres, they ran 2,700 head of cattle. As C. L. Sonnichsen observed in *Cowboys and Cattle Kings*, “To a stockman from West Texas . . . the Flint Hills are simply unbelievable. He can hardly imagine that there is that much grass in the world.”

Typical Flint Hills landscape with little bluestem in the foreground. (Photo by Gary Sneed)

In early June of 2010 I was driving by the site of that year's Symphony in the Flint Hills with a visitor from Australia. My friend's son operated seven cattle stations in the Kimberley, a cattle-raising region at the northern end of the state of Western Australia. (The Kimberley is about the size of Kansas and Nebraska with a population of fewer than 35,000 people.) The acreage of these seven stations totals three million acres (or, as Pete Burton says, "Three and a half, when the tide's out"), on which he runs sixty thousand Brahma cows. As we drove, Pete suddenly asked me to stop; he wanted to take a photograph of the pasture we were driving by: "I can just show a picture of this grass to our cows and they'll get fat!"

Those Australian cows in the Kimberley were allotted fifty acres each, nearly ten times more than a cow here would require. Early on in the big Texas-to-Kansas trail drives that followed the Civil War, Texans discovered the ability of Flint Hills bluestem to put weight on cattle quickly and cheaply, particularly during the summer grazing season. Today cattle are trucked to the Flint Hills from many states for summer grazing, some from as far away as Florida.

The Flint Hills stretch from Marshall and Washington Counties in the north down through Riley, Geary, Pottawatomie, Wabaunsee, Morris, Marion, Lyon, Chase, Greenwood, Butler, Elk, Cowley, and Chautauqua Counties.

Ranching here is different from that in other parts of the West, where huge, self-contained ranches concentrate on keeping cow herds and raising calves. There are plenty of cow-calf operations in the Flint Hills as well, but the major business here, the one that made the Flint Hills famous, is pasturing transient cattle, that is, cattle raised elsewhere, brought here for the summer grazing season, then sent on to feed yards for further fattening before being butchered. That's why throughout the Southwest the Flint Hills are known as Steer Country, not Cow Country. In earlier years, when most of the summer cattle in the Flint Hills were from two to four years old (today yearlings predominate), they would often go directly from the pasture to the packing houses of Kansas City, Chicago, or Omaha. For those older cattle, the grass was as good as corn for marbling beef.

Three figures are crucial to ranching here: the landowner, the cattle owner, and the custom grazier (or pastureman, many of whom are women), and each has specific duties. The landowner, many of them living outside the Flint Hills region, is responsible for paying property taxes and for major capital improvements, such as new fences, cattle pens, or ponds and water systems. The cattle owner is responsible for providing transportation to and from the pasture, as well as for any special dietary or medical needs. The pastureman prepares for the season by patching fence in the spring, burning the old grass, receiving the cattle, looking after them during the grazing season, providing salt and access to water, repairing water gaps after rains, and gathering the herd for shipping when the season ends.

Besides pasturing transient cattle, the other two major elements of Flint Hills ranching folklife are a mix of farming and ranching and the annual spring burning of last year's dead grass. Because of an annual rainfall of over thirty inches, and because the creek and river bottoms here have the same deep, rich soil as other parts of the former tallgrass prairie, farmers produce in the bottomlands abundant crops of corn, alfalfa, soybeans, and milo. But unlike the song "The Farmer and Cowboy Can Be Friends" in the musical *Oklahoma*, in the Flint Hills the farmer and the cowboy can be and often are the same person, someone equally adept at riding a tractor one day and riding a horse the next.

Long before white settlers arrived in Kansas Territory in 1854, the native peoples here, and throughout the Great Plains, had burned the prairies. One of the reasons for this aboriginal burning was the same as the reason today's ranchers burn: bison were as attracted to the fresh green grass of a newly burned prairie as cattle are. Interestingly, as strong opposition to annual burning increased from the time of settlement through the mid-twentieth century in both the general public and among range scientists, the practice effectively ended everywhere in the Great Plains except in the Flint Hills. Here, despite advice against it, farmers and ranchers continued to burn. In the words of the late Wabaunsee County agent Darrold Marlow, "I knew I was supposed to advise against pasture burning, but I couldn't help notice that those who were burning had fewer trees and weeds and better grass in their pastures, and their cattle did better. So I just kept quiet."

From the mid-twentieth century on, especially with the establishment of the Konza Prairie Research Natural Area south of Manhattan, scientific experiments have proven the efficacy of controlled pasture burning, both in weight gains in cattle and in the health of the prairie. Today prescribed prairie burning is being conducted in other parts of the ranching West, thanks to the merging of science and Flint Hills folk practice. Moreover, the new growth of prairie grass will sequester as much or more carbon as was released during the burn, so Flint Hills pasture burning does not contribute to climate change.

Clovis spear points have been found in the Flint Hills, which means that humans have been here for some twelve thousand years. In historic times the Kanza Indian tribe occupied the northern part of the Flint Hills, while the Osage were active in the southern part. The modern history of the Flint Hills can be divided into three eras, based on how cattle have been brought into the pastures here: the Open Range or Trail Drive Era, from the opening of Kansas Territory in 1854 to approximately 1890; the Railroad Era, from around 1890 to the mid- and later 1960s; and the Trucking Era, from about the end of the 1960s to the present.

There is no doubt that the Flint Hills are cowboy country, of both the rodeo and working varieties. Of the ten world champion rodeo cowboys who have come from Kansas, five have lived in the Flint Hills, while two of the three Kansas teams to have won the World Championship Ranch Rodeo, held annually in Amarillo, Texas, have been from the Flint Hills. The annual Flint Hills Rodeo at Strong City began in 1937 and is the longest continually held rodeo in Kansas. In 1940 Marge Roberts, also of Strong City, won the last women's saddle bronc riding contest held at the Cheyenne Frontier Days rodeo, while her two younger brothers were both world champions: Ken (bull riding in 1943, 1944, and 1945) and Gerald (all around, 1942 and 1948). Other champions from the Flint Hills region are saddle bronc rider John McBeth, steer wrestler Joel Edmondson, and steer roper Sonny Worrell.

Although ranchers and cowboys have always appreciated the utility of the Flint Hills, in recent years the wider public has become more aware of them, not just for their role in beef production but also for their beauty. Tourism in the Flint Hills is a growing industry, stretching back at least as far as the now defunct Flint Hills Overland Wagon Train, which offered a two-day, overnight camping experience in covered wagons, held at various times in

Greenwood, Butler, Chase, and Morris Counties. Today, and for the past decade, thanks to such entities as the Flint Hills Discovery Center in Manhattan, the Pioneer Bluffs Foundation near Matfield Green, the Flying W Cattle and Guest Ranch near Cedar Point, and the Symphony in the Flint Hills, which has held concerts in Chase, Butler, Geary, Wabaunsee, and Morris Counties, many thousands of visitors have been exposed to this wondrous place. In 1996 the Tallgrass Prairie National Preserve was established on the old Spring Hill/Z Bar Ranch north of Strong City, attracting visitors from all over the country and foreign lands as well.

Artists and photographers have also discovered the beauty of the Flint Hills. That beauty is subtle, not spectacular; calming, not exciting. It doesn't so much overwhelm viewers as lead them into quiet contemplation and a sense of calm and oneness with the expanse of grass and sky. *National Geographic* photographer Jim Richardson, who published a pictorial feature in that magazine in 2007, compares the green of the Flint Hills to the emerald hues of Ireland. Larry Schwarm's pioneering photographs of pasture burning garnered first prize and a book from Duke University's Center for Documentary Studies.

In recent years many other excellent photographers have captured the essence of the Flint Hills in their work, as have literally dozens of painters, both those from the area and many others from beyond. Their work can be viewed in studios such as Louis Copt's in Tecumseh or Judith Mackey's in Cottonwood Falls, or in art galleries and museums throughout the Flint Hills region, from the Strecker-Nelson-West Gallery and the Beach Museum of Art in Manhattan to the Coutts Museum of Art in El Dorado. Chase County alone has three art galleries: Pioneer Bluffs, The Bank in Matfield Green, and the Symphony in the Flint Hills Gallery in Cottonwood Falls.

So many artists have been capturing the beauty of the Flint Hills on canvas, in fact, that it is drawing national attention. Art critic Henry Adams published an article in *American Art Review* in 2016 suggesting that there is now a Flint Hills school of landscape painting, on the order of the Hudson River school that was a major factor in nineteenth-century American landscape art. Capturing the beauty of the Flint Hills, Adams says, requires "a form of painting that does not simply repeat formulas from other places, but responds specifically to the Flint Hills."

It is good that the beauty of the Flint Hills is being recognized by artists, photographers, and others from beyond the region, but it is equally gratifying that Flint Hills residents themselves are coming to realize just how special this area is. A few years ago, a hunter driving through southern Chase County met a cowboy along an open-range pasture road and stopped to talk. The city dweller, sweeping his arms in a wide arc, said something about how pretty the

Flint Hills were in autumn. The cowboy, after contemplating the view, said, "You know, I've worked on ranches from Montana to Mexico, and this is the prettiest place I've ever seen." He paused, then added, "But you have to love grass."

We here in the Flint Hills do love grass, for we live in the largest expanse of native tallgrass prairie still existing anywhere in the world. The rolling landscape and big skies of the Flint Hills are a national treasure. Theirs is a quiet beauty, one that leads to contemplation. If you want to have your breath taken away by rugged spectacle, go to the Rocky Mountains or the Grand Canyon; if you want a chance to catch your breath, come to the Flint Hills.

MY FLINT HILLS

Into the Hills

If, as Wordsworth says, poetry is emotion recollected in tranquility, then the Flint Hills are for me an epic poem. Or maybe they are an anthology, a gathering of poems of various sorts and kinds. A lifetime spent in the Hills—running cattle and burning pasture and riding fence and hauling water and making hay and checking salt and shocking kaffir and breaking horses—is surely an epic romance. A drive through the Hills on a spring day, or after a thunderstorm in summer, or a walk along the Verdigris or the Walnut or the Cottonwood during the changing leaves of autumn, or a snowy winter picnic in the shadow of Sugar Loaf or Teterville Hill or Jacob's Mound—these are sonnets in a sequence of tallgrass, limestone, and flint rock. The cowboys of the Flint Hills, the cowgirls, the ranchers, the farmers, the farm wives, the cattle buyers and horse traders and oilfield workers—these are characters worthy of a Chaucer or a Hardy or a Robinson. A day spent shipping cattle or riding pastures is, for me, a carpe diem lyric made literal.

I have spent some days like that, written some lyrics with a horse and a rope and a pasture full of cattle, grass brushing the bottoms of my stirrups and clouds billowing overhead. My story, however, unlike my father's or my uncle's, is not an epic of the Hills, for I have not lived all my days amid horses and cattle, windmills and ponds, coyotes and meadowlarks. Oh, I have kept these things near me, but my living has been made in the classroom, students for my companions—students and Chaucer and Marlowe and Cather.

But I have never been far from the Hills, even with a hemisphere in between. Bodmin Moor reminded me of the Flint Hills, and so would have the Scottish Highlands if only the mountains had been lower and rounder. But the Highlands were, like the Flint Hills themselves, open and green and fresh to the smell. At the other end of the island a farmer in Cornwall, turning fodder with a pitchfork, spoke to me in a voice that sounded so nearly like

Chase County that homesickness shivered through me. Australian spinifex is not Kansas bluestem, but Down Under they also burn off the dry grass to bring out its vitality, just as we do here in the Flint Hills. The hills of Argentina in Los Potreros Estancia in Cordoba Province look like the Flint Hills, only the rocks there sparkle of silica, not flint. The thousands upon thousands of horses and cattle and sheep roaming the unfenced mountain meadows of Kyrgyzstan made me think of the Texas cattle that covered the unfenced Flint Hills in the days of the Old Chisholm Trail. No matter where I travel, the Hills are never far from me.

I remember an August day in 1989, some quarter of a century, and half my life, after I had left my boyhood home. Josh, my son, then a teenager, was nearing the end of a summer job at Cassoday with Carl Grunder and his wife, Susan—hauling hay, driving a tractor, helping with cattle. Carl is a few years younger than I, reared a farmer a few miles southwest of our home place. But he's since turned rancher, leasing grass and running cattle, as do many of the farmer-stockmen of the Flint Hills. Josh had called to see if I could come help ship and look for strays; Carl was shorthanded and the cattle had caused some trouble when they were sorted earlier that week.

I drove down from Emporia early the next morning and ate some of the breakfast that Mother had fixed. Josh and Dad were out calling the horses in. Josh and I saddled and loaded, drove the mile to Grunders, then followed them to the pasture.

The steers were on a soil-bank pasture, the old Coffelt place a few miles east of Cassoday, near where the flats give way to the Hills proper. The loading pens were across the road north in the southwest corner of the Raster pasture. The old wooden-floored barn that had stood a few hundred yards north when I was Josh's age, where the Young boys, the Watkins brothers, Al Plummer, and I used to meet horseback to go camping down in the Hills, had long since rotted down. As on the Coffelt, only the outline of a storm cave amid some trees marks the site that once housed a pioneer family.

The yearlings had done well on this grass; we learned later in the morning, after the trucks had weighed their loads, that on average each steer had added 267 pounds to the 560 each had carried in the spring, some three pounds for each day they had been eating the protein- and calcium-rich bluestem. There were five of us (the owner was along, riding one of Susan's horses), and we had no trouble rounding up the cattle, most of them on the east side of the pasture, and driving them the mile or so to the pens. On the west side of the pasture, however, was a dead steer, gruesome evidence of the difficulty of the previous day's trouble. This steer had strayed into a neighboring pasture and did not want to leave. He had been alive, though winded and overheated, when they left him the evening before, but the combination of excitement, running, and August heat had been fatal. A death such as this is upsetting to both pastureman and owner. But it happens; it's part of the risk a cattleman takes.

The steers were penned and loaded without incident, and Susan left for El Dorado to buy cattle at the weekly auction. Carl was still three head shy, but he had seen them in the two-section pasture that bordered his to the south, so we got on our horses and headed toward what I had always known as the Harsh Hill pasture. When I was young and had helped Frank Klasser (pronounced *CLAY-zure*) ship cattle, we had always driven through the eastern side of this large pasture, then across its northern end and into the Prewitt Hill pasture before coming out on the Watkins Flats and then onto the township road at the corner of the Lake pasture, named after Fox Lake, built by the Santa Fe in the early 1920s to provide water for its steam locomotives. Since then parts of the Harsh Hill have sold and it has been cross-fenced. I don't know who owns the western portion that we were riding for strays. The Vestrings had it leased and were looking after the cattle in it.

When we were about halfway to the gate, we met Bob Vestring in an old rust-colored Chevy pickup, and, as is customary in the Hills, he stopped to visit a while. He asked Carl if he had a key to the gate (he did), and I asked Bob when he started locking gates. Gate locks are a relatively recent introduction into a countryside where one has customarily had the right to ride into his neighbor's pasture to look for strays, or to ride across it to get from one pasture to the next. Cattle theft is always a threat, although not an overriding concern, but the chief impetus behind gate locking has been the "sportsman," the coyote hunter who leaves gates open, the fisherman who strews pond banks with litter, or the sightseer who tosses out trash to keep the floorboards of his SUV clean. Bob said that he finally decided to put up chains and locks when beer cans and other trash began to show up in the middle of remote pastures that, like this one, were a mile or more from the county road, which itself is a back road that is several miles from the main road, which in turn was still miles from the nearest paved highway. Population, in other words. Too many people coming into the Hills without respect for beauty or for property rights or livestock or consideration for others. I'd like to know that I could get on a horse and ride cross country from Rosalia to Madison, or be able to stop my car along a gravel road in the middle of the Hills and climb over the fence to look at a plant or a rock or a long-abandoned storm cellar, but this access is being closed to me, and others like me, by road hunters and night fishermen and dirt cyclists and whoever else scatters his way through the landscape. "Leave a gate the way you find it" was an early lesson I learned from Dad. People are closing gates in the Flint Hills by leaving them open.

Bob commented on Josh's gray horse. Lots of stockmen in the Flint Hills like to have a light-colored horse for driving cattle. Or, more precisely, for leading them; cattle will supposedly follow a gray or a white horse more readily than they will a darker-colored one, whether because they like their looks or merely because such a horse is more visible, I don't know. Frank Klasser thought he needed a white horse to lead cattle with, and I remember the big-headed, pink-assed, ornery horse that he bought for just that reason. He wasn't much of a cow horse, but then Klasser wasn't much of a cowboy; he was a cattleman, and I respected him for that, but he didn't want to see you get a rope down or unnecessarily chouse cattle, and a youngster likes the excitement of cowboying. Klasser was not one of those people who look like they are part of the horse when they ride, which made this old pony's favorite trick an especially unnerving one. Whenever Klasser crossed a stream, the horse would act like he was dying for a drink, so Klasser would give him some slack in the reins and the ornery cuss would grab the bit in his teeth and jump out of the water on the run. Klasser would haul in reins as fast as he could while trying to hold onto the saddle horn and swearing at the same time. The horse might not have been that good as a cow horse, but he was a hell of an actor. Klasser might have known the horse couldn't really be thirsty, but he'd stretch down for that water so yearningly, and the drive into the Cassoday stockyards was such a long, dry one that Klasser, as least once each shipping day, it seemed, would give in and give him some rein. It was always a good show. Still, the cattle did seem to follow Old Whitey on the drives to town, and Bob recalled an old gray workhorse of his father's that, he said, smelled different from the other horses. The milk cows even tended to stay closer to him in the pasture than to the other horses.

Vestrings didn't have this pasture when I was helping drive cattle through it years ago, but they did lease the Henley pasture, which bordered it on the south. I recall once, probably around 1960, when my sister and I were helping Bill Rose, who worked for Vestrings, look for strays. I think we were actually helping Raymond Prewitt ship, or maybe spray, but he was missing a couple of head so the three of us were riding through the several thousand acres that made up the Henley. I was on a bay horse that Dad had recently traded for (he usually kept a few head around for trading stock), a well-made, quick-actioned gelding that probably weighed about ten and a half. He usually handled pretty well until you really needed him and then he'd get high-strung and couldn't see a cow if she ran into him. "What he needs," Dad said, "is to rope a bull off of him and turn him loose."

I'd never done anything like that before, but when we came upon one of the Prewitt steers (fat two-year-old Texas cattle) and tried to separate him from his Vestring buddies, Old Bay (I don't remember now just what his name was) started getting prancy and dancy.

"That horse looks like he needs some schooling," Bill said.

It's embarrassing to have a horse not know what to do, even if it's a colt, and the bay was old enough to know better.

"I'd like to rope that steer and let the two of them have at it," I said.

"It's all right with me," said Bill (who didn't own either the steer or the horse), "but you might get your horse hurt." The steer didn't weigh that much less than the horse.

By that time I was mad enough at him that I didn't care. "He isn't worth anything anyway if you can't do anything off of him," I said. I cinched up, tied my reins in a knot, and built a loop. I was, of course, tied on hard and fast (this was back in the old silk-manila days when we didn't know what a nylon was or anything at all about dallying), then took out after the steer. The bay stuck his head up in the air and didn't follow worth a damn, but as we got down into a draw among some trees, I got close enough to catch the steer and pulled him to a stop. Then I slacked the rope, got off, and walked away a few steps.

The steer stood looking at the horse, who had decided to put his head down to the ground and start eating grass. That's when I picked up a flint rock and threw it, not at the horse (who should never have taken his eyes off the steer), but right into the ribs of the steer. He grunted and took off, nearly jerking the bay off his feet. The horse jumped and ran to the north, the steer paralleling him, the rope between them clearing brush as they ran toward the head-high stump of a small dead elm tree. When the rope hit the stump and broke it off, the steer veered to the east, and this time he did jerk the horse down. Hard. And actually dragged him a few feet. When he got up this time, the horse had his eyes and his ears pointed at the steer. I threw a couple of more rocks at the steer, but now each time he jumped, the horse would turn to face him, keeping the rope tight.

So I got back on and Bill heeled the steer. Rita took the head rope off and we finished riding the pasture, taking the strays with us. Old Bay was not the best cow horse we ever had, but he worked a lot better after that, and Dad sold him for a pretty good price.

On this day, helping Grunder, I was riding a big red roan I'd had for a while. He was a little hard-mouthed and whinnied like a colt when the other horses were out of sight (an irritating habit), but I figured he'd be a pretty good cow horse if he was just ridden enough (as, in fact, he turned out to be). But that's true throughout the Flint Hills—and the West in general. A horse doesn't learn much about cattle when he's riding in a gooseneck; it takes wet saddle blankets.

After we left Bob Vestring and rode into the two-section pasture to look for the steers, Josh and Carl went off to the east, and the cattle owner and I split off to the west and south. The morning was as cool and cloudy as the previous day had been hot and sunny. I'd call it an unusual August day, but about the only thing unusual about Kansas weather is that it's usually unusual.

The north part of the pasture was flat, but as we rode south we hit the breaks. The texture of the land is one of the things I love most about the Flint Hills: riding along a flat pasture and seeing it finger off into ridges that become hills by giving way to draws and canyons, which in turn lead into more ridges and hills; finding a way through the layers of limestone that break out along the rims of the hills like a row of stone on a castle wall, some of the boulders big enough to serve as a slab foundation for a small house; hearing the click of horseshoes on side hills covered with loose, sharp-sided rocks, small chunks of irregularly faceted chert thinly enveloped, except for one or two surfaces, in lime; then coming out onto a sweeping valley floor a quarter of a mile wide totally devoid of rock.

And grass everywhere: big and little bluestem mixed with Indian grass and switchgrass growing tall in the valleys; bluestem on the hilltops, with buffalo grass on the poorer soil or covering the trails where cattle, or tires, have worn down the tallgrass; bluestem and side oats grama filling every crevice in the rock-strewn hillsides. Wildflowers—forbs among the grass—vary with the season. Some of these plants, such as buffalo beans or shoestring, are legumes and help enrich the soil; others, such as buckbrush or musk thistle, crowd out the grass. Along the streams are thick stands of timber—elms, walnuts, thorny locusts, huge oaks, and stark sycamores lining the banks of clear-running creeks. The pasture we were in was far from a creek, and it had not been overgrazed so there were no red cedars or hedge trees growing on it, but in the dry, gravelly bottom of a draw, a little north of a boggy area where a spring oozed to the surface, a willow tree grew. It had, in fact, been growing there for many years, judging from its size, but in its earlier years the cattle had rubbed its trunk into a grotesque curl, giving it the appearance of a timberline tree in the mountains.

As is true throughout the plains, the atmosphere in the Flint Hills can play funny tricks. I remember one foggy morning in the Scott pasture, several miles east of where we were on this day, looking southwest and seeing the huge oil-storage tanks of the Skelly refinery at El Dorado, twenty-five or more miles to the southwest looming on the horizon, seemingly no more than five miles away. Somehow the refraction of the light through the mist had thrown a mirror image of the tanks through the sky and projected it—upside down—onto a grassy hillside in the middle distance. On this morning there were no optical illusions, no mirages, but once, about mid-morning, out of a high overcast sky a number of billowy, white clouds sped low over the hills from the north, looking every bit as I imagined billows of smoke from an Indian signal fire might have looked. The atmosphere was heavy with the smell of grass, trampled weeds, and manure, but visibility was crystalline, despite the cloud cover: on the Teterville Road some three miles to the north, utility poles with their electricity-bearing wires were clearly visible (the poles, not the wires) against the backdrop of a blue-gray sky.

There had been, when we first arrived at the pasture, hot winds, strange for that early in the morning. Then cool winds blew in as we finished loading, and when we got to the pasture to look for strays, there was no wind at all. Suddenly, fierce gusts came up, wind that curled the brim of your hat against the crown or, if you ducked your head to the side, bent it down toward your cheek. I could see distant lightning, then hear rumblings of thunder that grew louder as the lightning drew nearer.

There is nothing more fearsome to a horseman on the wide prairie than the lightning of a thunderstorm. Getting wet doesn't matter; what does is that you on your horse are the tallest thing around, and lightning likes tall things. Cottonwood trees draw lighting, I have been told by old-timers in the Flint Hills, because their roots go all the way down to water. A cottonwood will grow where no other tree will, they say, because it will hunt out that water and send its roots right down to it. They draw lightning because, like high-pole gates or cowboys on horses, they are the tallest things around—and lightning likes tall things.

I had never been particularly alarmed by lightning until a few years ago when we (Dad, Josh, and I) were moving some cows to a pasture a couple of miles northwest of the home place. A storm blew up, but we kept going through the rain because we wanted to finish the job. We pushed the cows into the pasture, but as we were leaving and drew within a few yards of the high-pole gate, I suddenly felt as if someone had slapped a hand down sharply on the crown of my rain-soaked straw hat, and instantly I heard a sharp, loud clap of deafening thunder. I do not remember any smell of sulfur or any tingling of skin, there was no synapse of electricity shooting between the ears of my horse, and the lightning did not even strike the gate pole. But it must have crashed no more than fifty feet in the air above our heads. We loped home, hunkering low, as if that would protect us. I have had a healthy respect for lightning ever since.

I don't like to spook, but as the lightning got closer I headed back to the trailer. As I came up over the hill, I saw that the others had had the same idea. Now, what good loping toward a trailer does when lightning is flashing all around I don't know. About as much good as hunkering down when you hear a sharp clap of thunder. But at least you feel like you're doing something, not just waiting to be struck. I, like most anyone who has spent much time around them, have known of cowboys who were struck by lightning. Some survived.

We sat in the pickup for a bit, then went back to the cattle after the storm passed. There were a few drops of rain, just enough to cool things off, but it looked like there were some good showers to the west. To the northeast I could see the road running toward Lapland, and to the east there was Round Mound Hill on the old Klasser place. Sugar Loaf, a dozen or more miles to the south, stood out clearly on the skyline. Eight or ten crows were perched on fence posts to the west, looking at first glance like the worn-out boots that ranchers place on their fence posts in the Sandhills of Nebraska. A coyote jumped up in the distance, full-tailed and mange-free. As we went down a slope farther into the pasture, we lost sight of the road and the named hilltops. There were no landmarks other than ridges of rock or ponds or trees along the bank of a distant stream. The fences ran straight with the world, but without the sun as a reference point they seemed sometimes to flow with the terrain and go off at crazy angles until you could again get your bearings and sight them straight once more.

The Vestring cattle were nervous, whether because of the weather or because that was the personality of that particular herd I couldn't say, and most of them moved along with us as we spotted our three strays and headed them northwest toward the gate. One jumped the fence into the pasture we had rounded up earlier, but joined with the other two when we drove them quietly through the gate and toward the pen.

I had jumped a fence of my own that morning, back into a world of memories triggered by the familiar sights in a pasture I hadn't been in for over a quarter of a century. Like the cattle we had sent that morning from the freedom of a pasture to the confines of a feedlot, I had long since left the pastures of my youth and been driven (by chance, by choice, and by the inevitability of life) to the holding pen of a workaday world of words—and of people, always people. But now, briefly, I was back in a remembered, if romantically remembered, world of cattle and horses and rocks and grass and stillness. There is only so much of a day that one can seize, even less that one can hold on to. The world of the Flint Hills, as with any real or imagined world, is transitory (frighteningly so), but maybe, sitting in my pen holding a different kind of pen, I can capture some of the poetry that is the Flint Hills, can fix it into a form as permanent as the flint rock itself.

The Flying H Ranch

The Flying H Ranch traces its origin to the homestead of my great-grandparents, William and Mary Ann Davison Hoy, who left Perry County, Ohio, in 1877 to settle in the Flint Hills near Cassoday.

Our Flying H brand was first registered by my grandfather, Frank Hoy, son of William and Mary Ann. One April some years before my birth, Dad Hoy (as all his grandchildren called him) noticed a Flying H on several hundred big New Mexico steers grazing in one of the pastures around Cassoday. He registered that brand on the right hip for cattle and horses, and we have kept that registration current ever since. One of Dad Hoy's original hand-forged Flying H branding irons today rests on the mantel above our fireplace.

When Mary Ann and William first arrived at Sycamore Township in northeastern Butler County, Cassoday didn't exist. Instead, there was a small settlement called Sycamore Springs, named after the water that gushed from the ground and entered the Walnut River about two miles west of the present town. The first settlers at Sycamore Springs arrived about 1860, and a post office was established in 1868.

The Hoys bought eighty acres in the southwest corner of Section 15/Township 23/Range 7, one mile west of present-day Cassoday. The property lies about a mile northeast of Sycamore Springs. They were the third owners of this land, the first being Samuel Slover, whose 1869 patent bears the signature of President Ulysses S. Grant. The Hoys paid Silas Finnefrock $900 for a farm that had a three-room house and a stable with limestone walls and a straw roof. These buildings, and the house, barn, and sheds that would later replace them, were located on the northwest corner of the eighty. The Walnut River crosses through the middle of the property, although the water from the river goes underground about a half mile east of the line, reemerging about a half mile west. Only during heavy rains does water run on this stretch of the river.

The Campbell family in front of their store and post office at Sycamore Springs, 1889.

Several settlers coming to Sycamore Springs temporarily lived in the stable on the Hoy farm until they found land of their own, while travelers passing through often sheltered there and were fed by Mary Ann. In 1882 one of those traveling families lost a baby to fever while camped along the Walnut, about a quarter of a mile south of the house. Mary Ann offered to let the family bury their child in the southwestern corner of the property, promising that the grave would remain undisturbed.

William Hoy, a Union veteran of the Civil War, was a quiet, easygoing man, a capable farmer-stockman, and active in the community, serving on the school board for several years, but his wife was more outgoing and outspoken. She was a midwife, helping deliver many babies in the area. She also, in addition to donating land for the local church, helped organize the first Sunday school in Sycamore Township.

In 1872 the Kaw Indians were removed from their reservation near Council Grove to northern Oklahoma, the Pawnee of Nebraska four years later. Members of both tribes often passed through the Hoy farm, where a trail made by their travois can still be seen. At one time a group of some 250 Indians camped along the nearby Walnut River for two days. A story passed down in the family tells how a small band stopped one day and asked Mary Ann for food. William (called Pappy Hoy by his children and grandchildren) had butchered a hog

The William Hoy family. From left: Mary Ann, Loretta (Etta), Frank, Daisy, Ethel, William.

earlier in the day, so Mary Ann gave them the lights and a troublesome rooster she wanted to get rid of. The Indians built a small fire on top of the storm cellar east of the house, cooked their food, and thanked Mary Ann as they left.

The Hoys had three children born in Ohio—Loretta, Daisy, and James (who died of fever four years after coming to Kansas)—and two born in Kansas, Frank and Ethel. Loretta (called Etta) married Frank Goodnight, a rancher from Englewood in Clark County and a relative of Charles Goodnight (the legendary Texas rancher who invented the chuck wagon and blazed the Goodnight-Loving Trail); Daisy married Herbert Robinson of Cassoday; Ethel married Clark Wright, a rancher from Wild Horse, Colorado. Frank stayed at Cassoday, helping his father with cattle, horses, and crops. As a youth he worked as a cowboy, loose-herding cattle in the summer near Jack Springs on the open range between Cassoday and Matfield Green. He was paid twenty-five cents a week by the cattle owners, who lived at Newton.

In 1899 Frank bought two hundred acres of land adjoining the original homestead to the north and east. There he built a small two-story house, a large barn, and several other outbuildings. After his father died, he added the original homestead to his holdings, in addition to another eighty acres a mile and a half northwest. Like many if not most early Flint Hills settlers, he was a farmer-stockman with a diversified operation. He kept a herd of stock cows (mostly Hereford, some Galloway), had a few dairy cows (selling cream and bucket-raising calves with the skim milk), occasionally ran some sheep, raised hogs for butchering, and grew corn, kaffir corn, hay, and oats. He used Percheron horses in the fields, and also stood a Percheron stud. Later, after switching to mules for farm work, he stood a Mammoth jack. He raised both draft and saddle horses, keeping a herd of some two dozen brood mares, and leased pasture for his stock cows. On occasion he would ship steers to the Kansas City stockyards, driving them to the railroad at De Graff, some twenty miles to the southwest.

In 1901 Franklin Pierce Hoy (1878–1952) married Glory Katherine Breidenstein (1881–1964), daughter of German immigrants who had lived near Rosalia and then De Graff before moving to Sycamore Springs (the forerunner of Cassoday). Frank and Glory's family included two sons—Kenneth and Marshall—and four daughters—Grace (who died as a baby), Jeruah (called Judy), Cleda, and Virginia. Kenneth, the eldest (and my father), was born March 16, 1904, at the Arch Bridge on the Breidenstein farm. Marshall came along three years and two days later, then the girls. Virginia, the youngest, was often called Tid. Kenneth and Marshall always called each other Kid. As a little girl Virginia tried to call them Kid, but it came out Tid, thus the nickname.

The two sons worked with their father until 1946. At that time Marshall and his wife, Berdine, and their two daughters, Judy and Ann, moved to Towanda where he managed Harry Wilson's American Quarter Horse operation. The family later moved to Hopkins Switch, northwest of El Dorado, where he raised registered Quarter Horses and looked after pastures.

Kenneth, like his father, spent his entire life on the Cassoday property his grandparents and parents had put together. In 1938 he married Marteil "Marty" Rice (b. 1910), from Conway Springs in Sumner County, who was teaching at Cole Creek School southwest of Cassoday. This union produced two children, James Franklin (b. 1939) and Rita Ann (b. 1942). Rita married steer roper H. L. Todd of Rexford in 1961, and Jim married Catherine Thompson of Chanute in 1965.

Upon the death of his mother (who died in 1964, twelve years after her husband), Kenneth inherited the original homestead of William and Mary Ann Hoy. Earlier, shortly after their marriage in 1938, he and Marty bought forty acres split by the Walnut River in Section 16, just west of that eighty-acre property. In 1956 they bought a quarter section, the old Fluke place, in Section 3, two miles north of the home place, and in the 1960s they added the northeast quarter of Section 16 to their holdings (the Ernst and Davidson eighties). In addition to this deeded property, they also leased over a section of pasture in three different locations within a couple of miles of the home place.

Jim's grandparents, Dad Hoy (Frank) and Grandmother (Glory).

Jim's parents, Kenneth and Marty.

Jim and his sister Rita,
headed to Countryman's Rodeo,
July 4, 1945.

At seven hundred acres the Flying H Ranch is small compared to the big ranches in the Cassoday area, and in the Flint Hills in general, but it is typical of many such operations throughout the Hills in an earlier era. We ran about a hundred cows, originally Herefords then later black baldies. When he was in his seventies, Dad bought a couple dozen heifer calves from a roping club, and those Brahmas formed his last herd of cows. Even after he lost his right arm in a baling accident in 1985, Dad could saddle and ride a horse to look after the cows in summer, and in winter, with Mother's help, he could feed them.

During the summer grazing season we kept our cows on leased upland grass, some on the Deaver pasture in Section 8, about two miles northwest of home, some on the Knab pasture a mile north, and some on the Mosteller. The latter pasture was about two and a half miles south, split by Kansas Highway 13 (now K-177) and the Santa Fe Railroad, which ran parallel to the highway. It was owned by a family who lived at Bern, in far northern Kansas.

In the autumn we would bring the cows home to feed during the winter. Usually we kept them in the Cowlot, a forty-acre pasture just west of the home place, and in the Cemetery pasture, the south forty acres of the home place. Alternately, we called the Cemetery pasture the Cave pasture because it was the site of a stone quarry and of a small dugout that had contained dynamite used in the quarry, the stone from which had been used in the construction of Fox Lake in the early 1920s. The lake, a mile east of Cassoday, was a project of the Santa Fe Railroad, which used the water for its steam engines, pumping it south to a water tower at Aikman, the high point between El Dorado and Chase County. That way locomotive engines going either north or south would be headed (very slightly) downhill after taking on water. There was also a set of shipping pens at Aikman. The dry bed of the Walnut River ran through both the Cowlot and the Cemetery pastures, and both contained large feed racks filled with loose-stacked prairie hay (Cemetery and Cowlot) or alfalfa (Cowlot) for winter feed, which was supplemented by kaffir corn. Later in the 1950s we began to feed protein pellets (and had a bumper sticker on the stock racks of our truck that read: "Don't feed 'em, Gooch 'em") rather than kaffir as a supplement.

Both the hay and the kaffir required hard summer work. In the 1940s Dad bought a tractor, first an iron-wheeled Farmall F-20, later replaced by an Allis-Chalmers WC. I vaguely recall Dad and Dad Hoy both mowing alfalfa with mules, but my memories of Dad cutting hay with a side-mounted mower on the WC are stronger. All the rest of the haying, however, was done with mule and man power. At a young age my sister and I took turns running a dump rake pulled by a team of mules, either two bay molly mules, Flossie and Tessie, or Andy and Mickey. Andy was a lazy brown horse mule and Mickey a full-of-go white mare mule, so I was constantly prodding the former and pulling back on the latter. After the raking was completed, Dad Hoy ran the go-devil (sometimes called a buck rake or a hay buck in other parts of the state) with Flossie and Tessie, and Dad operated the Jayhawk stacker with Andy and Mickey.

In the mid-1950s, after Dad Hoy's death, Dad bought a Farmhand stacker that mounted on a tractor. With that machine he could go into the hayfield and gather up a load, then take it to the stack and dump it, thus eliminating the need for the Jayhawk stacker and the go-devil. With either machine, once the windrows had been gathered, we would then rake the scatterings.

While still living at Cassoday, Uncle Marshall stacked the hay into tall conical stacks at the edge of the alfalfa field, or into long loaf stacks in the feed racks. After he left Cassoday to move to Towanda (perhaps in no small part motivated by a desire to escape hay stacking!), the stacking was done by various men in the community hired for that purpose, until I got old enough to do the job. I soon began to lobby for a hay baler because loose-stacking hay is hot, dusty, hard, itchy work. Every forkful has to be moved into the right place and carefully tromped down if a stack is to be made correctly so that it sheds rainwater. Moreover, Dad Hoy was a stickler when it came to stacking hay. In his opinion a good haystack "should split a raindrop," half a drop running down one side of the stack, the other half down the other.

In 1957 we did get an Allis-Chalmers Roto Baler and an Allis WD tractor with a hand clutch with which to run it. In summertime we would wrap up prairie hay into small round bales that we would pick up in winter with a team of mules pulling a hayrack. We continued, however, to loose-stack alfalfa with a Farmhand stacker for several years more. As late as the mid-1970s Dad would hitch up our team of long-legged buckskin mules (Andy and Mickey were long gone by this time) and head south three miles to a prairie hay meadow we baled on the shares. Those mules could walk a good six miles an hour with an empty wagon, half that with a full load.

We also continued into the early 1960s to grow kaffir corn to feed our cows in winter. Kaffir is a grain sorghum that has long since given way to shorter-stalked, bigger-headed milo. In the fall Dad would cut the six- or seven-foot stalks with a single-row corn binder pulled by three mules, collecting several bundles into the accumulator before dumping them in windrows. We would then shock the bundles into tepee-shaped shocks where they would stand until we picked them up in a hayrack during the winter. When Dad Hoy was still alive, we would sometimes cut the grain heads off into a wagon with a guillotine-like blade. These he would use to feed his pigs and chickens. Or we would grind them with a hammer mill to feed a steer for butchering. The headless bundles were then placed into lengthwise, horizontal shocks to be fed to the cows later on.

One of the pleasures, for a kid, of feeding kaffir was killing mice. As the last few bundles were pitched onto the hayrack, the mice that had taken up homesteads under the shock would scatter and our dogs (Hank, Shep, and Speck) and I would go after them. Or I would dig into their burrows with my pitchfork, and the dogs would jump on them as they ran out. Then I would trot on up to the next shock where Dad was already pitching bundles. He never complained about my tardy arrival because he hated mice. On one memorable occasion Dad suddenly threw down his fork and grabbed his Lee Riders just above the watch pocket. He was yelling, jumping, and squeezing hard. It seems a mouse had run up between his pants and his long underwear but had been stymied by his belt. It more nearly resembled hamburger meat than a mouse when Dad dumped it on the ground. His aversion to mice, by the way, resulted from a time he had ridden over to northern Greenwood County to help Dow Gilbreath ship cattle. He had arrived in late afternoon and was camped for the night in an abandoned oilfield shack near Kenbro. He was awakened in the middle of the night by a mouse chewing on his hair; he hated them ever after.

Another pleasure of kaffir feeding was seeing the large flocks of prairie chickens that would fly up from the kaffir-corn shocks nearly every morning where they had been eating grain, which we didn't begrudge them because several times a winter Dad would put the .22 rifle into a canvas case and hang it on the hayrack when we went to the field. He would leave me in charge of the mules while he crept up on the birds, carefully keeping behind shocks so they wouldn't see him. Usually he would shoot one chicken and the rest would fly, but I recall one time when he shot one that was on the very top of the shock. Two other birds were on that shock, but they didn't fly as the dead bird tumbled past them, so Dad picked off another one, giving us two prairie chicken dinners on that trip. In those days, flocks of forty chickens or more were common; today we will jump maybe one or two birds a summer while riding pastures.

I recall only one time that Dad planted any wheat. We harvested both oats and wheat with a mule-powered grain binder, then shocked and threshed the bundles. One of our neighbors, Richard Goering, provided the separator for all the farms in our area, going from one field to the next, with neighbors helping one another until all the grain had been threshed. We also raised corn on occasion, but oats were a staple, planted every year to provide feed for the horses and mules.

During the winter we would keep up a saddle horse or two and one team of mules for use in feeding. The rest we turned out into the Funk pasture, a section of grass just northwest of our property. There they would stay, fending for themselves until mid- or late March. The pasture belonged to Karl Harsh, a man we helped each year with cattle, so he allowed Dad this perk. The horses would stay in good flesh all winter, eating the old grass and getting water from the snow. In March, however, they would start looking for the new growth of cool-season grasses and begin to lose weight, so we would bring them home to eat hay until the bluestem began to green up a few weeks later.

We rarely fed out cattle but would instead sell weanling calves or yearlings, which we usually hauled in our one-ton 1951 GMC truck to the livestock auctions at El Dorado or Emporia, or to the stockyards in Wichita. Only once did we take steers to Kansas City, and that was when we did full-feed a stock-car load. I suppose we drove them to the railroad pens in Cassoday, but I don't remember doing that. I do remember all our family, along with Karl and Eunice Harsh, going to Kansas City for a late fall holiday, staying at the Dixon Hotel and eating at the Golden Ox.

Each winter, usually just after Christmas when the weather was dependably cold, we would butcher a steer. In his mind Dad would draw an imaginary X from its ears to its eyes, shoot it in the middle of the X with a .22 rifle, then hoist it on the haymow pulley (later with the Farmhand stacker) for bleeding, gutting, and skinning. I vaguely remember the hog butcherings at Dad Hoy's, but Dad was allergic to pork, so we never had it on our table. I clearly remember the smokehouse just east of Dad Hoy and Grandmother's house with hams hanging from hooks and the strong odor of curing pork. I also remember Grandmother rendering the hog fat, as well as the doughnuts she made with the resulting lard.

I don't recall the actual Percheron (or "*PER chun*," as he and Dad pronounced it) stallion that Dad Hoy stood, but I do remember one time when a neighbor came by with a mare for breeding, and I was sent from the barn to be with Grandmother at the house. I had no idea what was going on, but my feelings were hurt when I had to leave the men and the horses at the barn.

I remember quite clearly, however, the Mammoth jack, named Old Black Joe, Dad Hoy kept for raising mules, both for our ranch and for neighbors. When I was very young, the ranch had twenty-five or so brood mares, in addition to the cow horses. We raised a few mules during my high school years, some intentionally and some when Joe got out and bred my father's best cow horse, Rusty. My mare, Star, also had a mule colt from that escapade. After that we used the mares for raising colts, breeding them to stallions owned by neighboring ranchers such as Buss Young, Wayne Rogler, and Wilber Countryman.

Probably our two best colts came from Wayne's stud, Sutherland's Firehair. Star had a small roan, blaze-faced mare, Jan, that I used for bulldogging at area rodeos. Rusty's best was a big dun gelding Dad gave to Rita. She called him Travis, but sold him to me as a three-year-old when she got married. I called him Buck, or sometimes One-eye. That nickname was the result of a large, round, walnut-sized, wartlike growth just above his right eye that was removed twice before it quit growing back. In the process of the second operation, however, a tear duct was cut. That eyelid drooped and constantly watered. But Buck could see more cow with that bad eye than most horses could see with two good ones.

In his younger years Buck lived up to his name. On one occasion he broke in two as I was riding along the timber just after a big snowstorm. I steered him into a deep snowdrift, as I had heard cowboys in the north country did, and that brought him to a stop. Another memorable episode was in the Deaver pasture. I saw a steer that needed roping, and just as I caught the steer, Buck ducked his head and cut loose. Dropping the dally wasn't an option because in those days I tied on hard and fast, just as everyone else did (except Dad Hoy; he dallied with a grass rope onto the nickel horn of his wide-swelled, high-backed Frazier saddle). The steer turned to the right and when he hit the end of the rope, it jerked Buck hard. He didn't go down, the steer got jerked around, and I managed to weather the storm. That was the last time that Buck ever bucked.

Buck was a big, stout horse but agile and athletic. I took him with me when I was in graduate school at Columbia, Missouri. Cathy and I rented a pasture where we kept our horses and ran steers in the summer. I won a team roping with Buck at Queen City and a calf roping at Williamsburg, but the most memorable occasion with him was at a rodeo at Pilot Grove. We had just unloaded and I was riding toward the arena when a camel (part of the rodeo clown's repertoire) suddenly stood up a few yards away. Talk about a spooked horse!

Getting back to the Flying H, in addition to raising an occasional colt, my father enjoyed trading horses, sometimes with neighbors, sometimes with a couple of traders who would come by at irregular intervals. In addition to working with our own cattle, Dad, Rita, and I often helped pasturemen in the Cassoday-Matfield Green area with receiving Texas cattle that arrived on the Santa Fe Railroad in the spring and shipping them in the summer and fall. Some of these ranchers included Karl and Neal Harsh, Raymond Prewitt, Wayne Rogler, Bob Zebold, Bob Vestring, John Berns, and Frank Klasser.

Some of our favorite times as youngsters were riding pastures with Dad. In my earliest memory Dad rode Taffy, a yellow buckskin mare, Rita rode Paint, her hard-to-catch spotted gelding, and I had a dun named Buckskin Joe. We always rode pastures after a rain in order to check for lightning kills, and to help pass the time as we rode, Dad would recite long narrative poems he had

Dad giving Jim a ride, 1940.

Rita on Paint, Jim standing on the ground, c. 1947.

learned in school—"Charlotte, the Frozen Girl," "Sheridan's Ride," or, our favorite, "The Ride of Jenny McNeal." Or we would plead, "Tell us about your dogs," which led to stories of coyote hunting. He and Dad Hoy kept greyhounds, and they hunted horseback, which gave the coyote much more of a sporting chance than hunting with pickup trucks and CB radios—and now with cell phones and GPS.

Our favorite of these stories was about the trip Dad and Dad Hoy had taken to visit Uncle Frank Goodnight, who lived on a ranch near Englewood on the Oklahoma border. It was in the autumn of 1923 and Dad was nineteen years old when Uncle Frank invited them to bring their dogs for a hunt in the sandhill country of Clark County. Dad said that they quickly jumped a coyote, but when they turned their dogs loose they ran only a few yards before sitting down, yelping and whining, and began to bite at the pads of their paws while the Goodnight hounds chased and caught the coyote while Uncle Frank laughed. He knew the shortgrass dogs were toughened to the sandburs, but the tallgrass dogs weren't.

The coyote hunt may have been anticlimactic, but the real gem of the story was the cattle drive. The Theis ranch was sending a crew to Canadian, Texas, to drive fifteen hundred Hereford steers to Clark County to put on wheat pasture. Dad, who was nineteen at the time, had bought a Morgan horse from the son of an Ashland druggist for $7.50, and his cousin Paul Goodnight loaned him a good cow horse. The drive took a little over a week, and the trail boss was an old open-range cowboy named Lon Ford, who well into the twentieth century still carried a pistol on his hip. Just like the old days the cowboys on this drive slept under the stars, sang to the cattle as they rode night herd, and ate around a chuck wagon. Ford had one of the steers butchered at the start, Dad said, and they had son-of-a-gun stew throughout the drive, with Dutch-oven biscuits, fried potatoes, and black coffee for breakfast. In 1923 this may well have been one of the very last Texas-to-Kansas cattle drives.

In the 1960s, after I had left home, Dad began cutting down the size of the cow herd. He had switched the cattle breed to Brahmas and planted the farmland back to grass, feeding protein pellets and baled hay instead of kaffir to the cows in winter.

In the 1970s Cathy and I bought sixty acres of grass that was the inheritance of one of my aunts. This pasture adjoined the Cemetery pasture at the northeastern corner. Around 1990 we bought from a distant cousin two hundred acres that adjoined that pasture to the east. After my parents died, we inherited the home eighty (the Cemetery/Cave pasture) and the two hundred acres across the road west of it, and in 2005 we bought the north quarter section (which my parents called Trail's End, because it was on a dead-end road that

Sign marking the conservation easement on the Flying H Ranch, at the Cassoday exit of the Kansas Turnpike. (Photo by Mark Feiden)

bordered Chase County) that my sister had inherited. We lease part of our grass to a neighbor and take in stocker cattle on the remainder during grazing season.

Across the exit from the Kansas Turnpike at Cassoday is an attractive metal sign commemorating the conservation easement that we placed with Ranchland Trust of Kansas in 2007. All seven hundred acres of our ranch, less about seventeen acres of carve-outs for buildings, will forever remain a ranch, a move strongly supported by our children and their families.

A note on conservation easements: Perpetual conservation easements are an excellent means of preserving both the ecology and the culture of the Flint Hills. Grassland placed in an easement can never be plowed or turned into housing or commercial developments—or disfigured with wind factories. An easement is a voluntary sale or donation to a holding agency of the development rights to that property. Besides Ranchland Trust of Kansas (an arm of the Kansas Livestock Association), other major holders of easements in Kansas are The Nature Conservancy, Kansas Land Trust, Sunflower Land Trust, and programs under the USDA. Under an easement the landowner retains all other rights except development, and the property remains under private ownership and on the tax rolls. Our ranch can be passed down to our children or sold, but the easement stays with it, no matter who owns the land in the future.

Josh on Molly dragging a calf, c. 1992.

Some easements are purchased by the holding agency, some are donated (as was ours), which results in certain tax benefits.

Our daughter, Farrell Hoy Jenab, is director of faculty development at Johnson County Community College and lives in Overland Park. Her two children are Henry, born in 1998, and Lucy, born in 2001. All three love coming to the ranch, riding, and helping with ranch work. Our son, Josh, his wife, Gwen, and their daughter, Josie, born in 2003, own the Flying W Ranch in Chase County, about twenty miles northwest of our ranch. The Flying W is an eight-thousand-acre working cattle ranch that hosts about four hundred cow-calf pairs year round and about 1,100 yearlings during the summer grazing season. It also has a guest-ranch component (flinthillsflyingw.com), offering lodging, horse and wagon rides, cattle drives, and other ranch experiences.

Kenneth and Marshall

My father, Kenneth Hoy, was born at Cassoday, Kansas, on March 16, 1904. His brother Marshall was born exactly three years and two days later. They began their lives about the time the first airplane flew, and they were 65 and 62, respectively, when the Man in the Moon was replaced by a man on the moon. By the time they died (Kenneth at age 92, Marshall at 81), home computers, music from CDs, and stock trailers were commonplace. In their youths ciphering was done longhand, music came from the Cassoday Cowboy Band at community concerts or from the Childers family band at barn dances, and you rode your horse from the barn to the pasture, even if that pasture was twenty to forty miles away.

Kenneth and Marshall were the eldest in a family of five. An early photograph, when they are approximately ten and seven, shows Kenneth seated with Marshall standing beside him, his hand on his older brother's shoulder, both boys dressed up for the portrait in white shirts and neckties. They were close and, although they occasionally would get a little irritated with each other (what brothers don't?), they remained close all their lives. Their wives and children easily distinguished one from the other, but many people, even those who had known them for years, mistook Kenneth for Marshall and vice versa. I remember once walking into the livestock auction at El Dorado one Saturday and one of the regulars there greeting Dad with, "Hello, Marshall. Kenneth just left a few minutes ago." When this sort of mistaken identity happened, as it often did, neither brother bothered to correct the speaker. Kenneth answered as if he were Marshall, and Marshall responded as if he were Kenneth. It was a bit amusing to hear these old cowboys when they were in their seventies and eighties calling each other "Kid," something they had done all their lives. In classic cowboy fashion (going back at least to Owen Wister's seminal novel, *The Virginian*), they each in the later 1930s married schoolteachers.

Cassoday Cowboy Band, c. 1908.

Childers Family Band. From left: Carrie with guitar, Maude with rattles, Joseph (father) with fiddle, Mary Ann (mother), Ivan with mandolin, and Clifford.

Kenneth (seated) and Marshall, 1914.

Kenneth married Marteil (Marty) Rice, and Marshall married Berdine Guggisberg. Each had two children: Jim and Rita for Kenneth and Marty, Judy and Ann for Marshall and Berdine.

I never asked Dad or Uncle Marshall how or why they became cowboys; that they were was just a fact of life, and they came by it naturally as natives of Cassoday, which Bruce Behymer (longtime agricultural broadcaster at KFH Radio in Wichita) always called "The Cow Capital of Kansas." Their father, Frank Hoy, in the open-range days of the late 1880s, worked as what was termed in the Flint Hills in that era a herd boy, loose-herding cattle in the Flint Hills during the summer grazing season, letting them graze up toward Jack Springs in Chase County during the daytime, then heading them back into Butler County at night. Dad Hoy, as did all farmer-stockmen in the area, had horses to ride, to drive, and to work. He rode a wide-forked, high-backed Frazier saddle with a nickel-plated horn. I remember seeing him use a rope only once, to catch a calf in a pasture, and he dallied his grass rope onto the horn when he caught it, this at a time when everyone else tied hard and fast. He also stood a Percheron stud, and later a Mammoth jack, after switching to mules for work animals. Kenneth and Marshall thus had plenty of horses to ride when they were growing up.

At an early age Kenneth and Marshall began breaking horses for neighbors at five dollars a horse. The story Dad told, and Uncle Marshall confirmed, was that when they had broken their first horse Dad Hoy let them buy a pair of boots with the money. Afterward when they got (or Dad Hoy got for them) a new horse to break, whoever rode it first to take the buck out of the horse got to wear the boots and the other brother had to wear regular shoes. Dad Hoy was too frugal to allow them to buy a second pair of boots. Not only that but as they got older and their feet grew larger and the boots grew tighter, they wanted to buy a new pair. Dad Hoy, however, thought that an extravagance since they could still squeeze into the old pair. So the boys decided to

Kenneth on Brutus, c. 1935.

Marshall on Commando, c. 1953.

Marshall saddling, Kenneth earring down, a Sturgeon twin helping with an unbroken horse for its first ride, c. 1935.

stretch the boots by pouring them full of oats and then filling them with water. They stretched, all right. Dad said that next morning every stitch of thread had popped loose. Their father's frugality might explain why, in later life, both brothers favored handmade boots. Kenneth had his made by Blucher, in Olathe, and Marshall by McDowell, in Wichita.

Their method of horse breaking was far different from that used by horse trainers today (as was their recompense; a trainer today typically charges $500 or more to ride a young horse thirty days). At first one brother, on horseback, would hold the new horse, perhaps twisting its ear to make him stand, while the other saddled him. Later on they built a saddling chute in the pole corral south of the barn. Once firmly in the saddle, the brother on the broke horse turned the unbroken one loose and the other brother rode until the horse quit bucking. Then both brothers would ride from the corral out into the nearby pastures. By the time they returned an hour or more later, the new horse was well on its way to being tamed and trained.

As they got older, Kenneth and Marshall started helping some of the big ranchers in the area at shipping time or when cattle arrived in the spring. The

Santa Fe Railroad did not build through Cassoday until 1923; the shipping points before that time were at De Graff in Butler County, Burns in southeastern Marion County, or Bazaar in Chase County. They became top pasture cowboys, often working for Dow Gilbreath of Madison, riding cross country and sometimes camping out overnight in oilfield shacks in order to help ship Dow's cattle out of the Matfield Green stockyards.

Some of the ranchers they helped around Cassoday, Aikman, and Matfield Green were Fred Burk, Karl Harsh, Grover Prewitt, Louis Vestring, John Berns, Holt Green, Mason Crocker, Billy Mercer, and Wayne Rogler. In later years they helped Frank Klasser in western Greenwood County, who shipped out of Cassoday.

The brothers traveled by horseback to compete at area rodeos in Newton, Dexter, Madison, El Dorado, and other towns. El Dorado held an annual professional rodeo for a number of years in the late 1920s and early 1930s, at one of which Marshall was awarded a pair of spurs as the best all-around cowboy. Dad said that he and Marshall would ride from their home to the Countryman ranch a few miles south of Cassoday, where Wilber Countryman would join them in leading their strings of relay horses to El Dorado. Marshall and Wilber often teamed up in the wild cow milking. Because Wilber was a left-handed roper and Marshall right-handed, whether the cow ducked right or left one of them was there to stick a rope on her right out of the chute. A panoramic photograph of the 1930 rodeo contestants taken by V. F. Brown shows twenty-eight dismounted cowboys, two rodeo clowns, and forty-four mounted cowboys and cowgirls, along with rodeo producer Mac McLain. Marshall, Kenneth, and Wilber are all in the photograph.

Both Kenneth and Marshall entered saddle bronc riding, wild cow milking, relay race, and bulldogging events, and Marshall also roped calves. When they rode to those out-of-county rodeos on their matching Mueller high-backed saddles with big swells (eighteen-inch for Kenneth, sixteen-inch for Marshall), they took advantage of their similar appearance to increase their chances of winning in the bulldogging contest. Marshall, who could jump equally well from either side of the steer, would sometimes bulldog both steers. Both brothers had black mustaches, wore black hats, and looked enough alike that they were often mistaken for each other.

Dad Hoy, Kenneth, and Marshall helped in the production of the pasture rodeos held just southwest of Cassoday in the 1930s. The roping, bulldogging, and steer-riding cattle and the bucking horses were all provided by local farmers and ranchers. Dad Hoy had a big buckskin mare that was nearly unrideable because, in addition to being a hard bucker, she would rear up high and

Marshall riding a bronc at the 1934 Newton rodeo.

sometimes fall over backward. Dad said that he drew her at one of these rodeos and had to be talked into getting on her by Marshall, who kept telling him, "You can ride her, Kid." He did, and won the bronc riding that year.

Dad quit rodeoing at age thirty-four when he got married, and Marshall quit the rough-stock events about the same time. For another thirty years, however, Marshall continued to rodeo and was considered one of the top calf ropers in the region, especially when mounted on his good buckskin horse Commando. When he was in his mid-sixties, he was the first calf roper out at a rodeo in Latham, tying his calf in fourteen seconds flat. That time held throughout the day's competition, and he won first place.

Marshall loved to rope, but Wilber Countryman may have loved it even more. One time the two of them were moving some of Wilbur Stone's steers from El Dorado to Rosalia, riding along at the rear of the herd and tossing their ropes at weeds and fence posts. Wilber was itching to cut a steer out of the herd and rope it. "What if the boss comes along?" Marshall asked. Wilber had a ready response: "Why, we'll just tell him we saw a steer that we thought needing roping, but after we got him caught we found out he didn't so now we're turning him loose." Typical cowboy thinking.

Like all young cowboys Kenneth and Marshall would rope anything they could. Velma King, whose family lived on an oil lease near El Dorado when she was a little girl, told me of seeing Kenneth and Marshall driving by their house on the way to work at Wilbur Stone's ranch. "Your dad or your uncle, one, would be sitting on the front fender," she told me, "and as they drove by they'd rope one of my mother's chickens for their dinner." Snitching chickens was apparently a minor misdemeanor in their eyes. Dad said that the ride from Cassoday to the rodeo at Madison involved a couple of nights camping, during which they foraged for chickens and garden crops at farms along the way. Little wonder that the reputation of rodeo cowboys wasn't too high back then.

One of my favorite stories about the youthful exploits of Kenneth and Marshall is about a particular Saturday night in Cassoday spent at Al Gennet's barbershop, which was also a de facto pool hall, pitch and domino parlor, beer joint, and outlet for bootleg whiskey. I suppose some of the fellows there had cars, but most of the crowd, at least the ones my father and uncle hung around with, were there horseback.

They were riding back home one night across pastures under the light of a bright full moon. The Sturgeon twins, or maybe it was the Plummer boys, were riding with them. Whether it was simply high spirits or perhaps a bottle or two of Prohibition beer, they got it into their heads to practice their rodeoing skills. Kenneth roped a steer and the others worked at rigging up a loose rope with which to ride him. Kenneth dismounted to help hold the steer because both the Sturgeons (or the Plummers, whichever it was) were younger and smaller than the Hoy brothers. Somehow in the moonlight and the confusion of an uncooperative steer, Kenneth's riderless horse spooked and jumped, dragging the steer across the grass. Like nearly everyone else in the Central Plains during that time period (in fact, from the 1860s to the 1960s), he was tied on hard and fast. The steer got jerked down, which further spooked the horse, and he took off, dragging the steer across the prairie. The other three gathered up their horses as quickly as they could and finally stopped the runaway. They figured the steer was dead, but after a little while he managed to catch his breath, find his feet, and stagger off.

The boys split up and headed for their respective homes, their high spirits well dampened. About a week later Dad Hoy and his sons were in town when they ran into the neighbor whose steer had been roped and dragged. In the ensuing conversation the neighbor remarked, "Frank, the damnedest thing happened. Lightning hit one of my steers the other night and burned the hair clear off of one side. Made him a little stiff, but it didn't kill him." Neither Kenneth nor Marshall breathed a word.

The first horse of Dad's that I remember was a yellow buckskin mare with black mane and tail that he called Taffy, but he used to talk about two of his earlier horses, Brutus and Cap. The latter, he said, was the only one he ever had that was a foolproof ground-tying horse; before he would move, he would starve to death with a bale of hay ten feet away, Dad said. Dad's best cow horse, in my memory, was a reddish-gray mare he called Rusty. I remember once in the Davidson pasture when she was still green broke, Dad was riding her with a piece bit in her mouth (he didn't call it a snaffle), and a headstall without a nose band. Something spooked her, she jumped and ran, and the bit broke, which left him holding reins that were essentially attached to nothing but air. I don't remember how Dad got her stopped, or if she just ran herself out, but he always rode a bridle with a throat latch and a nose band after that. And a solid-bar grazer bit.

Marshall stood a stallion and raised good-quality registered Quarter Horses, whereas Kenneth (who also raised an occasional colt out of one or another neighbor's studs) got a lot of pleasure from trading horses. Both brothers were good judges of horses and also good at matching them with young riders, a trait they put to good use when acquiring horses for their grandchildren. For example, when our daughter, Farrell, and son, Josh, were in early grade school, Dad bought them a half-Welsh pony named Rebel. Rebel was big enough (and tough enough and ornery enough) for me or Dad to ride, but better suited to a kid. If Rebel got irritated, he would sometimes nip, a trait Josh and Farrell could readily attest to, but he knew when to control the urge. Once when Dad was saddling him, Rebel whirled his head around, teeth bared, as he felt the cinch jerk tight, but when he saw who was doing the jerking, he just as quickly whirled his head back to the front and glared. He was as smart as he was ornery, and he knew better than to mess with Dad.

The girl who had owned Rebel before Dad found him didn't like giving other kids rides with her, so she had taught the horse to buck if she put her hand behind the saddle and placed it on his back. One of Josh's favorite things to do was to make him buck, so every once in a while he would reach around and put his hand on Rebel's back just to spice up the ride.

Another horse Dad got for our kids was a full-sized cream-colored buckskin called Creampuff. He was as easygoing as Rebel was lively. We kept both kid horses in a corral each night, and every morning when Farrell and Josh would go down to let them out, they would stand on the gate and jump onto Creampuff's back as he came out, Rebel following. Farrell was usually in front, Josh behind, and without saddle or bridle he would walk up to the house and they would slide off.

Dad usually kept a little trading stock around, a horse or two he would pick up at a good price, take the buck out of (if they had any in them), then he would ride them until he could sell them at a profit. Or trade them for another horse, usually getting a little boot in the deal. Two of the last horses Dad

Josh making Rebel buck, c. 1981.

picked up, when he was in his mid-seventies, were a bay he called Kenny and a sorrel named Andy. He sold Kenny after a year or so, but he kept Andy, who was a little on the jumpy side, but a good pasture horse.

Both Kenneth and Marshall kept a mid-sized cow herd, as well as looked after pasture cattle that belonged to other people. They were excellent pasture cowboys who always knew how to be in the right place at the right time to handle cattle as calmly as possible. They each had excellent riding and roping skills, but they would cowboy in such a way as to only have to run a steer or get their rope down on rare occasions. And when working cattle in a pen, they never turned their horse's rump to a cow.

Their cowboy reputations extended well beyond the Cassoday area. In those days before pickups with stock racks (and well before stock trailers), cowboys had to ride to the pasture being shipped, arriving while it was still dark. They would then round up the big Texas steers and hold them in a corner while the Kansas pastureman, the Kansas City livestock commission man, or a representative of the Texas owner would cut out a few railroad-stock-car loads of the fattest steers, then count the rest back into the pasture. A good cutter on a good horse would bring just the steer he wanted, but sometimes he couldn't separate the one he wanted and he'd bring two or three, telling the herd-holders, "Turn back the brindle," or "Just the one in the middle." A

Kenneth doctoring a calf Marshall is holding, with Marty looking on, c. 1938.

little of this was okay, but too much and the brothers had a sure cure: they'd just turn them all back to the herd. After a few times of this, the cutter got the message and would bring just the one he wanted.

Back in 1938 Kenneth and Marshall had an adventure at the Santa Fe stockyards in Cassoday that, along with a photograph my mother took, has lived on in family lore. I have heard the story from both brothers, but Uncle Marshall could spin a better tale, so here is his version:

> The Teters were bringing in a bunch of cattle from out east of town, Greenwood County, and this one old renegade gave them a lot of trouble, a big old Brahma steer with untipped horns. He must have been a four- or five-year-old. They choused him around and finally got him across the tracks, but they couldn't get him into the pens. Your dad and I were hanging around the yards, and when that steer jumped the fence into the Oliver pasture and headed north, old Jim Teter asked us if we thought we could get him in. Heck, we thought we could do anything. So we had someone call home and

tell Dad to get in the truck* and drive up Highway 13 while we headed after the steer. By the time we got within sight of him, he was already across the county line, three or four miles north in the East Frew pasture, but he had slowed down and was heading down into a little canyon. So I told Kenneth to come in behind him after I loped around to the far side so I could rope him when he came out. He ran with his head up, so it wasn't very hard to catch those high horns. Kenneth roped his heels and we tied him up. By that time Dad was there with the truck, but there wasn't any good place to load him, so we had to drag him a hundred or so yards to the nearest ditch. Dragging him on the grass like that burned the hair off his shoulder just like a brand.

When we got back to the yards, somebody asked us how we were going to get him turned loose—he was fighting mad. Dad drove into the big pen on the northwest and Kenneth tied the rope on the steer's horns to a post and hollered at Dad, and he drove out from under him. While that steer was still bouncing with all the wind knocked out of him, we jerked the ropes off his horns and feet, then jumped up on the fence—along with everybody else. Old Jim Teter started yelling about how rough we were treating his steer, but I just told him: "What the hell are you complaining about? Your cowboys couldn't even get him in the yards."

Along about 1978, in addition to running their own cows and looking after others, Kenneth and Marshall were asked by the Flint Hills Overland Wagon Train to go along on the wagon rides as outriders, supposedly to open gates, but really because they were genuine Flint Hills cowboys who added a lot of color to the expeditions. The Flint Hills Overland, for some quarter of a century, went out into the hills on overnight camping excursions that gave tourists a taste of pioneer travel. I particularly remember one night on Glen Kirk's ranch west of Eureka when Marshall's grandson Rick, my son Josh, and I had gone along. We were in our bedrolls beside Marshall's stock trailer, and Dad and Uncle Marshall were telling stories.

Sometime around 1:00 a.m. (an insomnia that did nothing to keep them in bed after 5:00 the next morning) their talk moved from the corncob fights in the barn on the neighboring Schuler farm to a big rat killing on their own place. The rats had made a network of burrows under one of the dirt-floored sheds, so Kenneth and Marshall got the Schuler boys to come over, and they took some pitchforks and clubs and started digging up burrows and killing rats.

*The truck Marshall referred to was actually an old Model T Ford touring car that Dad Hoy had bought new in 1915. The rear seat had been replaced by a wooden platform. That car sat under an elm tree just north of the granary at our house, and my sister and I would often sit in it and play like we were driving.

Jim Teter's outlaw steer in the Santa Fe stockyards at Cassoday, 1938.

About three hundred of them, or so they recalled some six decades after the fray. The hero of the day was a terrier dog that would grab a rat, shake it dead, then grab another and shake it, all so fast that the dog literally collapsed from heat exhaustion. So the boys threw water on him and the dog jumped up and went right back to killing rats as fast as he could.

There was a pause in the storytelling on this cool July night, then Kenneth asked, "Was that our dog or was it Schulers'?"

"I don't remember," Marshall replied, "but it was our rats." Laughter broke out from the other side of the trailer where some eavesdropping campers had just been repaid for being kept awake by the storytelling old cowboys on our side.

As recounted in the previous essay, when he died in 1996 Kenneth may have been the last cowboy alive who had driven cattle overland from Texas to Kansas when, in the fall of 1923, he helped trail fifteen hundred steers from Canadian, Texas, to Englewood, Kansas.

Kenneth remained at Cassoday his entire life, spending most of it on the farm his grandparents had settled on in 1877. He raised Hereford cattle, later switching to black baldies. His last herd was of Brahma cows, raised up from roping calves he bought from a roping club in the area. In 1946 Marshall moved from Cassoday to Towanda to become foreman of Harry Wilson's Quarter Horse ranch. Five years later he moved to Hopkins Switch, northwest of El Dorado, to become a pastureman on Don Wilson's ranch. He also bought some land of his own and ran his own Angus cow herd as well as continuing as a pastureman. In 1985, at age eighty-one, Kenneth lost his right arm to an Allis-Chalmers Roto Baler. Until he fell and broke a hip five years later, however, he continued to ride and, with the good help of Marty, to look after his cows. He traded for a little blue mare he called Misty, bought a lightweight saddle, and took off the back cinch. He could literally saddle that little mare with one arm and be mounted before I had my own horse saddled. His last horse was a registered gray Quarter Horse he called Fibber.

Marshall died in 1988 at age eighty-one and is buried beside his wife in the Cassoday cemetery. Kenneth died in 1996 at age ninety-two and is also buried beside his wife in the same cemetery. All four graves lie together in a row in the cemetery that Mary Ann Hoy, Kenneth and Marshall's grandmother, had given to the community back in the 1880s, a fitting resting place for these two Flint Hills cowboys.

In 2013 Kenneth and Marshall were inducted posthumously into the Kansas Cowboy Hall of Fame in the Working Cowboy category.

Grandma Breidenstein and Grandma Hoy

In 1998, anticipating the birth of our first grandchild, Cathy and I dusted off one of the family heirlooms in our house, Great-grandma Breidenstein's rocking chair. Although its design is somewhat unusual and it was brought over from Germany in the nineteenth century, I really doubt it would command much of a price at an antique store nor be worth dragging to a taping of *Antiques Roadshow*. But it is solid and reasonably comfortable for a wooden chair. She may even have rocked me in it, although I was only seven months old when she died. But it is a nice link to the past.

We have the memorial album from Grandma Breidenstein's funeral that my mother passed down to me. This book is in itself a noteworthy artifact, documenting as it does Kansas funeral customs of over eighty years ago. Embossed with the name "Breidenstein" on the cover, a replica of Italian hand-tooled leather, the album was prepared by the Arnold-Kirby Funeral Home of El Dorado. Inside, the biographical information of birth date and place, death date and place, and time and place of the funeral service is all inscribed in a beautiful calligraphy of black ink.

There we learn that Katherina Breidenstein was born on March 7, 1852, in Lauterback, Germany, and that she "entered into rest" at 12:20 p.m., July 31, 1940, in her home in Cassoday at age eighty-eight. E. E. Elliott, minister of the Methodist churches at Cassoday and Rosalia, conducted the service, which was also at her home, on August 4 at nine in the morning. Among the six pallbearers were my father and his brother, Kenneth and Marshall. Harry Cameron and Nina Harader sang three hymns, including "The Old Rugged Cross," and three young women in the community were flower bearers.

Some fifty-odd names are recorded as having come to the home to express sympathy, most of them from Cassoday and surrounding towns, but some from as far away as Saint Louis and Washington, Missouri; Lawton, Oklahoma; and Santa Monica, California. Grandma Breidenstein was one of the old-time pioneers in Butler County, and from the looks of a couple of the shaky signatures in the guest book, not many of her generation survived her. It stirred my memory to see the elaborate swirls and flourishes of my great-uncle Leo Westerhaus's signature in the album; even as a child I was always struck that the work-toughened hands of this old railroad section foreman could write so beautifully. Asters and gladiolas predominated among the flowers, along with carnations.

One section of the album is reserved for press clippings, and here are included death notices and obituaries from four newspapers, including the *Kansas City Times*. Also included is a poem, "I Shall Remember," by Jane Sayer. This little four-stanza tribute to the poet's mother has been altered, probably by Aunt Lilly (Grandma Breidenstein's maiden daughter who cared for her in her final years), to fit her own mother; in the line that reads "Mother wore a white shawl in a rocking chair," the word "white" has been marked out and "blue" penciled in.

In a separate envelope stuck in the back cover of the album is another clipping from a newspaper two years earlier telling of the reporter's visit to the house on the occasion when Aunt Lilly had fallen and broken her leg. "It would require skill to tell the fascinating events of Grandmother Breidenstein's 86 years," the reporter said, as she described Grandma reading good books while sitting "in the same low chair in which she rocked her babies." The same chair in which we rocked her great-great-great-grandson, Henry. And also his sister Lucy and their cousin Josie.

I don't really remember Grandma Breidenstein, but like many childhood memories, photographs and oft-repeated stories have supplanted, and become even more real than, actual experience. I sure don't remember Grandpa Breidenstein—he died in 1905 when my father was only one year old. He was seventy-seven at the time of his death, his widow fifty-three. They had been married thirty-four years.

August Breidenstein was a native of Neidershed, Germany, where he had been a smelter. Like many land-hungry immigrants, he came to America to farm and was living in central Illinois when he met Katherina Fiedler, one of four daughters born to Katherine Stilgerbauer and Henry Fiedler in Lauterback, Germany. (In our library sits a black wooden trunk with "Maria Fiedler," one of the daughters, and "Bremen—New York" stenciled on the front.) The family arrived in New York in the spring of 1869 and immediately went to Illinois. August and Katherina were married on New Year's Day 1876 at Beardstown, where they farmed before moving to Kansas in 1886. Like many later settlers on the plains, they arrived not in a covered wagon but by train, shipping out their household goods, farm implements, horses, mules, chickens, and even a dog in a boxcar. They also brought five children, leaving their older son and eldest daughter in Illinois.

I wish that their original Kansas homestead was still in the family because Grandpa Breidenstein's first farm was a few miles southeast of Rosalia, near the Dunne ranch, in one of the prettiest areas of the Flint Hills. But like many settlers at that time, he was a farmer, not a rancher, and was more interested in buying good crop land than in tallgrass prairie. I remember Aunt Lilly telling how the land agent reacted when her father asked what those white things were on the hillside of the far side of the tract. "Why that son-of-a-bitch," he ranted, "I told that man to get those sheep off of there!" August went ahead and bought the land, but the "sheep" were there the next day, and in fact they are there still—big chunks of Flint Hills limestone.

During their first week on the place, in late March, another new settler decided to burn off the old bluestem so he could build a house, but he hadn't had experience with the forty-mile-per-hour winds that give prairie fires a life of their own here in the Hills. Only the help of neighbors who had been there longer saved the Breidensteins and half a dozen other new arrivals.

Because there were no trees on their place, Grandma planted castor beans to give her children shade for playing. She also planted a garden of flowers that was admired by all her neighbors. Her love of flowers carried over into the names of her five daughters: Rosa (rose, the one who stayed in Illinois), Lillian (lily), Glory (morning glory, my grandmother), Daisy, and Ivah (ivy).

August's first crops looked good, until the last of June when a hailstorm cut everything to pieces. The sorghum sprouted again, however, and appeared to be heading for a good crop of molasses, but then some free-ranging hogs got into the field and stripped it bare. They ate so much, as it turned out, that they all died. Then the coyotes ate all the chickens and turkeys, and Aunt Ivah led all the children into the "summer complaint" of chills and fever. Grandma nursed them all back to health, but three years later son Suel died in Illinois, as did son Charles in Kansas a few months after that.

This was about the time that the family moved to a farm along the Walnut River southwest of Cassoday, where Glory was courted by and wed to Frank Hoy, my grandfather. Grandma Breidenstein lived the rest of her life at Cassoday. When she died, she was buried alongside her husband in the cemetery given to the community by my other great-grandmother, Mary Ann Hoy.

For many years we also had Grandma Hoy's wooden rocking chair, a more prosaic piece of workmanship. It had been painted a number of times before

The Breidenstein sisters: Lillian, Glory, Ivah (with doll), Daisy, and Rosetta.

we stripped it to its natural color. One of the round slats (can a slat be round?) on the back is not original, but it is old. I remember my father telling me how his father went to the timber and cut a slender, straight (well, nearly straight) hickory branch to replace the piece that had been broken.

Grandma Hoy was born Mary Ann Davison in Perry County, Ohio, on December 20, 1844, in the same area as my great-grandfather, William Hoy (1841–1912), who was three years older. They married in the fall of 1869 and lived in Ohio until they moved to Butler County, Kansas, in 1877, where they bought eighty acres split by the Walnut River one mile west of present-day Cassoday. It is also the same distance northeast of Sycamore Springs, the original settlement in the area and a landmark and stopping place for travelers ranging from American Indians to settlers and traders on what is known locally as the Old California Trail. Three distinct traces of Indian trails, made by the dragging of travois, are still visible on the home place, one in the pasture just north of the house and two in the pasture south of the Walnut.

Grandma Hoy was apparently a hospitable woman, and, according to family lore, she was also a forthright one. It is said that no traveler was ever turned away hungry from her door, and if they needed a place to sleep, they could bunk in the rock stable near the house. At least two families lived in that stable until they were able to find a place of their own. She was also a midwife, reputed to be good at forecasting a baby's time to be born. If neighbors saw

Grandma Breidenstein, 1939.

her purposefully driving her buggy in the direction of some pregnant woman's house, they knew that a new birth was imminent.

In 1882 a pioneer family, camping for the night on the Hoy farm, lost a small child to disease. Grandma offered them a burial site, but when the grieving mother expressed concern that the grave would soon be lost in a sea of grass, Grandma assured her that she would fence off that corner of the pasture. She then gave two acres at the site for a cemetery and for the building of Sycamore Springs Methodist Church, stipulating only that no charge be made for burial plots. In 1906 the church was moved to its present location in Cassoday, while in the 1990s Cathy and I gave two more acres to be added to the cemetery. The Cassoday cemetery lies along County Road 150 (also known as First Street Road, a forty-mile straight line into Newton) at the southwestern corner of the home place.

Mary Ann Hoy died on August 20, 1940, at age ninety-six and is buried beside her husband in the lasting gift she gave to her community.

CATTLE

Changes in Flint Hills Ranching

Especially around shipping time I often get to thinking about the differences between the cattle that used to come into and go out of the Flint Hills by rail and those of today that arrive and leave on trucks. There are several differences, both in the cattle themselves as well as in the way they handle.

Back in the Railroad Era of Flint Hills history most all the summer cattle were steers from Texas at least two years old, many older. Black Angus were making inroads against the then dominant Herefords in local cow herds in the mid-1950s, while the first Charolaise I remember came in around 1960, maybe a little before. Most of the steers we saw around Cassoday when I was a kid came from South Texas and were straight Brahma (technically Brahman, but generally pronounced brahmie) or Brahma-crosses, a mix of whiteface and/or Shorthorn with the humped and droop-eared kine of India.

Along about 1970, roughly when railroads quit hauling cattle not only to and from the Flint Hills but throughout the West, yearlings were replacing the older steers on summer grass. At about the same time heifers became more common in Flint Hills pastures, which is logical when you stop to think about it. By the time a heifer is a two-year-old, she's either hamburger or having her first calf, so naturally most of the two- and three-year-old cattle in that earlier era would have been steers.

Another major change in cattle was the influx of "exotics," of cattle from many other parts of the world (although mostly from Europe). I remember the good old days when dairy breeds outnumbered beef breeds two to one. Dairy farmers had half a dozen breeds to choose from (Ayrshire, Brown Swiss, Guernsey, Holstein, Jersey, Milking Shorthorn), while Flint Hills cattle ranchers were generally content with Hereford, Angus, and Shorthorn. Although early-day livestock journals sometimes mentioned Brahman, as well as Devon, Galloway, and British White Park cattle, and even less occasionally ran a photograph of an

Black Angus cows and calves on a Flint Hills pasture. (Photo by Mark Feiden)

old Texas longhorn as a reminder of the bad old days when cattle were bony and tough, it was the three British breeds that predominated in the Flint Hills from the Open Range Era to almost the end of the Railroad Era.

The invasion of the exotics began with the importation of Charolaise in the later 1950s, although American ranchers had been doing some experimenting along the way with Brahma crosses, resulting in Brangus, Braford, Santa Gertrudis, and Beefmaster. Just as the pendulum had swung from the lanky longhorn to the squatty baby beef of the 1950s, so it began to swing back again to a stretchier animal with less body fat and more muscle. As hybrid vigor, a bigger frame, and leaner beef became more desirable in commercial herds, the search continued for the best exotic bulls to cross with the three British breeds or black baldies (a Hereford/Angus cross).

By the 1970s the floodgates had opened wide. By this time ranchers were even thinking of Charolaise as nearly an old-line domestic breed as the new waves of exotics came pouring in: Chianinas, Belgian Blues, Fleckviehs, Gelbviehs, Salers, Limousines, Simmentals, Blonde d'Aquitane, Murray Greys, Maine-Anjous, Wagus, Watusis, and on and on. Many new Brahma crosses were being experimented with: Simbrah, Gelbrah, Braunbrah, Brahmousin, Charbray. At about the same time the Texas longhorn was brought back, touted as the "domestic exotic" that produced lean, low-cholesterol beef (as well as easy calving). In the early 2000s bison were being commercially

A longhorn and a Shorthorn cow on the Flying W Ranch. (Photo by Mark Feiden)

marketed, also for lean, low-cholesterol meat. A bison-cattle cross (Beefalo or Cattalo), which had been around since the later nineteenth century, was revived. In all, there are over 250 recognized breeds of cattle worldwide.

Where will it all end? It probably won't. As long as there are cattlemen the search for the perfect beef animal will continue, and that search will never end because there is no one cow that is best for every geographical, climatic, and economic situation.

Along with yearlings of many different breeds (and myriad crosses thereof) came a new way of transporting cattle. Not only had the railroads willingly ceded cattle hauling to trucks, but along the way in the 1960s someone, somewhere invented the triple-decker trailer to pull behind a semitruck. Initially we called this trailer a "possum-belly" or "potbelly" trailer because of the lower deck. The latter name stuck, and today you'll hear cattlemen refer simply to "pots."

Instead of forty-five head of aged Texas steers on a railroad stock car, a truck could haul seventy-five to eighty yearlings. And instead of giving each larger, older steer five acres of grass for a six-month season (mid-April to mid-October), each yearling got about half that. Then, following some experiments at Kansas State University and elsewhere, many Flint Hills ranchers began to double-stock yearlings. (Double-stocking is also referred to as intensive early-season grazing.) In other words, in the spring they would put twice as many cattle in a pasture as normal but would leave them in for only half as long. Thus the cattle would be in the pasture from late April until the end of July or early August, a time when the grass is at its most nutritious, the normal rainfall is higher, and the grass grows fastest. When in late July the grass starts putting its energy from the sun into the roots instead of the leaves, the cattle are gone. With a late summer rain or two, the grass will grow and be ready to burn the next spring.

Back in the Railroad Era, if a rancher had a 2,500-acre pasture to fill, he would receive five hundred two-year-old steers all in one shipment of a dozen stock cars. Those cattle would then be driven horseback maybe as far as twelve or fifteen miles to their summer home, and as soon as they were in the pasture, their heads would drop to the grass. After three months of eating that protein- and calcium-rich bluestem, shipping would start in mid-July, but only the fattest steers would be taken, say, four carloads at twenty-five head per car, leaving four hundred steers in the pasture. The sign that steers were fat enough for market were knobs of fat bulging out on either side at the tops of their tails, as big as softballs, sometimes almost as big as volleyballs. Then a few weeks later another draft of the fattest would be cut out and driven to the stockyards, that process being repeated until by mid-October the pasture would be cleared. Thus over the next three months those steers, which had already probably been gathered a few times in Texas before coming to Kansas, would have been rounded up several more times in Kansas.

According to Jack Hurlburt (a cowboy, veterinarian, and poet), who worked on ranches in many western states, the Flint Hills had the best ranch cutting horses in the West. In Texas or Montana or Arizona or any of the other big ranching states, cutting horses got used during the annual roundup and just a few other times during the year, but in the Flint Hills cutting horses got used maybe three or four times a week during the three months of shipping season. They were well practiced.

Today that same 2,500-acre pasture would hold around 750 to 800 yearlings for a full season, a thousand or more if double-stocked. (Many ranchers determine how many cattle they pasture by weight, so numbers vary.) Instead of being driven to the pasture from the railroad, they would be hauled directly by truck to it and dumped out, with most of them immediately hightailing it for the far side. After three months every head of double-stocked yearlings would leave by truck on the same day rather than being parceled out a few loads at a time over the last three months of the six-month season. Moreover, the trucks would come back to the pasture to get them so that rarely would the yearlings have to be driven more than a few miles to get to a set of pens. Or portable pens might be set up in the pasture where they had spent the summer. Thus at a minimum they might have been gathered only twice in their short lives: once when they were brought in with their mothers to be weaned (and maybe wintered in a backgrounding pen) and once when they are to be loaded onto the trucks to go from summer grass to a feed yard.

Shipping by truck or by train was different for cowboys as well as for cattle. Back in the railroad days we would get up at 3:00 or 4:00 in the morning (depending on how far we had to go to help ship), do our chores (i.e., milk three or four cows, separate the cream, feed the bucket calves, catch the horses, saddle them, and load them onto the truck), get to the pasture while it was still dark, find a ditch to back into to unload the horses, then push the cattle to a corner of the pasture, hold the herd while the fattest steers were being cut out, drive them into the Santa Fe stockyards, weigh them, put them in holding pens, go down to Opal's Café to eat dinner, and then, when the train arrived, lope back to the yards and load the steers. Then while Dad rode back with the rancher to get our truck, my sister and I would lead Dad's horse as we rode back home, bringing in the milk cows on the way, and do the chores. We'd usually finish up by early evening. Next shipping day, same routine.

With trucks we get up about the same time, but the only chore is to catch and saddle horses and load them into a trailer. Milk cows and bucket calves, while maybe not completely a thing of the past, are rare. We're still at the pasture when it's dark, but instead of pushing the cattle into a corner, we push them into a set of pens in the pasture, or a neighboring one, often by 7:00 or 7:30. A cell phone call to the trucks, which have been waiting out of sight, and they soon arrive. We count cattle off into drafts for loading into the four compartments of a potbelly trailer (half a dozen to the front, two dozen to both the upper and lower levels, half a dozen to the rear is a typical load), send the trucks on their way, and we're home by noon, sometimes before or a little after.

Of the various changes from the Railroad to the Trucking Eras, the switch from aged steers to yearlings is probably the most interesting. As I said, those older steers came mostly from Texas, where they had usually been rounded up a few times during their lives, traveled together on trains to Kansas, spent the summer together in the same pasture, then rounded up again several times during shipping season. No wonder they had a strong herd instinct.

A significant change that occurred when trucks replaced trains was the pencil shrink. "Shrink" is the term stockmen use for the loss of weight in cattle that occurs from urination and defecation. Back when steers were walked several miles from the pasture to the stockyards, they would have been urinating and defecating all the way to the scales. Thus there was no need for a pencil shrink because the weight they carried by the time they got there was pretty much all meat and bone. Today, however, when cattle are loaded onto trucks right in the pasture, that natural elimination of weight is lost, so buyers usually demand a 2 percent pencil shrink. That is, if a steer weighs 500 pounds, the buyer will pay on 490. I remember that Wayne Rogler hated to have to drive cattle down the highway to the Cassoday yards because he thought that made them eliminate more than driving through pastures. Of course, the wet spots and cow piles that readily show up on pavement are hidden by grass, so the weight loss would have been the same whether that elimination occurred on asphalt or bluestem.

The yearling steers and heifers found in today's summer pastures come from all over the place. Many are still trucked up from Texas, some come from Mexico (both Old and New), some from Oklahoma or Colorado or other parts of Kansas, but many are cattle raised east of here—Missouri, Iowa, Mississippi, Kentucky, even rarely places like Florida. These eastern cattle, especially, were seldom raised together. Instead a cattle buyer puts together a herd from several different livestock auctions. Thus often these young cattle have spent only a few days, a few weeks at most, with their pasture-mates before they are turned out into a Flint Hills pasture to be together for three months in the summer, where they will be rounded up only once, when the season is over. They don't know how to act like a herd.

Working with yearlings that, because of age and different geographic backgrounds, haven't acquired a fully developed herd instinct is like having a job supervising a bunch of rambunctious, rebellious, and/or sullen teenagers. Working with those older Texas steers that were all raised on the same ranch, on the other hand, was like supervising a group of young adults, lively but responsible.

Add to this mix the influx of exotics over the past few decades, and it's little wonder that yearling cattle can be more difficult to work with. Consider that most of the exotics are European breeds, cattle that for centuries had been developed on small farms in small numbers and carefully tended, almost like members of the family. Each night they were kept in a barn and each day taken out to graze. In many cases the cattle even shared a dwelling (animals below, people above) with the humans. Several years ago Cathy and I stayed at a bed-and-breakfast on a cattle farm on the Isle of Hoy in the Orkneys, just north of the Scottish mainland. The four dozen or so cows there were fat and tame. Our host walked out among them, placed his arm around this cow or that, and called her by name. He didn't keep them in the house, but he did put them in a shed each evening.

I recently learned that there are federal laws in Germany that cattle being hauled by truck have to be unloaded and fed and watered something like every five hours. Here, back in the Railroad Era, cattle had to be unloaded for rest and feed only every thirty-six hours, while today a truck loaded with yearlings in South Texas could be unloaded in a Flint Hills pasture in fifteen or twenty hours with no stops along the way.

Introduce these pampered breeds from Europe to the ranching West in large numbers where they have to fend for themselves, whereas the cattle breeds (both English and Spanish) already here since colonial days had for generations wandered the range scrounging for food and fighting off predators, and it's no wonder that the exotics are more difficult to handle; their DNA hasn't had enough time to adjust. It's like turning a bunch of carefully monitored and chaperoned teenagers loose with no supervision in Fort Lauderdale on spring break.

In my admittedly limited experience, Limousines have been the most difficult cattle to handle. The ones I have worked with were flighty, wouldn't herd up, and either ran at the sight of a horse or challenged you and tried to run past you. At a talk I gave recently, where I lamented the difference between those older Texas steers and today's "rebellious teenager" yearlings, a man from Germany came up afterward and said, "You know why Limousines are so difficult to work with, don't you?" "Why?" I asked. "Because they are French."

Cultural prejudices aside, what is the remedy for cattle that do not have a fully developed herding instinct? My great-uncle, Frank Goodnight, used to say with only a little exaggeration that it took one cowboy to drive one steer, two to drive two steers, three to drive three steers, but four cowboys could drive a thousand. That's because once you reach a critical mass of bovines, they tend to stick together and follow a leader, whereas two or three are more likely to wring their tails, throw their heads up, and take off in separate directions. The late Andy Olson told me (as recounted in *Flint Hills Cowboys*) about late one afternoon driving a bunch of thin, weak steers from the railroad stockyards at Dwight or White City to a pasture south of town. Many of those thin and weak steers played out and were dropped off along the way. It was dark when they got to the pasture, but the next morning the cattle left behind on the road had followed the rest of their herd and were in the pasture.

One spring Josh received several hundred Limousine heifers from Texas to pasture. He had brought a portable chute for unloading, but many of the heifers leaped out, barely touching the chute. (One trucker opined that if the heifers knew they weren't getting off in Texas, they wouldn't be so eager to leave the truck. Little did he know how much they would love Flint Hills grass!) I don't think they'd ever seen a horse. Every time you rode into the pasture, they'd start running, even from half a mile away, and they'd still be running when you left. Josh was naturally worried about how he was going to get them penned for loading at the end of the season without a lot of trouble. So he decided to "break" (i.e., train) them.

A few days later Cathy and I joined Josh and Gwen and pushed the ones that had not started running at the sight of us after the wilder ones. We headed them for a corner, and they split around us in every direction. We didn't fight them, we just got behind the tail end and pushed them after the runaway leaders. We tried putting them in a corner, but they broke and ran. After a couple of hours and several more times around the thousand-acre pasture, even the wildest ones were worn down enough that when they got to a corner they paused long enough for us to push the slower cattle into them and mill them around. Then we backed off and rode away, leaving the herd alone in the corner to come out at their own volition.

At shipping time they were still full of life, but the leaders didn't try to break away. Those heifers came together, walked out the gate and down the road, and went into the loading pens without a hitch.

Then there were some Florida heifers Josh and I were helping with in the early 1990s. They weren't wild and didn't try to run, and we had no trouble gathering them into a herd, but when we got to the gate, they just stood there and wouldn't go out. The rancher we were helping tried to push just a few through the gate so the others would follow, but still the rest just stood inside and watched. We finally got them onto the road, but I bet it took fifteen or twenty minutes to do it. Many of those heifers, by the way, had bob tails and/or ears, probably from getting them frozen when they went through a Kansas winter, but Josh maintained that alligators had bitten them off.

Wild Cattle and Outlaw Steers

In the later 1980s a friend was telling me about helping ship wild cattle from a pasture in southern Chase County. He said that a dozen cowhands (both men and women) had worn out two or three times that many horses, not just trying to get these cattle into a set of shipping pens, but literally trying to get them out of the pasture where they had been summered. Coincidentally, a couple of weeks later I was talking to another friend who was regaling me with stories of trying to ship a pasture full of wild cattle. I thought at first that he had been in on the Chase County roundup, but this pasture, he said, was east of Cassoday in northeast Butler County. It was part of the Vestring ranch and had been filled with cattle from South Texas.

In 1990 I was talking with Bob Vestring and he told me about that roundup. The cattle, he said, were from the Jones ranch near Falfurrias, a ranch that apparently has developed a reputation for unruly cattle, even in Texas. These steers, which would run at the sight of a horse, had been rounded up in Texas by helicopter. In their summer pasture in the Flint Hills they didn't see many horses, either, and would run if they saw even a pickup driving into the pasture. So when September came and it was time to ship, Bob assembled a crew of hands who were well mounted and knew how to handle cattle. I forgot to ask just who all was helping, but one man he did mention was Bud McLinden, who had probably looked at as many cattle from the back of a horse as anyone active in the Flint Hills in his day.

There were something like four hundred head of these steers, but after a full day the crew had managed to get only about a third of them into the pens some half a dozen miles away. Most cattle are gregarious and will "bunch up," that is, come together and stay together when they are moved. But these steers, Bob said, went off in every direction as soon as they saw the horses. If you got close to them, they would charge your horse. Or they would throw their heads up, put a nine in their tail, and run to the far end of the pasture—and then keep on running. They jumped fences like steeplechasers. The running didn't bother the Brahmas among them, but a couple of whitefaces died from heat stress. One cowboy was injured and a horse permanently lamed.

A couple of days later after another try (they got about sixty head this time), Bob called Joe Payne of Webb City, Oklahoma, and asked him to bring his cow dogs. Payne's dogs had been used on outlaw cattle from Florida to New Mexico, and he guaranteed success. But the Jones ranch steers scattered just as much for the dogs as they did for the cowboys—two hundred steers running two hundred different directions, six of them with dogs dangling from their tails or their muzzles.

After that it was back to the cowboys, some on horses, some in pickups, some on three-wheelers. It took three weeks to get the last steer caught and shipped. The final thirty or forty were roped and dragged into stock trailers one at a time—some of them miles from the pasture where they had spent the summer.

I couldn't help but wonder how the old-time drovers would have handled a bunch of cattle like this. Probably no better than their modern counterparts, but at least the old longhorns ran together when they stampeded, not scattering off in every direction. Moreover, longhorns were used to the sight of a horse—and hadn't been chased out of Texas by helicopters.

Back in August of 2003 I had a little fun helping catch the last dozen steers out of the Schoolhouse, a rough Chase County pasture that had been shipped a couple of weeks earlier. The cattle, which had come out of Alabama, had never seen a horse until they got to Kansas, but they sure knew trees and how to use them to elude pursuit, nor did it take them long to learn how to navigate the rocky slopes of the Flint Hills. The Schoolhouse pasture is probably a section in size, but it has some extensions and uneven borders because of a creek on the east side and the ruins of some stone walls and buildings on the west. Three draws run through it, two the full width of the pasture and one through the southeast corner. Every stream is thick with trees, and in many places the slopes running down to the draw are too steep and rocky for a horse to climb safely. The southwest corner is brush-covered, much of it in thick blackberry brambles. In other words, this pasture is tailor-made for cattle that don't want to be penned up.

Shawn Rogers, the pastureman, had spent quite a bit of time on horseback out there during the summer, but the cattle still spooked every time they saw a mounted man. So, hoping to make things go more smoothly, he had my son bring a crew to rope half a dozen of the wildest steers a couple of days before shipping. We didn't catch nearly enough, though, as later events would prove.

The cattle had been fed protein pellets for a couple of weeks, so on shipping morning Shawn was driving the feed truck for the cattle to follow. We had to take the steers out of the northeast corner of the pasture, where the creek formed a kind of point where the fence met the road. Unfortunately, he was driving too slow, and some of the wilder steers in the lead got suspicious and headed back at us going full speed, taking the whole herd with them. During the second gather about three dozen of the 240 steers escaped down one of the wooded draws, so we took what we could get to the pens.

After roping four of the remaining steers, and with the heat of the day coming on, we left the remainder for another day. Three other days, as it turned out. I got in on the last day's activities, the count still a dozen or so short. About ten of us arrived at 5:45 in the morning, and as soon as it was light enough we started combing the draws. Eight head ran to the blackberry corner, and five came right back out. Cattle were flying, horse hooves were pounding, and ropes were whirling. Four of that first bunch got caught right away, the fifth shortly after. Tied-down steers were in every part of the pasture, waiting to be loaded in a trailer.

Then we went back to the blackberry patch and flushed out the other three steers. Two got caught on the south side of the pasture, but a Charolais I was helping chase down the middle draw just seemed to disappear—not exactly into thin air, but in thick timber. At that point a couple of riders, along with one of the owner's friends with a tranquilizer-dart gun, went to a neighboring pasture where they darted one steer amid a herd of llamas. (Yes, llamas.) The rest of us went to an adjoining soybean field and CRP patch and roped two steers that were hanging out there.

We learned, by cell phone (what in the world did cowboys do before cell phones?), that another steer had been found in a pasture to the south that was being shipped that day. That left only one animal uncaught, the elusive Charolais that had disappeared on us earlier. The whole bunch of us started riding both sides of the north draw, some on the ridges to watch the steer should he break out ahead of us. Nothing. Then we came back up the middle draw. About halfway, a hundred yards from where we last saw him, Gwen, riding along the clifflike slope on the south, spotted the steer in a small thicket where he had undoubtedly dropped out of sight three hours earlier. How could a nine-hundred-pound steer, and a whitish-colored one at that, disappear in a small thicket? Well, cattle, as big as they are, can be pretty elusive.

Several years before that I was helping gather a pasture east of Cassoday. The cattle were headed toward the gate when I spotted a lone steer off to the southeast, maybe a quarter of a mile away, trotting down a draw away from the gate. So I loped out after him, gaining ground quickly. As I went down a little depression and came up the other side, suddenly there was no steer in sight. What the hell had happened to him? Had I ridden past him? I looked back to where I had come from. No steer there. I rode on along the draw, which was neither very deep nor wide. I had ridden maybe fifty yards when I saw the steer, not in front of me but off to my left side. He was lying in shallow water at the bottom of the draw, body straight, belly down, hind legs under him, forelegs stretched out in front, neck and head extended low, nostrils just above the water as it flowed slowly past. I had never before seen a bovine in that exact prone position. If I hadn't seen it, I would hardly have believed anyone telling me about it, just as I could hardly believe we hadn't earlier seen that Charolais lying there in the Schoolhouse pasture. The point is, if a steer wants to hide, he can be pretty good at it.

My descriptive powers can't do justice to the wild chase that ensued with the Charolais. He refused, naturally enough, to leave the timber, running back and forth in it, but with ten riders, he wasn't able to again vanish from sight. Finally, Gwen got a rope on him in a clearing but couldn't get her dally before he again hit the trees. Fortunately, someone else was able to jump off his horse, grab the rope, and wrap it around a tree before he got away. Then Josh and I dragged him out into the open and into a trailer.

Having to rope 20 percent of a pasture is not a very efficient way to ship, but it is a lot more exciting then trailing cattle that are running after a feed truck.

So far I've been writing about other people's wild cattle, but we've had a few of our own on the Flying W Ranch. I suppose it was about 2000 when Josh and Gwen had bought a bunch of drouth (my preferred spelling of "drought") cows at a good price, and most of them were a good buy. But there were several that were not only hard to pen but would actually run when they saw you coming and even try to hide. At one point, Josh said, they were after seven of these cows. They caught two, but in roping them the other five hit some timber with a stream running through. After putting the two they had caught into a corral, they went back to look for the others. It was wintertime and a cold day. They knew that the cows had to be in the timber, but they couldn't find them. Then, Josh said, he noticed some steam rising out of a deeper part of the stream. All five of these cows had gone into that hole and were completely under water with just their noses sticking out. The Vestring steer would probably have done the same if the water he was in had been deeper.

The lengths those five cows went to in order to hide, Josh said, reminded him of a pastureman he knew in the southern Flint Hills who was three steers short when he shipped. For several weeks he combed the pastures in the area, especially the brushy and timbered ones, but without success. He did occasionally see reasonably fresh manure in one pasture, but no sight of his steers. There was an old abandoned farmstead in this pasture—a storm cellar, the foundation of a house, and an old barn with the doors missing or hanging by a hinge. Seeing some fresh sign near the barn one day, he went inside. Suddenly there was a commotion in the haymow above his head, and his three steers came running down the stairway to the mow and out of the barn. They would apparently come out at night to graze and drink, then retreat to the haymow during the day.

But back to the Flying W and the drouth cows. The two worst cows and their calves escaped from the pasture and managed to cross the Cottonwood River and a highway, ending up at a ranch a dozen miles away. Josh got them loaded up and took them to the sale barn at El Dorado, I think it was, on a Thursday. Sale day was Saturday. That fall Josh had been having Carl Grunder buy cows for him, and on that Saturday evening Carl drove in really pleased that he had been able to pick up a couple of cows at El Dorado at a good price. That's right, he had bought and brought back those same two Josh had just gotten rid of. They spent the week in a corral and were back at El Dorado the following Saturday.

For two years in a row, back about 2010, Josh and Gwen pastured some helicopter cattle from Texas, like the ones Bob Vestring told me about in 1990. Not only would they would run at the sight of a horse or a pickup, they would not even come to a feed truck. In fact, Josh said, they spurned his attempt to even give them protein pellets. If the steers had run into a corner, Josh would keep some distance out, then augur out pellets in a quarter circle from fence row to fence row so that they could come up to eat after he had driven away. Instead, he said, he would watch from the rearview mirror as the steers would come out of the corner, make a wild leap over the line of feed he had laid down, and head at a run to the other side of the pasture.

Josh got a crew together about three times that summer trying unsuccessfully to pen the steers, but the only time we got them all in at the same time was on the fourth try. Thankfully, that was the day we shipped them.

Our luck wasn't so good the following year. On shipping day, August 1, we had all but about thirty head of the 1,200 steers just about penned when about ninety-five broke away and drew those other thirty with them as they headed to the east side of the 2,400-acre Lewis pastures. By the time we got after them, they had laid down over an eighth of a mile of fence and were hightailing it across the neighboring Morrill pasture, which is probably over two and a half times larger than the pasture they had escaped from. The Morrill had already been shipped, so we went back and loaded what we had, which meant that two trucks left empty.

We waited a couple of days to give them a chance to settle down, then about ten or twelve of us went out to see about getting the wild bunch in. And they were wild. We could never push more than three or four into a bunch. They just wouldn't stay together. I think we had about half a dozen in the Lewis pens the first day we went back to get the runaways and were headed in with two more when one of them took off at a run to the south on the Morrill side of the division fence. Pudge and I were after him at the high run when suddenly a horse hit Pudge on the right hip; Flint, with Gwen also in hot pursuit, had run into us. Pudge stayed on her feet and I stayed on her. I don't know about Flint, but Gwen hit the ground and Pudge's hoof grazed her head, her wide-brimmed straw hat absorbing most of the blow. Gwen didn't lose consciousness, but it took a little while before her talk made much sense. Fortunately, Cheryl Bailey, who is a trained EMT, was helping us that day, and she took over. Cathy wanted to take Gwen to the emergency room, but Gwen resisted and was back on her horse after an hour or so.

We ended up with about seven head in the Lewis pens that day. I went out several other days as well. One of the more memorable was when three of us encountered four steers in the southeast part of the Morrill. We started for them, intending to drive them to the Morrill pens, which were on the northeast corner of that pasture, close to the Santa Fe tracks and about a quarter of a mile west of K-177 highway. Instead of moving away from us as a group, all four actually ran right at us, trying to butt our horses or run under them, then split off running in four different directions. We got three of them roped, but lost track of the fourth.

If there were three of us, one would rope a steer, another would heel it, and the third would tie three (or sometimes two) legs. If there were two, then one headed the steer, the other heeled it, and the header tied him up. If you were by yourself, then you had to jerk the steer down and tie it yourself, harder but not impossible, especially if you had a horse that knew what he was doing. At some point you let the people driving the pickup know approximately where you had left a steer, and then someone on a horse would pull the steer into the trailer. This is not only time-consuming, but also rougher on the animal than driving it into a set of pens.

Unless, that is, the day is hot and the steer does a lot of running before submitting to being driven. Death from heat exhaustion is not uncommon for a steer being chased in the middle of the summer. We didn't kill any of these steers from running them, but one steer did kill himself. I wasn't there that day, but Josh said they had gotten three or four steers into the Lewis pens. They were not putting any pressure on the cattle; in fact, they were off their horses outside the pen, and Josh was headed on foot for the pickup and trailer when one steer made a run and tried to jump the pipe gate. His head hit the top pipe and he fell back dead. Helicopter cattle might not be born crazy, but some of them sure turn out that way.

We ended up getting over fifteen in the Lewis pens all told, and maybe twenty-five in the Morrill pens, ten in the Lincoln pasture pens to the south, and a few more in pens in other pastures. Altogether we penned about fifty-five head and roped about seventy from August 1 to December 20 when the last steer was captured. He was in the South Frew pasture on the Chase County side of the Butler County line, fifteen or more miles from where he had spent the summer.

Sometimes a pastureman is unable to deliver all the cattle he or she has been caring for during the season, either because of death, theft, or simply losing track of them. Dead animals he doesn't have to pay for, but the others he does. In this case Josh and Gwen accounted for every single one, but it wasn't cheap. Gwen estimates that counting for the two empty trucks they had to pay for at shipping time, along with the mileage they accrued in picking up cattle in various pastures, hauling them to a sale, hiring cowboys to help find and pen or rope cattle, and other expenses, it cost the Flying W an extra ten thousand dollars in expenses.

I was probably about fifteen or sixteen when I got to help with three genuine outlaw steers. This was back in the mid-1950s when the prolonged drouth and low cattle prices were about at their worst. Frank Klasser had a ranch a dozen or so miles southeast of Cassoday where he summer-pastured Texas steers. He preferred two-year-old Herefords, didn't particularly like Brahmas, and didn't want to mess with cows and calves, but by this time in the decade he couldn't afford to be choosy.

On this particular spring he received several hundred head of steers in one shipment, all from the Welder-McCann ranch in southeastern Texas where they had scoured the brush in order to get every steer they could find. These cattle weren't purebred Brahmas, but they all had plenty of ear, lots of dewlap, good-sized humps, and long legs. Half or more might have been two-year-olds, but the rest were older. Many of these steers had escaped from earlier roundups, while three in particular Jake Jordan, the ranch foreman, had labeled genuine outlaws. They were at least a dozen years old, maybe older, he said, and had eluded at least ten earlier roundups. One was a muley cream-colored steer, one a light red with big, tipped horns, and the third a dark red whose wide-sweeping sharp horns had never been touched.

The cattle made the train ride to Kansas thin but strong. Klasser liked to handle his cattle quiet and easy without running, but these steers left the yards and headed for the Hills on the trot. They slowed down after a mile or so, the crew got them into Klasser's pasture without any trouble, and it was big enough, the grass good enough, the fences strong enough that none of them strayed. But Klasser worried and stewed all summer about how he was going to get those outlaw steers back to the stockyards and onto the train.

In addition to not liking noise and Brahmas, Klasser also didn't like ropes. One time at the Cassoday yards, Slockie Brazel was helping count cattle up the alley for loading, and as the right number went past, he would toss his rope out sideways to scare the others back. He wasn't trying to rope anything, just separating cattle with it, but when Klasser spotted Slockie doing that he blew up, cussed him out, and picked up a board. Brazel threw a couple of rocks, guns were mentioned on both sides, and when Klasser went downtown to phone the law, Brazel mounted his horse and rode off. Despite his animus about lariat ropes, however, when it came time to drive the outlaw pasture back to the stockyards, Klasser not only had a crew half again the normal size, he also made sure that Uncle Marshall, one of the top arena and pasture ropers in the area, was among them.

As it turned out, no ropes were needed. The cattle strung out nicely for the trek back to town, moving quickly with a light-colored Brahma in the lead, the three outlaws not far behind him all the way to Cassoday. They crossed the railroad tracks without a fuss and headed into the pens, where Klasser had made sure to have the gates open all the way to the back. By the time the lead cattle hit the end of the pens and headed back toward their entry point, the drags were safely inside and the gate closed.

As usual, we weighed the steers, then went to Opal's Café for dinner before heading back to the yards to wait for the train. When it came in, I took a position on the loading platform (as the younger hands customarily did, allowing our elders to stay mounted and drive the cattle to the cars), helping to swing gates, place the bullboards, and punch the cattle up the chutes.

The three outlaws stayed together as they came up the chute, just as they had stayed together in avoiding a dozen roundups in Texas, just as they had grazed together in the Flint Hills all summer, and just as they had walked together to the stockyards earlier that day. As each passed beneath me on their way into the cattle car that would take them to the Kansas City stockyards and ultimately to a packing plant, I reached out and touched each outlaw's back, knowing even then, years before trucks and yearlings and double-stocking, that the Flint Hills would never again see their like.

The Outlaw Steers

The cattle that now graze upon the grass
Of the Flint hills are mostly yearling steers and heifers,
Tame and small compared to those that came
Up in railroad cars from Texas in springtimes past,

Aged steers, whose lanky frames filled fast
With the rich bluestem, transforming sun and rain
Into protein for the hungry in cities far away
From the pastures where we played at work under vast

Skies that seemed as endless as our days.
But, as our youth, so too the Big Beef Steer
Gave way, as had the longhorn of the open
Range, receding into memory's haze.

Through sequent waves of imperceptible change, I recall
A time when in my youth I saw, and touched,
A moment that divided past and future:
The last of the big steers, shipped out in the fall.

It was in the later fifties, two-year-old steers
Still filled the Bluestem, but tastes were changing,
And tender feedlot yearlings would soon replace
The heartier grassfed beef upon the tiers

Of market shelves. And there had not, for years,
Been any of the four- and five-year-olds
My father and uncle yarned about, cattle
Driven miles from railroad shipping pens, and fears

Of blackleg, fever tick, and worse. But then one spring
Welder and McCann, combing the cactus and the brush,
Had shipped up from Victoria, in a herd of eight hundred
Head, three outlaws, steers that had taken wing

During previous roundups—some eight years, or ten;
They were big, these brutes, with an eye not wild but aware
And calculating, and Klasser, the pastureman, was worried.
How would he ever manage to keep them in?

But they didn't test his fences or his cattle guards,
Although they eyed him carefully each time he rode
His white horse onto Round Mound Hill to get a count
And fret anew about getting them into the yards

At Cassoday. I remember him pointing them out—
A cream-colored brindle muley, a reddish-yellow steer
With long, tipped horns, and the red one, sharp horns never touched;
They grazed together all summer, each one watching out

For the others. Usually about eight of us gathered cattle
For Frank Klasser, but that fall there were a dozen
And more when it came time to ship the outlaw
Pasture, capable hands all, armed for battle

With rope and spur, though Klasser hated a rope—
And a rodeo cowboy. But Marshall and Kenneth Hoy
Were there, Peanuts Prewitt and the Youngs, Buss and Jim—calf ropers
And cow milkers in arena and pasture. If there was a hope

Of getting these cattle to the yards without a spill,
These men, along with Toad and Strut and Cliff,
Could do it, with us younger ones, Jay and Richard, Rita and Jim,
To follow the drag through the gates and up the hills

Through the flats, and into the cattle lanes that led
Past the lake the Santa Fe had built to water the thirsty
Steam engines that pulled the stock cars from Aikman through Cassoday
And on to Matfield and Bazaar, the pens that fed

The grassfat steers to the Kansas City yards
By the thousands. The outlaws never took the lead
But stayed together, a length behind the light-
Colored Brahma that led all the way, setting a hard

And steady pace past the Harsh Hill pasture spring,
Where we got our last drink before the iced tea at Opal's
Café, then past Watkins, no other house along
The way, and that a mile off the trail that would bring

Us from the pastures to the lanes, the cattle strung out thin
Until we neared the tracks and the men in front
Slowed the leaders to bunch the herd for crossing
The rails—always touchy, for who knew when

A train might approach, causing the herd to spill
Back the way they had come. But we're lucky, no trains
Today; and, luckier still, the big outlaws
Follow the lead steer without pause or snort up the fill

And across the tracks, wing fence on our left, and through
The gate. By the time they pass through half a dozen
Openings and bounce off the back fence of the last pen
The drags are in the yards, the gate clapped to

Behind them. Klasser goes into the scale house with Jake,
Foreman for Welder-McCann, and the commission man,
Weaver, while we help draft off bunches of twenty
To push into the alleys, where the older hands will take

Them to be weighed, then back to the pens to await
The cattle loader. It's nearly two when we ride
To Opal's; ten hours since breakfast, roast beef and gravy
And corn, ice cream and pie to fill our plates.

But Frank barely touches his meal; he toys with his pie,
Not daring to breathe easy until the outlaws are on
The cars. Jake Jordan regales us with tales of Texas,
Of the pasture for horses, the little one, ten sections in size,

Behind the ranch house back home—but he knows it took
Only three thousand acres of Kansas grass to fatten
These steers that had grown nothing but tall on twelve thousand
Acres in Texas. The train whistles in and we look

To our horses, loping back to the yards to take our places
For loading; the older hands stay on their mounts,
A nod to custom, and deference to their skill,
A badge of status they wear without a trace

Of arrogance. They cut out twenty-five
At a draft, pushing them down the alleyway;
The younger, stouter hands wrestle into place
The bullboards and wings before the steers arrive

To be crammed into cars that in the spring
Had held half again that many. Our job was best,
We thought, to punch the steers on up the chute,
Reach over with a spur to rake the back of a straggling

Or reluctant steer. No stragglers as the first
Draft hits the chute, the Brahma lead steer coming
Up the ramp, the outlaw three still on
His tail. No need to hit them with a burst

Of yells or prods. And as they climb the ramp,
As alert as when they dodged a dozen Texas
Gathers, as calm as if still grazing Kansas
Grass, as purposeful as if approaching the damp

Bank of a stream for a drink, I feel a sense
Of sudden awe. Never again will cattle
Like these grace the Hills, these atavistic three—
Reminders of a time when plow and fence

Had yet to scar the plains. And I am there
To watch them scramble toward the railroad car
Laden with their mortality. They pass beneath
My outstretched hand; I reach bare palm to hair,

Touching each in turn, their backs firm
With fat, their coats coarse but smooth to the touch.
They neither flinch nor start, but ignore my hand
With regal aplomb, as if they had come to terms

With all there is to know of life. I see
Them disappear into the car, swallowed
Up into a general swirl of horns.
The door slides shut and is fastened, the wings swing free,

And the brakeman signals the next set of cars into place.
The outlaws are gone. And so now are most of the men
Who pushed the cattle down the alley that day,
Gone the way of steam engines and stockyards, small trace

To mark the passing of an age. Yet even now
A whiff of creosote, or manure long dried, or pungent
Gourd brings to my mind as real as life
Itself, the day of horse, stockyard, and steer.

Liggett Cattle Drive

In the past few years we have several times driven some of our cows from Flying W pastures near Clements down to the Flying H near Cassoday in the spring and back again in the fall, a distance of eighteen or twenty miles one way, depending on which pasture we leave from or are going to. Before the railroad made its way to Cassoday in 1923, my father and uncle (and all the other cowboys and cattlemen here) had to go to Bazaar, Burns, or De Graff to pick up cattle in the spring and return them in the fall. In my grandfather's day, it was Newton, forty miles to the west. Even after 1923 cattle drives of over a dozen miles to the Cassoday stockyards (or those of other Flint Hills railroad shipping points) were not unusual.

Really long drives to or from the northeastern Butler County Flint Hills, however, have been rare for decades. In the early 1930s the Crocker ranch, complete with chuck wagon, overlanded cattle from northern Oklahoma to Matfield Green, but the last long drive that I'm aware of took place in 1942, shortly after the beginning of World War II. In March of 1993 Teresa Stovall wrote an account of that drive, based on an interview with the youngest of the participants. On October 25, 1942, Gwynn Liggett loaded four horses with saddles and gear, five men with bedding, and cooking gear and enough food for a week onto a 1936 Chevrolet truck and headed south to Kay County, Oklahoma, near the little (now ghost) town of Hardy, a few miles southwest of the little (now ghost) town of Maple City, Kansas.

They were headed there to drive some 475 Hereford cows that Liggett had bought to his ranch a few miles from Rosalia. He had paid a hundred dollars a head for them, a pretty good price in those days, but these were pretty good cows, and they were heavy springers. That is, they were not only pregnant but about to drop their calves. The men arrived at the Oklahoma ranch as evening approached, threw a tarp on the ground, and spread out their blankets for what rest they could get before starting the drive to Kansas the next day.

Besides Gwynn and his son Blaine, the others on the drive included Van Haines, Buck Piper, and young Keith McGregor. Haines was the most experienced cowboy on the drive, McGregor the greenhorn. It was his job to drive the truck and take care of the baby calves that were born along the way. He also did most of the cooking, although everyone was relieved when Liggett took over that chore. Gwynn had been divorced a few years earlier and thus had picked up more kitchen experience than the others. They had a campfire every night but cooked on a Coleman camp stove. The menu was generally bacon and eggs for breakfast, sandwiches and pork and beans for other meals.

Liggett had made arrangements with landowners along the way so they could trail across pastures and bed the cows down in a pasture each night, eliminating the need for night herding. When a calf was born during the daytime rather than at night, the men would stop to give it plenty of time to get licked off and to its feet, nurse, and gain a little strength, then they would load it in the truck and turn it out at night to be with its mother. Some two dozen calves hit the ground during the short week the drive lasted, all of them arriving safely.

Although not a cowboy himself, McGregor occasionally got to ride Gwynn's horse while the boss drove the truck, especially if it was cold and raining. (It's not for nothing to be owner and boss.) Each morning the men would load the calves, gather the cows, and start north, averaging a little over eleven and a half miles per day. When they reached Beaumont, they left the livestock there and spent that last night in their own beds, going back the next morning for the last leg of the drive.

On Halloween Day, the cows and their babies, born and yet to arrive, reached their new home, thus ending one of the last long cattle drives to the Flint Hills.

Checking Brands

Back in the mid-1990s I ran into Jess Miser in Cottonwood Falls. He had recently read a newspaper column I had written about shipping cattle on the railroad, but, he said, "You forgot to tell about checking brands." He went on to tell me of the time he and three other cowboys were shipping steers from the Santa Fe stockyards at Bazaar and were looking for a stray they knew was in the herd because they had seen him in the pasture. They had to run the cattle down the alley twice before they could spot the brand on the stray.

"Every time you shipped," Jess said, "you always checked the brands to make sure you weren't putting somebody else's cattle on the train." If you didn't, then the brand inspector at the Kansas City stockyards would probably catch them anyway. Which seems to me a little different from nowadays when those who ship first all seem to have their count, while the poor guy who empties his pastures last is likely to come up short. Not that people don't still check for brands, but I don't think they're always quite as meticulous as they used to be.

I recall a *New Yorker* article from the early 1990s by John McPhee about brand inspectors out in Nevada. That was about the time our son had just gotten back from working on a big Colorado ranch near Pueblo. One of the more interesting people he had met in his time out there was the state brand inspector, who traveled around from ranch to ranch in the fight to keep rustlers unemployed. I had never paid that much attention to brand terminology, relying instead on lengthy descriptions or making a drawing in the dirt if I had to describe a brand. I knew about "flying," of course, but Josh filled me in on such arcana as "connected" and "backwards" and "over" and "under."

Our brand, the Flying H (which my grandfather had seen on some New Mexico cattle being pastured near Cassoday), is a simple one—a couple of slanted lines arching out at a forty-five-degree angle from the tops of the H to make wings. And because our iron is large, it doesn't blotch like a smaller one can when it's applied to the cow's hide. There isn't anything much more frustrating than riding through a pasture full of spooky steers on a cloudy day trying to spot a dim brand. That's when you wish the owner had used a big iron and burned the brand on plain and easy to see. (I much prefer looking for a stray steer in a pasture full of heifers anyway—or vice versa.)

But maybe checking brands won't be that much of a problem in the future. I was talking to a rancher from Saskatchewan's Cypress Hills a while back, and he told me that up there they had begun implanting computer chips under a cow's hide and could scan a herd with an electronic device to tell not only ownership but the entire genetic and performance history of every animal in the herd.

In Australia this technology is mandatory, I was told by a squatter (rancher) who runs seven cattle stations (ranches) in the northern part of the state of Western Australia in the Kimberley. (About a hundred of his calves each year are eaten by crocodiles, he said. At least that's something a Flint Hills rancher doesn't have to worry about.) We were sitting around the table after supper one evening when he got a phone call from a cattleman in the Northern Territory who was getting ready to send a boatload of steers to Indonesia (a literal instance of shipping cattle) and had six steers belonging to the Western Australia cattleman. "Do you want me to hold them back or reimburse you the average price for each?" he wondered. "Go ahead and sell them," my host told him. After hanging up he told me that the other man's cattle were bigger than his, so he'd get a good price and not have to drive to Darwin to pick up his cattle. And how did the NT man know about the WA steers? Not from a brand but from computer chips in their ears.

Weaning Calves

I don't think many cattle raisers would put up much of an argument against the notion that calving season, whenever that season might come, is the most stressful time of their year. Here in the Flint Hills most cow-calf operators seem to favor spring calves, with the mother cows actually dropping their babies in late winter—February and March. Some still have fall calves, but it seems to me that the tendency for calving in the fall, then having to feed the mothers for producing milk as well as for maintenance, began to go out of fashion about the time that screwworms ceased to be a problem in the spring.

Most people with a cow herd will put the bulls out in May, hoping that all the cows will be bred within a few weeks so that the calves will come in a bunch nine months later and not be strung out over several months. Either way, when the babies start to drop, the rancher (and/or spouse, kids, hired hands, and anyone else on the place) goes on twenty-four-hour alert because every lost calf puts a dent in his pocketbook at weaning time.

For the mother cow, once she gets past being a first-calf heifer, calving season becomes almost routine. For her, as with the calves, the big trauma comes at weaning time. There isn't anything much noisier on the farm now that John Deere tractors have a full set of cylinders than a pen full of calves with their mothers hanging around outside, both sets of animals bawling nonstop. In fact, it seems that all you have to do to start a chain reaction of bawling is ride into the cow pasture any time after Labor Day. Cows that have been quiet and tractable all summer will suddenly start bellering and running at the sight of a horse as soon as the weather turns cool, or so it seems.

Portable pens have made calf weaning a quieter time. No longer does the herd have to be driven to the home place for sorting, which means less noise around the ranch house. Sometimes, particularly if you don't wean the calves when the sign of the moon is right (Toad Griffin always said not to wean when the sign was in the throat), the cows and calves will beller for a couple of weeks. Around home we didn't pay much attention to the moon sign because we would generally sort off the calves, then load them up and haul them directly to the Emporia or the El Dorado livestock auction (or maybe to both, since one was on Friday and the other on Saturday), letting the new owner put up with the noise. The cows would bawl around the empty pens for a couple days, then get over it. If the calves remained in sight, however, the mother generally mourned longer than the baby. That's because by weaning time the calves are big and not getting much if any milk anyway, so they're ready to be on their own.

In February of 2019 Cathy and I made a trip down to the Hill Country of Texas to visit my sister and brother-in-law, who live in Johnson City. Rita's daughter was there, too, and Kim was bemoaning the invasion of Hill Country by rich city people who were buying up property and building big houses, people who have no clue about cattle. Kim said that the previous year she and her husband had gotten a call from the local humane society. It seems one of the newcomers had lodged a complaint about them for mistreating their cows. They knew the cattle were being abused because of the constant bawling. What they obviously didn't know was that when calves are weaned, both they and the mother cows tend to complain about it.

Why Shipping?

Nan Broad, a friend from Australia who is as interested in the history of the cattle business there as I am here, once asked me why we in the States talk about shipping cattle when we don't ship them, we truck them. Maybe, she suggested, it was because our prairies are like a sea of grass, a comparison that has become almost a cliché with both fiction and nonfiction writers. In the Kimberley and the Northern Territory, they often sell cattle to Indonesia and the Middle East, so they do indeed transport those cattle by ship, but in order to get their beef-on-the-hoof from the interior to the coast they use trains (as we used to do) or trucks (as we do now) or by driving them overland (also as we used to do). Stockmen Down Under distinguish among the terms droving, shipping, trucking, and railing, depending on the mode by which they are transporting their cattle.

Here in the Flint Hills, and across America as far as I've been able to find out, we ship our cattle, even though we are actually trucking (or sometimes trailering) them. You'd have a heck of a time getting a boat, not to mention a body of water, big enough to haul even one steer, let along several hundred, anywhere in the Flint Hills—or Montana, or Nevada, or any other cattle-raising area except maybe ranches on the West Coast or the Gulf of Mexico.

So why do we ship cattle when we are actually trucking them? I think the term became common in an earlier day when a major mode of mechanically moving large numbers of cattle, as opposed to driving them overland, was by boat. In the years before trains, for instance, cattle would have been driven to a port, then loaded onto a boat to be moved to a major market. I have seen an old film documenting the early cattle industry in Hawaii that shows paniolos (Hawaii's cowboys) swimming cattle out into the harbor, where they were then lifted one at a time by a crane onto ships to be sent to mainland markets.

So even though we no longer ship cattle by ship or ship cattle by train, we do still ship cattle by truck.

And then there is the "throwing" of cattle, which has nothing at all to do with a bulldogging contest in a rodeo. In the Trail Drive Era cattle would be thrown off the trail for grazing or thrown onto a bedground for the night, things we don't do today. But we do still say things like "I threw that stray heifer into Jones's pasture," or "When you've sorted out the sick ones, throw them into the brome grass south of the house." We don't, of course, literally throw them, but that's the term that we use.

No wonder English is a hard language to learn.

HORSES

Catching Horses

One disadvantage with some, not all, horses is getting them caught so you can saddle and ride. Some horses are easy to catch. You can just walk up to them in the corral, or even in the pasture, halter in hand, and they will just stick their nose into it. But in my experience those horses are extremely rare. More often you need to shake a can of oats before they will come up to be caught, and even that doesn't work lots of times; you have to get them into a small corral.

For instance, my current cow horse, Pudge, loves to work cows. She'll lay her ears back at them when you're sorting in a corral, she often reaches out to nip a laggard cow's rear end when you're driving them to a pasture, and she will often alert me to a cow in timber or down a draw well before I can see it. The only thing she loves better is feed. If she's anywhere close enough to hear me when I call the horses, she'll come on the run, the first one in the corral. Once there with her nose in a feed trough, catching her is easy.

Except in the summer when there are pastures to ride, cattle to doctor, and especially when it's time to ship. Then she is hard to catch. To be more precise, she can be almost impossible to get into the corral, no matter how much I shake the feed can. Sometimes I have to shut the other horses in an inner corral, put some feed in the trough in the outer corral, then hope that she'll be tempted to come in and that I can sneak around the barn and get the gate shut before she sees me and takes out. The only solution is to get the horses in about sunset and shut them up overnight so they'll be in the corral next morning.

Maybe it's genetic; her mother, Molly, also loved to work cows, but could be difficult to catch in the wee hours of the morning. When you have to be at the pasture when it's barely light enough to see ten yards ahead, you have to call the horses in when it's still pitch black. I remember one early morning when I chased her (on foot, of course) all over the pasture (a small one) with a feed can and a flashlight when she wouldn't come into the corral. I was just

Jim and Pudge dragging a calf to the branding fire on the Flying W. (Photo by Gary Sneed)

about to give up when she stopped running and actually came up to me. It was as if she were playing a game and once she had proven that I couldn't win, she decided it would be more fun to chase cows than to stand around in the pasture all day.

When I was a boy back home, the horses would come in when called, except for my sister's. Interestingly, my mount back then was often a little bay mare, while my sister Rita's was a big, tall paint gelding, a pacer. She taught Paint to stretch out so he was lower to the ground and easier to get on. She could not, however, teach him to be caught, even with oats, if he didn't want to be. Paint was so bad you could hardly drive him in if you were horseback. Finally, Dad attached about six or so feet of heavy log chain to a leather strap and buckled that onto his front ankle before turning him loose. That slowed him down enough that he could be driven into the corral the next time Rita wanted to ride.

I've known of ranchers who had a cow dog trained to bring the horses into the corral. We often kept a horse in the barn overnight so we could drive the others in the next morning. As noted above, I call mine in with oats (actually little protein pellets). My son and his wife and daughter use a four-wheeler to run the horses into the corral when they're needed. But how did cowboys catch their horses back in the days of the open range?

At the time of the Texas-to-Kansas trail drives, and before, there were no corrals on the open range. Rather than using a bucket of oats to lure horses into a barn with a feed box and manger, cowboys back then roped the mount they were going to ride that day. The remuda would be driven into a large corral and then into a smaller one, where each cowboy would step into the corral and, on foot, as the horses ran by in a large circle, throw a hoolihan loop over the head of the pony he wanted. On some ranches, rather than each cowboy, one man, often the foreman, handled all the roping. The cowboys would call out the mount they wanted to ride, and the roper would catch it and turn it over to the cowboy.

But how did this work when the hands were out on roundup with the chuck wagon for months at a time, miles away from ranch headquarters? Or on the big trail drives? In both cases, from what I can tell, there was one designated cowhand, often a youth, whose job was to handle all the horses being used by those who were working, or driving, the cattle. He was called the horse wrangler or, particularly in Texas, the horse jingler. He would herd the horses all day, and early each morning he would drive them up to the chuck wagon and into a makeshift corral made of a few lariat ropes, one of which was tied to a wheel of the chuck wagon. The remuda would stand inside this temporary (and flimsy) corral while the cowboys caught their mounts. The horses could easily have jumped (or in some cases even stepped) over the ropes, but they didn't because, I suppose, they had been trained not to.

One glaring error in movie or television depictions of cattle drives is that the actors always ride the same horse all the time. Think of the old television series *Rawhide*, which gave Clint Eastwood his boost toward stardom. The overarching plot of the show was a cattle drive heading to Sedalia, Missouri, but despite eight seasons on the air, they never seem to have gotten there. I think it was because in every one of the 217 episodes the cowboys ride the same horse, whereas on a real cattle drive (or on an open-range roundup) each cowboy would have had eight or ten horses in his string. Each day the wrangler would herd the horses while the other hands handled the cattle. Early each morning, while the cook fixed breakfast and the trail hands were getting a last bit of sleep, the wrangler would ride out to the remuda and, as noted above, drive them to the chuck wagon.

What kept the horses from straying during the night? Horses are herd animals, and they are also political animals. In any group of horses, a few will be leaders and the rest will be followers. The followers will naturally stay close to the leaders. Perhaps the leaders were hobbled so that they could not get far. Or sometimes a bell mare might have been used. The other horses would tend to stay close to the bell mare, so called because she wore a bell around her neck. The wrangler could also hear the bell in the early morning when he went to gather the remuda.

In South Texas and Mexico some vaqueros catch their horses in an open corral without roping them. I have seen a 1973 photograph taken on the Chaparrosa ranch near La Pryor, Texas, that shows a string of at least forty horses standing close together in a straight line, their sides almost touching one another, their rear ends backed against a corral fence while one vaquero stands at the midpoint of the line calmly looking at them, a bullwhip in his right hand dangling onto the ground. Several other vaqueros are walking up to the horses to catch the one they want to ride. The technique is called *formando*, something I'd like to see in real life. It would make catching your mount for the day easy, but I bet it's not so easy to train the horses to line up that way.

Speaking of catching a horse to ride, I've often wondered how in the world those consummate horsemen, the Great Plains Indians, managed to catch their horses. I'm no authority on Plains Indians, but I do know that they were extremely skilled riders. If you can ride a horse bareback with a heel hooked over a hip while you are leaning over the opposite side and shooting a bow and arrow at an enemy under the horse's neck—well, that's skill. Personally, I think that would be impossible, but that's how many nineteenth-century observers described what they saw. I do know that the Cheyenne were described by contemporary Euro-Americans as the best light cavalry in the world and that other contemporaries thought the Comanche were even better.

But right now I'm more interested in how they caught their horses, not how well they rode them. George Catlin, whose paintings from the first half of the nineteenth century are among the best early documentations we have of Plains Indians, in one image shows some Comanche catching wild horses. In the foreground is a brave, on foot, with a mustang he has just caught with a rawhide lariat, bracing as he pulls the horse to face him. In the background is the horse he has ridden to catch the mustang, while a couple of other Comanche chase other mustangs in the distance.

I can understand how the Comanche or Kiowa or cowboys could chase and rope wild horses out on the plains, even though it wouldn't be easy to do. But I'm puzzled at how the Indians caught the horses they had already captured and trained to ride. They had no permanent corrals, and I've yet to read of any temporary ones they used. I have read that Indian men often kept a horse staked outside their lodges so that it would be ready for immediate defensive use if their village was attacked, but how did they catch that horse out of the herd of scores or hundreds of head that grazed on the perimeter of the village?

Plains Indian wealth was determined by horse ownership, so even a village of sixty or seventy men, women, and children might well have had a horse herd (usually looked after by young boys) of a couple of hundred or more. If a man wanted to gather a particular horse, say, for a buffalo hunt, how did he do it? Say he mounted the steed staked outside his tepee and rode out to the horse herd, either by himself or with several others. Then what? Rope another horse (which would cause many if not all of the other horses to run)? Or would several men go out and help one another by forming a kind of human corral? Did they use hobbles on selected horses in the herd, hoping that the less spirited animals wouldn't run away? Even so, could they just walk up to their horses out in the open with a catch rope in hand and pass it over the neck of the horse they wanted to ride? Most gentle horses I know, let alone the skittish ones, don't quietly let you walk up to them. In fact, most will run from you in a corral or round pen for at least a little while before facing up and submitting to a halter. Out in an open pasture? You're going to need a feed bucket to catch even the most gentle, dead-broke horses, and Indians didn't have oats.

Maybe some old-timer back in Indian country observed a brave catching a mount out of the herd and wrote about it, but if so I've yet to discover that article. Or maybe some keeper of oral tradition knows how it was done in his or her tribe, but, again, I haven't seen a written account. Until then, it will remain a mystery to me, but I'd be glad to hear theories.

Horseshoeing

Every year at the National Cowboy Symposium in Lubbock, Texas, the Texas Farriers Association has its annual meeting. I don't know how many members there are, but a couple of big tents are filled, one with samples of and promotional pitches for horseshoeing equipment and one where the contests for horseshoe making and horseshoeing itself are held. Contestants come from as far afield as England, and it is truly amazing to see how quickly a plain old piece of steel bar can be turned into a finished horseshoe. Even more amazing is the skill and speed with which a horse is shod.

It's sure a lot different from the way I used to do it. I learned to shoe horses (a real farrier would dispute that claim) from my dad. I don't ever recall a single time that a professional horseshoer ever set foot on our place. Dad bought cold shoes and pounded them into shape on an anvil attached to a tree stump just outside our shop. Sometimes he bought shoes with small corks already on them, and sometimes he bent them on. He also had to widen the nail holes with a punch so the horseshoe nails would fit in properly. Only when I started to rope calves did he use flat plates, which allow for a smoother, sliding stop. Nowadays I don't know anyone who uses corked shoes.

I think I was a teenager before he picked up a hoof nipper somewhere, probably in a box of junk at a farm auction. Until that time he took off however much hoof had to be trimmed away with a rasp, and not a very sharp one at that. In fact, I think I still have the rasp he used, and it is mighty dull. Neither did he have a hoof pick. A pocketknife was what he used to clean the mud and manure out of a horse's hoof, and he clinched nails with a hammer and a small square chunk of steel.

Dad's shoeing jobs weren't pretty. The nails didn't line up in a nice row on the hoof wall; some were close to the bottom edge of the hoof, and some were high up the side. In fact, he occasionally put a nail in a little too deep and had to pull it out, bend the tip slightly with the little saddle hammer he used for shoeing, and drive it in again. But I don't recall many of his horses ever throwing a shoe in less than five or six weeks after being shod, and even that was rare. Also, unless he was going to be riding out in the Hills, he often would put shoes on only the front hooves, which worked well for our pastures, which weren't as rocky.

I did buy a pair of clinchers, hoof nippers, and a hoof pick when I started putting shoes on my horses. My work wasn't scientific, but I did learn pretty quickly from the sound of the nail being pounded whether or not it was going in too deep. Nor was the finished product very pretty, but my horses didn't stumble, and they didn't get graveled. One time when I was rodeoing with my future brother-in-law, who lived at Rexford out in western Kansas, I volunteered to put shoes on either his bulldogging or his roping horse, I don't recall which. A day or two later he had them replaced by a professional. That's when I realized the difference between how I did it and how it should be done.

Horseshoeing is one of the hardest, sweatiest, most painful, most frustrating tasks I've ever undertaken. Real farriers have some tricks (techniques, they call them) to ease the strain, to minimize the risk of injury, and to handle recalcitrant equines. I, on the other hand, have a deep scar on the ring finger of my right hand where Buck, probably the best all-around horse I ever owned, jerked a nail almost to the bone. Buck weighed close to 1,300 pounds, and he must have put well over half that weight on whichever leg I picked up to work on. I've never sweat so much in my life, or used such bad language, as I did when shoeing him.

I haven't put a full set of shoes on a horse for, gosh, at least a dozen years. And I don't miss it, although I did replace a thrown shoe last summer, and it felt pretty good. But putting one shoe on one hoof is a lot different from doing four. Turk Harsh, on the other hand, one of the old-time cowboys at Cassoday, was still shoeing his own horses when he was in his early eighties. They made them tougher back then—tougher than I am, anyway.

In a Western movie it's always easy for the hero to know by the tracks when Indians are in the area because they ride barefooted horses. The cavalry, on the other hand, always rides shod horses. Custer, notorious for keeping his troops in the saddle for long periods (which earned him the nickname "Hardass"), is said to have taken ten farriers with him on his campaigns. Considering the weight of horseshoes, I wonder how many pack horses it took to carry them.

What about on ranches in the early days? Certainly in rocky country horses would have to be shod, but what about in sandy country? Why go to the trouble and/or expense of shoeing if rocks aren't a problem? Who did the shoeing? I know that the big cattle stations in Australia, many of which were great distances from the nearest town, had not only blacksmiths but storekeepers and gardeners on the payroll. In America was each cowboy responsible for his own shoeing, or did the ranch employ a blacksmith? Or did they take horses into the nearest town? A town of any size at all would likely have had a blacksmith, as well as a livery stable that might also have had a resident farrier.

What about horses on trail drives? Were they shod or not? I have never read an account by any old-timer that talks about this subject. Andy Adams, in his novel *The Log of a Cowboy*, accurately describes a trail drive that went from the border of Mexico to Montana. The remuda had 142 horses, ten for each cowboy and a dozen for the trail boss. Say a set of shoes lasted two months, each of those horses would need three sets (twelve shoes) for the six-month drive. If each horse started with a fresh set, then two changes during the drive would require 1,056 new shoes for the chuck wagon to carry. That's a heck of a lot of extra weight in addition to all the flour, bacon, and beans necessary to feed the crew, not to mention the bedrolls of all the trail hands. The only reference to shoeing in the book occurs when the cook takes the chuck wagon into Ogallala to replace the shoes on the mules that pulled it.

A three- to four-month drive from Texas to a cow town in Kansas or Nebraska with, say, a hundred-horse remuda would require at least one change of four hundred horseshoes. I have seen in the Buckaroo Hall of Fame in Winnemucca, Nevada, a small, round anvil carried in the chuck wagon so that horses could be shod during the months spent away from ranch headquarters during roundup. Did chuck wagons on the way to Abilene or Dodge City carry a similar anvil? I also wonder when ready-made horseshoes became available. If shoes back in the Trail Drive Era had to be made from scratch, then a chuck wagon would also have had to carry a portable forge as well as an anvil.

When my son took a job on a Colorado ranch in the early 1990s, he was told that he'd have to do his own shoeing, so I gave him a necessarily crude (considering my limited abilities) crash course in the fundamentals. He took a couple of horses with him, one a green-broke three-year-old that was touchy about his feet, to say the least. We stopped in Dodge City on the way out and I got ahold of Buck Jones, an old bronc riding acquaintance turned racetrack farrier, to shoe the colt. It took massive amounts of liquid halter and heavy twitching to get the job done. Buck allowed it was the worst horse he had ever had to work with. For subsequent shoeing on the ranch, Josh had to throw the horse and tie his legs to get shoes on.

Most of the horses used on ranches and trail drives back then were not nearly as gentle as horses are today, so changing a set of shoes would have been a time-consuming job. Horseshoeing was sometimes a spectator sport, probably not so much for trail-driving cowboys as for town loafers. Turk Harsh once gave me an old photograph showing a young horse thrown (Turk is one of the rope holders) and tied down with the Cassoday blacksmith ready to attach the shoes. A dozen or more men are standing or squatting by the door of the shop, enjoying the excitement. Fun for them, if not for the blacksmith.

Horse Traders

My early years coincided with a cultural change that saw the used car salesman take the place of the horse trader as a symbol for someone of questionable veracity. "Would you buy a used car from that man?" took the place of "If you bought a horse from a trader, you got cheated."

My father liked to trade horses, but he wasn't a horse trader. That is, he didn't travel the countryside with a truckload of horses, stopping in at farms and ranches to see if he could work up a swap. Instead horse traders came by our place every once in a while, and he would look over what they had to offer. Then he might have me and my sister run in our small horse herd for the trader to look over. Sometimes Dad would swap one of his horses for one of the trader's, but more often he would try to sell the trader one of his own that he didn't particularly like, or maybe one he had picked up at the local sale barn or bought from a neighbor.

One of the traders that made irregular visits to our place was named Jimmy Shaw. He was the son-in-law of an older trader who also came by once in a while, although I can't remember his name at all. Dad referred to Shaw as a "little gypsy," and he was small of stature and swarthy of complexion, although I don't know if he was Romany by ethnicity or just by lifestyle. Gypsy culture, both in Europe and America, was originally a horse culture, and many of them did indeed travel the countryside with a string of trading stock. When Cathy and I made our first trip to England back in 1967, we saw two or three gypsy encampments with wagons and horses. I recall my grandfather talking about how gypsies would camp in their wagons by the creek on our place while they attempted to trade horses with him and the neighbors.

One time some young traders stopped in driving a two-ton truck with half a dozen horses in the back. Dad wasn't interested in buying any of them, but he did have one he wanted to sell. He was a young pale buckskin gelding we raised out of Buss Young's palomino stallion, Ranger. I forget what we called him, but he was big and stout with a bowed-out Roman nose. That wasn't a real strike against him (any horse that works well looks good, no matter his color, pedigree, or conformation), but by the time this horse was three he had gotten scarred up by wire, bitten by a rattlesnake, and stung by bumblebees. Dad had decided he was just a hard-luck horse and was ready to get rid of him.

These traders that had stopped by were a long way from home—Minnesota, I believe. Dad priced the horse to them for around $400. By the time the bickering was through, they wrote a check for $300, loaded the horse, and drove out of the yard. Dad was feeling pretty good about the deal until he noticed that on the part of the check where you write out the amount, they had written "three" instead of "three hundred." The number part, $300, was okay. Dad thought maybe he had been snookered, but the bank honored the full amount and the check didn't bounce, so everything turned out okay. And Minnesota was probably too far north for rattlers or bumblebees, so the horse found a good home.

About twenty years ago I sold a nice mouse-colored gelding (grulla is the official name of the color) to a man from up that way—Wisconsin, I think it was. He was a nice-enough horse, Ready Money bred, but not that good on cows. Josh had used him on some ranches he had worked on, and had him out at the Flying W, which he and his cousin had started a couple of years earlier. I don't remember just how we came in contact with this fellow, but he was wanting to take a horse home with him and Josh didn't have any he wanted to sell just then so he suggested I might sell Smoky. I had better horses to ride and was ready to sell this one, if I could get a good price. Horses were selling at this time, around the late 1990s or early 2000s, for a lot more than when I was a kid, by the way. Anyway, I met this guy at the Flying W pens and had the horse saddled when he drove in. I rode Smoky around the round pen a little bit, then turned him over to the potential buyer. We had done some pasture roping on Smoky, and I said, "You can rope on him, too," and ran a yearling into the round pen and handed the guy a rope. It was pretty obvious by the way he held and threw the nylon that he wasn't a roper, but he did hit the rear end of the steer with his loop a couple of times. Josh said I should ask at least $4,000, so I did and was pleasantly surprised when he agreed without even attempting to bargain. I had paid around $500 for him as a weanling colt a few years earlier. When he pulled out with the horse in his trailer, we were both happy, which is the best way to end a horse trade.

The key to a successful horse trade, as all horsemen know, is to be on the side of the deal that draws boot. In other words, never trade even up, but try to get a little money in addition to a new horse. Or trade one horse for two. Often (inevitably?) the horse you got from the trader would have a hidden flaw—hard to catch or a stump sucker or windbroke or had a lameness that didn't show up because the painkiller he'd been doped with hadn't yet worn off.

One of my best friends from home was Jay Young. We were always trading something or other, from goats to saddles. I still have the Fred Lowery roping saddle made by Veach Saddlery of Trenton, Missouri, that I got off Jay. Sometimes he'd come out ahead, and sometimes I would, but we enjoyed the arguing back and forth. On our last horse trade, we both came out well. I had a big dark-bay gelding called Hector that was good in the pasture that I swapped for a sorrel mare we called Cinnamon. She was a decent cow horse, but she was outstanding at throwing good colts.

One of those colts, Hunter, was a sorrel mare that was a top cow horse that I traded to my son, not for another horse but for a promise. Josh was recently out of high school and doing day work here and there. We were helping Chris Locke, I believe it was, ship some steers southeast of Rosalia, and Josh and one of his friends lit up cigarettes as we neared the pens. He wasn't really a smoker, but at the age when kids try out various vices. I told him, "If you promise not to smoke, I'll give you this mare I'm riding. But if you ever light up another cigarette, I'm taking her back." He quit, and never gave me a reason to get my good mare back.

Among the other colts that Cinnamon had was Molly, who in turn became the mother of the favorite of all the horses I've owned. This filly colt was out of Jay's Jag Tyree stud, a gray. For the first few months this baby was sorrel, but she shed off gray. I named her Lucy, but then our daughter had a little girl and named her Lucy, so I changed the little mare's name to Pudge, who matured into one of the best all-around cow horses I've ever owned. Anyway, I've digressed a bit, but if it weren't for that last trade I made with Jay, I'd have missed out on some good horses.

During the four years I was in graduate school at the University of Missouri, Cathy and I rented a pasture outside of Columbia where we ran steers in the summer and kept our horses year round. Dad would occasionally send a young one over for me to ride, one he'd picked up at a horse sale or in a trade. Naturally, they usually had a flaw, one that could sometimes be cured with a little riding and sometimes not. One of those that couldn't was a nervous, high-headed bay gelding that I sold to a local trader who thought he was getting a good deal. Soon after, however, he unloaded him at a horse sale after tranquilizing him. Beware of a horse with droopy eyelids.

One lesson I learned from Dad was that when you reach the point in a deal where you're ready to make an offer on a horse, make it low: "Don't worry about insulting the owner," he'd say. Another was to not be shy about putting an outrageously high price on a horse that you don't really want to sell. The other guy might reach for his checkbook, and you better get enough money to make up for the disappointment of losing the horse. I lost the best cutting horse in the central Flint Hills that way when I was only four or five years old. Dad had a good young gelding named Tony he intended to be mine when I got older. One day Gwynn Liggett from Rosalia came by, saw the horse, and tried to buy him. Dad named a price he thought would scare Gwynn off, but instead he got out his checkbook and loaded the horse. Gwynn changed the horse's name to Smoky and started cutting on him, and for the next twenty years I saw the two of them winning contest after contest at rodeos in our area.

That reminds me (I don't know why) of the time around 1950 that Cliff Cannon was at Wilber Countryman's Fourth of July rodeo, roping off a good, and good-looking, buckskin gelding. A man attending the rodeo wanted to own the horse, and he offered Cliff a good price, which Cliff turned down. He kept raising his offer until he hit a thousand dollars, this in the day when a hundred would buy you a damn good horse. Cliff wouldn't sell, and Wilber's observation was, "That's when two fools met."

Some of Dad's other techniques were, if you can, to get the other guy to make the first offer, whether selling or buying. He might offer to sell below what you thought you might have to pay, or, conversely, he might offer to buy at a higher price than you might have been about to ask. Either way, it gives you the advantage to buy for an even lower price, or sell at a higher. Another of Dad's ploys when buying a horse was if the seller's price was too high, just turn and walk away. If Dad didn't get the horse, he didn't get him, but should the other guy call him back, Dad knew he'd get the horse at a lower price.

When I was about eight years old, Loyal Bowman, a bachelor who lived southeast of Cassoday, wanted to buy Dan, a big dun horse that Dad didn't particularly want to sell. Loyal, by the way, had an interesting way of talking that is hard to reproduce in writing. I remember him telling Dad one summer, "Kenneth, between the cheench bugs and the blackbirds [emphasis on "cheench" and "black" with a distinct pause after each word], I'm not going to get any kaffir this year." (Chinch bugs were a common pest in those days.) Anyway, one reason Dad was reluctant to sell was because he knew Dan was too much horse for Loyal, who was a farmer, not a horseman. But Loyal insisted, and Dad sold him for I think $300.

A couple of weeks later we were in town and Loyal came up and wanted to sell Dan back. He was obviously afraid of the horse, which was indeed more than he could handle. So a few days later Dad, Rita (my five-year-old sister), and I drove down to the Bowman place. Dad bought Dan back for half what he had sold him for, then added insult to injury by first throwing the kid saddle on him and then lifting Rita up onto the horse. "You can't put that leetle girl on that horse," Loyal protested. "She can ride him," Dad said. And she did, all the way home.

Horse Thieves and Vigilantes

I recently ran across *Lynchings in Kansas, 1850s–1932* by Harriet Frazier. Of the 206 lynchings she documents, almost all of them occurred in the nineteenth century, and only four in the twentieth. The majority of these were for horse theft (ninety-three), and the next highest number (seventy-seven) for murder. Interestingly, horses were much more highly valued than cattle with only two rustlers executed by vigilantes.

Of the ninety-three lynchings for horse theft, eleven occurred in Flint Hills counties with a total of twenty-one men executed. Lyon and Wabaunsee Counties each dispatched one thief, Geary and Morris two each, three in Riley, and four in Greenwood, while Butler County vigilantes hanged or shot eight men for stealing horses. All eight of Butler's occurred near the town of Douglass in the south end of the county, and all within a month toward the end of 1870. Those are the official records that Frazier documented, but local lore often comes up with larger numbers.

For instance, the two volumes the Greenwood County Historical Society published in 1986 and 1990 tell of three brothers from a farm near Madison (no names were given) who had been to Neosho Rapids up in Lyon County, and when they returned that night they found the corral gate open and all their horses, except the ones they were riding, gone. Next morning they saddled up and started tracking the missing stock. A day or two later the brothers rode back into the barn lot with all the missing animals. When their father asked where they had found the horses, the boys said they were downstream along the Verdigris River. He asked if they had seen anyone, and they said no. The next day a man rode into Madison with news that he had found two men hanged in a big cottonwood tree southeast of town along the Verdigris.

The pervasive thefts in Greenwood County, unchecked by official law enforcement, eventually caused a secret society of vigilantes to be formed. Some members of the group, on the watch for suspicious activity, determined that a druggist in Madison was in cahoots with the horse thieves. They spread the word, surreptitiously, to gang members that they should meet at the drugstore that evening. Of the nine suspected thieves in the gang, eight showed up at the rendezvous where they were immediately surrounded by twenty-five vigilantes. Dispensing with the formalities of a trial, the vigilantes took the thieves to a stand of trees near a sawmill where a large timber had been placed between the forks of two trees and hanged them forthwith. Then the vigilantes rode back into town and told the sheriff that there were eight men at the sawmill that needed burying. A ledger found in the drugstore, by the way, recorded each of the horses that had been stolen and how the money had been divvied up among gang members.

About the same time in Lyon, the county just to the north, horse thievery was equally rife. In one particularly audacious theft a family of movers set up camp along the Cottonwood River near Soden's Grove at Emporia. In order to secure their team of "the best four-year-old mules I ever saw" (in the words of Royal Wolcott, an Emporia resident who died in 1934), the owner locked chains around their necks then passed the chains through the spokes of the wagon wheels and locked them. Next morning, in spite of these precautions, the mules were gone. And so were the wagon wheels. The thieves had carefully jacked up the back of the wagon, removed the wheels, then led both mules away simultaneously so one wouldn't nicker after the other, all this without wakening any of the family members asleep inside the wagon. The wagon wheels and the chains, cut off the mules' necks, were found several hundred yards away. Royal said that he never in his life saw a more surprised look on a man's face than when the owner crawled out of his wagon that next morning.

A few years earlier some strangers were selling horses at Sixth and Commercial in the heart of Emporia. A hunter stumbled onto a herd of horses hidden along the Neosho River north of town and alerted the local vigilantes, who set up a watch over the next few days and saw the same strangers leading in stolen horses one and two at a time. Once sure of the guilt of the gang, the vigilantes slipped out at midnight and formed a half circle around the thieves' campsite. One shot was fired into the air, which caused all the thieves to jump out of their bedrolls, and immediately twenty vigilante shots rang out, killing all the thieves.

In one particularly cruel incident a horse thief took a team of good workhorses from a barn, leaving two horses of far lesser value in their stead. Then he set fire to the barn, assuming that would cover up his crime. He was caught, however, because the two nags he had put in the barn were shod and the good team wasn't.

Of all the Flint Hills vigilante action against horse thieves, that which occurred near Douglass is the best documented. In fact, it is the subject of a 1992 book, *The Violent Years: The Founding of a Kansas Town*, by J. Mark Alley, and of a doctoral dissertation written in 2003 at the University of Kansas by Lisa Miles Bunkowski, *The Butler County Kansas Vigilantes: An Examination of Violence and Community, 1870.*

By 1870 horse theft was becoming all too common in southern Butler County. For instance, an article in the *Walnut Valley Times* reported that thirty-two horses had been stolen on August 8 from Wichita and Douglass. Editor T. B. Murdock, commenting on all those stolen horses, suggested in an editorial printed in April of 1870 that "Lynch Law should be put in force." A month later he noted that protective societies were being formed, and he further advocated that some of the thieves should "pull hemp without judge or jury. Hanging is the only effectual remedy for horse thieves, and the quicker applied the better."

In May the bodies of two unidentified men, apparently killed by horse thieves, were found between El Dorado and Wichita with a note on one body on which was written: "Beware of Horse Thieves." The tables were turned by an owner who went looking for three horses that had been stolen from him. A few days later he returned with the horses, commenting: "Them thieves won't steal any more horses."

In early November P. W. Crawford was in Wichita when several men claimed his mule and took it away from him. Crawford went to his camp and, bringing his two sons (William and James), went back to Wichita, found his mule, untied it, and started leading it back. They were overtaken by Douglass residents George Booth, James Smith, Jack Corbin (a former scout for Custer at the Battle of the Washita), and another man (probably Jack Ledford or Booth's brother Lewis), who demanded the mule back as well as the horses they were riding. They beat the elder Crawford with their pistols, while the two sons raced back to camp, armed themselves, drove off the thieves, and rescued their father. The next night the thieves returned and stole all three work teams belonging to Crawford.

On Election Day, November 8, Crawford was in the Douglass House hotel, where votes were being cast. When Corbin walked through the lobby, Crawford asked who it was and said that he was one of the men who had beaten and robbed him. Some Regulators (the name the area vigilantes had adopted) heard him. Both Booth brothers were also in town that day, and that night they and Corbin rode back to Lewis's home, while the drunken Smith rode his white mule into a saloon before starting to his own house later.

While some of the Regulators lay in wait along Smith's route home, a group of the others went to Lewis Booth's house. The masked vigilantes knocked on the door, and when Lewis's wife Jennie opened it, they forced their way in and seized the three men. Taking them to the woods near the Walnut River, they put a noose around Corbin's neck and hoisted him up and down a few times until he named some of the other thieves in the area. Then they hanged him for good. The two Booth brothers begged for bullets instead of hemp, so the Regulators told them to make a run for it, then cut them down in a hail of bullets. Meanwhile James Smith was shot at Slayton's Crossing as he rode into the ambush the other group of Regulators had set.

Storekeeper William Quimby, Michael Drea, Dr. James Morris, and his son Alexander, a druggist, were all suspected of stealing horses or at the very least being sympathetic to horse thieves. Shortly after midnight on December 2, a couple of hundred Regulators took the four men from Quimby's store and walked them south of town to a sawmill where they had placed a log between the forks of two trees (which seems to have been a popular form of makeshift gallows in the Flint Hills). After extracting a confession and the names of others involved in the syndicate, the vigilantes strung them up.

All told, eight horse thieves were lynched at Douglass in just under a month. And that was the end of widespread horse theft and vigilante action in that part of the Flint Hills.

Winter Horses

Winter in the Flint Hills is a movable feast, or famine—sometimes mild and gentle, sometimes fierce, usually a mix of both. I remember Christmas time at Dad Hoy and Grandmother's house with all the cousins. Sometimes we were huddled inside for warmth, sometimes outside having snowball fights, and sometimes playing in the sun with bees buzzing.

The winter of 2018–19 fit into the miserable category here in our part of the Flint Hills. It was wet with rain and mud, several periods of snow (but never more than three or four inches at a time and on the ground for only a few days at most), much of the time with temperatures in the twenties, and a few days close to zero. And wind? Strong and constant, it seemed. On those days when the ice was too thick on the pond for the horses to break on their own, it meant bundling up and going out to break ice.

February of 2014 was another bad one with eight inches of snow covering the ground and several days in a row of single digits with nights below zero. It wasn't all bad, however, because when the grandkids came to visit one weekend they had great fun playing on the frozen pond. We didn't have skates big enough for our fast-growing teenage grandson, but the girls took to the ice like ducks to (unfrozen) water. We have a nice slope for sledding just east of the house, which they also enjoyed. Out in the level hay meadow south of the house I used to use a horse to pull them on the sled, but I had bought a Polaris Ranger a little while earlier, so now we hitch the sled to it. Two advantages: (1) I don't have to saddle a horse and get her sweaty, and (2) the ATV goes a lot faster and doesn't get tired. The kids love the speed, but there's no windshield and my face gets a lot colder than when I'm pulling them with a horse.

When my sister and I were that age, we would sometimes tie the sled behind the hayrack when Dad would go out to fill it with kaffir corn bundles or hay from the haystack to feed the cows. It was a slower ride, but still fun. Dad

A winter cattle drive on the Flying W Ranch. (Photo by Mark Feiden)

liked feeding on snow, which gave the old girls a nice, clean table to eat from. When the snow melted, however, their tabletop turned to mud.

I wondered how feeding protein pellets on snow works, which is what ranchers use today, along with the big round bales of hay, which they unroll on top of the snow (or the grass, if there's no snow). So I asked Josh and Gwen, who had taken in (this was in 2014) some six hundred yearlings to winter just before the cold weather hit. They said that pellets work better in snow than on grass because the cattle don't have to root all the way into the ground to get a mouthful. I asked how the steers were doing. A few had been under the weather, they said, but because the cattle had come from Iowa, they arrived with long, shaggy coats and were already used to cold weather. Years ago I worked on a ranch that brought in some Mississippi steers right when winter began. With their short hair they had a lot more trouble adjusting to the cold, which kept me busy doctoring half a dozen or so a day for several weeks.

Breaking the ice: often these words mean relieving tension in an awkward or dangerous situation, opening up conversation to prevent an altercation. Or you might tell a joke or say something self-deprecating at a meeting, for instance, just to loosen up the crowd. Often when I am interviewing an old-timer, I will take along a photograph of an 1890s roundup or a 1930s rodeo just to get him talking. In other words, you open things up and get things flowing when you break the ice.

When I'm breaking the ice for the horses, however, I think that the person who first used that expression must have been chopping ice on a river or stream, not a muddy-bottomed pond half empty because of drouth. You might open up a hole in the pond ice, but there is sure no flowing going on. If there's anything much colder than chopping through four or five inches of ice with the temperature in single digits and the north wind well into double, I can't think of it at the moment. It seems no matter how far down on my forehead I pull my ear-flapper cap and how far up my face I wrap my neck scarf, I still manage to get hit by those little slivers of ice and sprays of freezing water.

Dad always carried an ax along on the feed wagon when the weather was cold. After pitching off the alfalfa or the bundles of kaffir to the cows, he'd head the mules toward the pond or the water hole in the creek. He'd usually chop two or three holes to give the cows multiple access points to the water, and I'd follow along with a pitchfork to throw the chunks of ice out onto the surface. At home we had a horse tank for the mules and a couple of saddle horses. When I was in high school Dad bought a propane heater to keep the tank clear, but before that the ice would sometimes freeze nearly to the bottom. (Didn't seem to bother the goldfish, though.)

We ran the rest of our horses in a section pasture half a mile north, kicking them out in later October after the cattle had been shipped and keeping them there until early spring. We never gave them a single bale of hay all winter, and we didn't break ice for them, either. If the ground was snow-covered, they would paw down to grass and get all the water they needed from snow while eating grass, and if the ground was open they would break the ice by pawing with their hooves if it got cold enough to freeze the stream. Interestingly, they never lost any appreciable weight until early March, when the cool season grasses began to grow and the horses quit eating the old grass. That's when they'd start to "gant up," and we'd bring them home and give them hay. Horses are much more self-sufficient than cows.

Here at home I keep a big round bale of hay in front of our horses all winter long, and I break ice on the pond as necessary. What's interesting is that, even with an open barn they can go into whenever they want, they will stay outside even during extreme cold or a snowstorm. You would think that with the wind howling they would have taken shelter in the barn, but the next morning they will be standing at the hay feeder, their well-insulated backs covered with a layer of snow.

It's a cliché to say it, I know, but I really don't think our winters are as snowy as when I was a kid back in the 1940s and '50s. It seemed that we fed on snow almost all winter long back then, and that the mud wasn't bad until spring was really ready to come. Be that as it may, January and February of 1979 gave us plenty of snow. For six weeks, with a break of about three or four days in the middle, we had to walk back and forth the eighth-of-a-mile driveway from the mailbox to our house. This next might sound far-fetched, but one afternoon we got a phone call from our neighbors telling us we had a horse on the road. The snow was so deep that the top wire of the pasture fence was only a couple of inches above it, and Rebel, the kids' half-Welsh pony, had walked over the hard-packed drift and out onto the road. A friend from Nebraska was not impressed by this story; he claimed that he remembered drifts so high that he and the neighbor kids would step over telephone lines on their way to school. I think he was telling the truth; a Texan might exaggerate, but a Nebraskan?

A few years back I interviewed an old-timer in Chase County who claimed that he had to walk to school through chest-deep snow, holding his hand up to the front pocket of his bib overalls to show just how deep it was. "Kids have it easy nowadays, though," he said. "The snow never gets any deeper than this," dropping his hand to his knees, which would have been about the height of his chest back when he was in second grade. Thus memory doth make unintentional liars of us all.

Still, he had a point. A snowfall with enough depth to let kids make snow angels, much less snowmen or snow forts, comes rarely anymore. One of our favorite winter recess games at Cassoday Grade School was fox and geese. I wonder how many schoolchildren today know the rules or have even heard of the game.

One of my favorite Kansas winter jokes is about the old farmer who, after eighty years of pitching hay, milking cows, feeding the bucket calves, and slopping the hogs, was finally persuaded by one of his daughters who had moved to southern California to retire and come there to live where it was always sunny and warm. He enjoyed the change in climate for a year or two, but then one February morning he walked outside, looked around, went back inside, and said to his wife: "Oh hell, another damn beautiful day."

I'll close with a favorite winter memory, which occurred during the middle of the 2017–18 winter. At the time we had four equines on the place, our two good gray mares, Pudge and Tica, twenty-year-old half sisters born about a month part; Artemis, a four-year-old dun mare; and PeeRoy, a miniature spotted donkey about nine hands tall (or, more accurately, short). Our granddaughter Josie gave him to us, and she called him Peewee, but years earlier Cathy's dad had given Josh and Farrell a wild burro BLM rescue animal that our kids named Elroy. Thus PeeRoy.

I was at the pond, cutting a hole in the two-inch-thick ice when the horses came up for a drink. I was about half finished when Artemis (named after the Greek goddess of the hunt; her mother we had named Hunter) came up, slightly hindering my efforts. Even before I had cleared the chunks from the hole with a pitchfork, Artemis was drinking, her front hooves two or three times slipping down into the cold water up to her fetlocks. After she finished, she came up to me while Pudge moved to the hole and, without getting her hooves wet, got her drink. Then it was Tica's turn. As with Pudge, she also drank without her hooves sliding into the water.

All three horses moved away from the pond and up into the pasture as the miniature donkey went down for his drink. It was sunny and wind-still and they were feeling calm and friendly. They stood as I rubbed their necks and backs, and as I did I noticed that Artemis was wet past her nostrils while Pudge and Tica had only the bottoms of their muzzles dampened. When PeeRoy came up, he had only the faintest bit of water on the bottom of his lips and, like the grays, none on his hooves.

So what? Probably nothing, but I found it interesting that the youngest, most exuberant of the equines was also the one least careful about getting wet in the cold, cold weather.

On a cold afternoon a couple of days later I looked out the kitchen window and saw Artemis running at PeeRoy, apparently chasing him. I thought he might not like that and was about to get bundled up and go out to put one of them in the corral. But then I saw PeeRoy, who was twenty or so feet in front of Artemis, suddenly turn and run past her, kicking up his heels at her as he went running by. Then Artemis whirled, jumped high in the air and kicked as she jumped, and ran past PeeRoy, executing several more perfect twisting bucks as she went past. Eight seconds' worth of those lively bucks and she would have scored a good forty points from the judges in a saddle bronc ride (and so would the rider, if he had been able stay aboard). Then PeeRoy ran and kicked past her, then she past him, each taking turns in what could only be described as a joyous frolic.

They must have made eight or ten such passes before settling down to the hay feeder. Johan Huizinga's book *Homo Ludens* posits the idea that the ability and inclination to deliberately play is a trait humans share with other animals. If he could have seen Artemis and PeeRoy playing, he would have had all the validation he needed for his theory.

SOME RANCHES

Rogler Ranch

Back in the early 1960s I worked for a while for Wayne Rogler on his ranch near Matfield Green. My father and I had often helped Wayne ship cattle out of both the Cassoday and Matfield stockyards. At the end of shipping season in the fall of 1961 Wayne asked if I wanted to stay on. He was getting some yearling steers from Mississippi to pasture for the winter, and I didn't have anything better to do, so I said sure. I had graduated from K-State that May, worked a few weeks on the maintenance crew on the Kansas Turnpike to get a little money, then spent the summer cowboying and rodeoing.

Until the yearlings came in, Wayne had me help out with various jobs, one of which was building some calf sheds out of railroad ties and curved sheet metal, kind of like small Quonset huts. Now carpentry is definitely not my strong suit, and those sheds didn't look like much, but they were still standing over thirty years later.

Wayne was an interesting man to work for. When you'd get there in the morning, he'd come out and give you instructions for the day. Then he'd likely change his mind two or three times before you could get out of the yard. One of the older hands on the place told me that it was best to jump right to work after the first set of instructions so that Wayne wouldn't have a chance to tell you to do something else. But one of the wiser hands gave the best advice: listen to all the jobs Wayne lined out, then start doing the one that sounded best to you.

So I was glad when the cattle arrived in late October, and I had a definite long-term assignment. We drove them to the West Frew pasture on the Butler-Chase county line about half a dozen miles south of the Matfield yards. It was a cold October with skiffs of snow, and it got worse in November. Between shipping fever and being suddenly transported from a warmer to a colder climate, those cattle got sick in droves, and I was put in charge of doctoring them.

Every morning I'd drive the dozen miles from home to Rogler ranch headquarters a mile north of Matfield Green, and Wayne would hand me a bottle of medicine (probably penicillin), a syringe, and a couple of needles and send me back south toward the Frew, which lay on the north side of the county line. Years earlier Dad had warned me about taking down a rope to throw at weeds (or heels) if we were helping ship Rogler cattle; Wayne, like most cattlemen, didn't approve of roping a cow unless it was absolutely necessary. He knew I was going to have to rope those sick steers in order to doctor them, but he never once mentioned it; he just handed me the medicine and sent me on. To tell the truth, I don't think he could bring himself to actually visualize what was going to happen out in that pasture. He just sent me off and shut his eyes to the rope hanging from my saddle.

I had two Rogler horses to use, both of them three-year-olds. Each had been ridden before I started working there, but they were a whole lot better broke after that fall. One was a pretty little sorrel Quarter Horse mare owned by Wayne's daughter, Mary Ann. I don't know what she had named her, but we called the mare Mary Ann. Very few people were allowed to ride her, so I felt good about that. She was a natural cow horse and really liked the work. My other mount was a bay gelding with thoroughbred blood the other Rogler hands had named High Pockets. He was tall, thin, and fast. He didn't take to cows like the filly, and at first he'd stick his head down and try to pitch while chasing a steer, which made the roping a little more exciting. But we never parted company and he soon got over it.

At the end of November I quit, not because of dissatisfaction, but because I wanted to go back to the Chicago rodeo. The year before I had gone with H. L. Todd, who later became my brother-in-law. The rodeo lasted something like ten days, and I won third place in the calf roping. In 1961 I didn't place in the average, but I did win enough go-round money to get me through the winter and spring without a regular job. Of course back in those days the cost of living wasn't all that much—a quarter would get you a gallon of gasoline, or a beer, or seven songs on a jukebox. And I hadn't yet gotten onto the idea of acquisition and getting ahead.

Tom Burton took my place when I went to Chicago, rising to the position of foreman a few years later, a job he held for the rest of Wayne's life and beyond, some forty-five years. There were times, in the midst of grading a seemingly bottomless pile of freshman comp papers, that I wished I'd not gone to that rodeo in Chicago.

One of the benefits of working on the Rogler ranch was the cooking of Mrs. Geer. She lived in a small two-story house, dwarfed by the Crocker house (a large Victorian two-story house, transformed into a near-mansion when pillars were later added to flank the front door) a hundred yards to the south and about two hundred yards across a brome grass lot to Wayne and Elizabeth's house to the north. She was an older woman, not a widow because her husband, Oss (probably short for Oscar, but I don't know for sure) Geer, worked at the sale barn in El Dorado. I don't know if they were divorced or what, but she lived at Matfield and Oss at El Dorado. She cooked breakfast, dinner, and supper for the unmarried men working for Wayne. Because I lived at home and drove to work each day, I only ate the noon meal and an occasional breakfast with the other hands. She was a good cook, nothing fancy, just good solid Flint Hills cuisine, heavy on the roast beef, potatoes, and gravy.

In later years I would often stop by to visit with Wayne, who was a font of information about early history in the central Flint Hills. I would also sometimes bring my Flint Hills Folklife class to meet with him for the same reason. Wayne knew every inch of ground in his part of the Flint Hills, and most of what had happened on it. I recall one time we were in his pickup on a high hill overlooking Matfield Green, and he told me that he could point out the spots where eleven men had died with their boots on. One of those places, near where the Cities Service Booster Station was located, was called Dead Man's Hollow, and Wayne said that as a kid it was pretty spooky to ride through there at night.

He had handled literally hundreds of thousands of cattle in his lifetime, from registered beef cows to longhorns and Brahmas. I particularly liked his story about some wild steers they had unloaded in the springtime at the Matfield stockyards. It helps to know a little about how railroad pens worked to appreciate this story. The loading platform is about four feet off the ground and about a foot and a half from the stock car, so you had to place a heavy piece of lumber called a bullboard (which weighed well over a hundred pounds) between the platform and the stock car so that cattle wouldn't step into the crack and possibly break a leg when you loaded or unloaded them. The door on the stock car was on rollers, and to keep the cattle inside the car while you put the bullboard in after sliding the door open, there was a four-foot-long, two-by-six-inch barrier board that fit across the door about chest high on the cattle. One end of the barrier board was attached to the door frame with a length of chain and could be firmly set into a slot, while the other end could be fitted into a slot on the far side of the door.

Normally when unloading you had plenty of time to put in the bullboard and remove the barrier board, but on this particular bunch of steers, Wayne

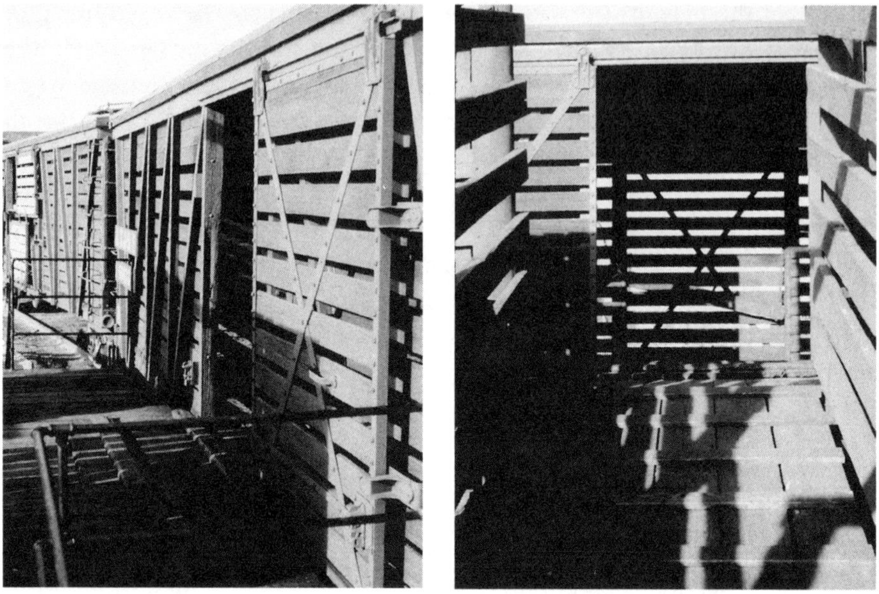

Left: Line of railroad cattle cars. All stock car photos taken at the Ranching Heritage Center, Lubbock, Texas. Right: Loading chute.

said, they had no sooner slid the stock car door open than these wild Brahmas began jumping over the barrier board and heading down the chute. When the wildest ones (about half the car) were out, the cowboys finally got the bullboard in place and the barrier board taken down, and the rest of the cattle poured out of the car and down the chute.

Then, Wayne said, just as the cowboys were about to toss the barrier board back into the car and take up the bullboard, they heard a clatter of hooves and looked over their shoulders to see the lead bunch of steers charging back up the chute. The men jumped out of the way just in time as the cattle ran back into the stock car. They had hit the back end of the pen, bounced off, and decided, I guess, that they wanted to go back home to Texas.

The Rogler ranch came to an end on the October 16, 2006, when what was left of it was auctioned off. At one time Wayne had run cattle on some fifty thousand acres of owned and leased Flint Hills bluestem, but by this time, thirteen years after Wayne's death and several months after his widow Elizabeth's death, there were only a little over four thousand acres for the auctioneer to work with.

The ranch had its start when Charles Rogler, accompanied by his friend Henry Brandley, had come into what is now Chase County and preempted a homestead in 1859. Charles Rogler left Austria at age seventeen, sent by his

Inside a cattle car looking out. Note bullboard in place between car and platform, and barrier board hanging down on the left side of the door.

father to America to find land for a new home. In 1868 he acquired legal title to the land he had first settled on nine years earlier. His first house was a log cabin, a replica of which his grandson Wayne constructed in 1960 and which still stands at Pioneer Bluffs, the home of Charles's son and Wayne's father, Henry.

In 1908 Henry built a two-story house, followed by a large barn seven years later. These impressive structures lie to the east of a large bluff, thus the name painted on the barn: Pioneer Bluffs. When the house was completed, Henry planted sixteen cottonwood trees along the walkway in the front yard, each one named for one of the sixteen U.S. presidents who had served at the time Charles Rogler built the original cabin. Today, only the Lincoln tree is still standing.

Charles Rogler died in 1888, Henry in 1972, and Wayne in 1993. In the later 1950s Henry retired and Wayne added the original ranch to his own holdings, which he had been putting together for several decades following his graduation from Kansas State Agricultural College in 1925. Later on he added a cow herd, but his original, and continuing, enterprise was pasturing Texas cattle for absentee owners on land leased from absentee owners—in other words, the classic mode of ranching in the Flint Hills. In his first year, about 1927, he pastured nine hundred steers. The following year the number was doubled, and doubled again the year after. At the peak, Wayne was responsible each year

Wayne Rogler standing on the bluffs, Santa Fe tracks (not visible) to his right, Pioneer Bluffs across the highway.

for the welfare of some ten thousand aged Texas steers grazing on some fifty thousand acres of Kansas grass.

Wayne was one of the most astute ranchers I ever knew, and I learned from him that a successful Flint Hills cattleman doesn't manage cattle; he manages grass. Take half, leave half, Wayne said, so you'll not overgraze and thus have enough old grass to burn the next spring. Perhaps even more important, Wayne valued the Flint Hills as much for their beauty as for their economic potential. Don Good, emeritus agriculture professor at Kansas State University, Wayne's alma mater, spoke at the auction and said that Wayne was a lover of the land and a lover of livestock. Wayne told me once that your pulse rate was guaranteed to slow down whenever you got out in the middle of a bluestem pasture in the Flint Hills. (As I often say, the Flint Hills don't take your breath away, they let you catch it.)

Wayne liked getting out into those pastures, sometimes in a pickup truck, sometimes in an Olds Cutlass, as recalled by Chase County extension agent Mike Holder. Mike sometimes accompanied Wayne on these drives. One time they got stuck on the far side of the ranch, down in a valley where the two-way radio didn't work and they had to walk several miles back to headquarters.

Someone asked Mike if Wayne had walked back, too. "Only far enough to point me in the right direction," he said.

I have fond memories of the Rogler ranch. I hated to see it broken up and only hope that the new owners will value tradition, grass, and the beauty of the Flint Hills as much as Wayne did.

At the 2006 auction a consortium bought the twelve acres containing Henry Rogler's house and the big barn, establishing the Pioneer Bluffs Foundation, whose mission is Flint Hills ranching heritage. Pioneer Bluffs sponsors many events that help educate the public about the Flint Hills, particularly the Prairie Talks that have featured many area ranchers telling about their family histories and ranching operations. Information about Pioneer Bluffs is available at https://pioneerbluffs.org/.

Clover Cliff Ranch

In the spring of 1860, just one year after Chase County was organized, a young man from the mining country of northwestern Virginia came to the Kansas Flint Hills and acquired a quarter section of land along the Cottonwood River valley just a few miles southwest of present-day Elmdale. The young Welshman, Jacob Blackshere, built a small, one-room stone cabin, bought longhorn cattle to graze the hills behind the cabin, and broke out some farm ground in the bottomland of the Cottonwood River.

By the following year Blackshere had control of eight hundred additional acres of land, but the unrest of the Civil War caused him to return to his home in Virginia (soon to become West Virginia). In his absence from the Flint Hills, he had arranged to have three rooms added to his cabin (a kitchen, a dining room, and a second-floor bedroom, also built from native limestone). Construction on the house was completed in the 1870s with the addition of four more upstairs bedrooms and a couple of downstairs sitting rooms to go along with the kitchen and dining room. A year after hostilities ended, Blackshere returned to his ranch, bringing with him his wife and their four children.

Upon his return he immediately upgraded his livestock by dispensing with longhorns and replacing them with five hundred Durham (Shorthorn) cows, imported from Scotland. In the early 1880s he began stocking Galloways, a Scottish breed of black, hornless cattle, but with thick hair. Today, Galloway cattle are rare in this country, replaced by another black, hornless bovine from Scotland, Aberdeen-Angus.

To complement his cattle operation, Blackshere also farmed the flat, rich soil of the river bottom. Besides introducing purebred beef cattle to this section of the Flint Hills, he is also credited with planting the first kaffir corn in Chase County. More important, Blackshere was the first man in Kansas to plant alfalfa, probably the best and most nutritious of all hay crops. In 1875 he paid

$32.50 to have a bushel and a half of alfalfa seed shipped from San Francisco. He soon had some 1,250 acres of rich bottomland devoted to this legume. According to the 1943–44 report of the Kansas State Board of Agriculture, Blackshere "made a fortune each year" by selling alfalfa seed.

In 1901 Blackshere hired some fifteen men, in addition to his regular staff of five, to help harvest the alfalfa crop. Some was loose-stacked with dump rakes, go-devils, and overshot stackers, and some was baled. In that year the ranch shipped a hundred railroad carloads of baled alfalfa to Kansas City for export to South Africa.

Paul Jantzen, author of *Clover Cliff Ranch: The Land and Its People* (from which I am acquiring much of this information), notes that the fragrant, purple blossoms of the alfalfa plant most likely inspired the name for Blackshere's ranch: Clover Cliff. Interestingly, in the many years I have been passing by the Clover Cliff Ranch on my way to my son's Flying W Ranch, I have noticed that those 1,250 acres are still being used for raising alfalfa, occasionally alternating with corn.

By the time of his death, in 1894, Blackshere had a ranch of over 4,600 acres and a house that was (and continues to be) a showpiece. People driving U.S. Highway 50 between Clements and Elmdale, and even local residents, often note and comment on the striking beauty of the large two-story native limestone house sited on a bluff that overlooks both the highway and the Cottonwood River to the south.

In 1907 Homer Lee and Kathryn (Baker) Prather moved from Missouri to a ranch in the Flint Hills of Greenwood County west of Madison. Five years later they bought Clover Cliff from the Blackshere family. In that same year (1912) poet Vachel Lindsay undertook a walking tour from Illinois to New Mexico, stopping at Clover Cliff in late June. There he applied (unsuccessfully) to help put up alfalfa hay, as he described in this excerpt from his book, *Adventures while Preaching the Gospel of Beauty:* "Back on the little hill, properly introduced by ceremonious trees, was the ranch house itself. And before it was my lord on his ranching charger. The aforesaid lord created quite an atmosphere of lordliness as he refused work in the alfalfa harvest to a battered stranger." Lindsay may well have appeared battered, working his way cross country by shocking wheat, cutting weeds, picking gooseberries, cutting firewood, and hoeing corn and potatoes. However, using a pitchfork to properly build a haystack so that it does not spoil when rain falls on it requires both skill and attention to detail. Apparently his somewhat disheveled appearance did not inspire confidence in Homer Prather. (I know about the proper stacking of hay, both the alfalfa and prairie varieties, from youthful experience, having learned under the tutelage of a grandfather who insisted that a haystack should "split a raindrop.")

The Prathers, keeping up with (and in many ways, leading) the times, made improvements to the house and outbuildings. The ranch was one of the first in the region to have a telephone and to use electricity, having had a generator installed in the early 1920s and hooking onto the highline when REA came to the county in 1938. Homer had died in 1921, and his widow, Kathryn, took an active role in ranch management, sometimes checking on the pastures in her electric-powered automobile.

After seventy-five years, the Prather era ended when Jim and Joan Donahue bought the ranch in 1987. In addition to continuing the cattle and alfalfa business, the Donahues opened the ranch to the public in 1993 by instituting a bed-and-breakfast operation in the main house and the two tenant houses. On at least two occasions I arranged for my Flint Hills Folklife classes to tour the ranch house and enjoy a meal that Joan had prepared for us.

In 2014 the Clover Cliff Ranch again changed hands. On February 13 the Donahue heirs sold the four-thousand-acre ranch, including the alfalfa-growing bottomland, the magnificent stone house, two other houses, a barn, and some haysheds and other outbuildings, at auction.

Jacob Blackshere had paid $320 for the original 160 acres that formed the foundation of the ranch. In 2014 that two dollars per acre mushroomed into $2,125 per acre for a total sales price of over $8.3 million. Happily, the new owners are Flint Hills residents who know the legacy of Clover Cliff. After all, Warren and Susie Harshman are neighbors whose own ranch borders Clover Cliff just a couple of miles to the west. They have continued allowing public access, in both the bed-and-breakfast and the large, well-appointed pavilion they built for weddings and other such gatherings.

Sauble Ranch

In late May 2006 I attended an unusual birthday party a couple of miles south of Cedar Point—the 150th anniversary of the Sauble ranch. As you might imagine, it was a festive affair. I don't know of any other ranches in the Flint Hills, or anywhere else in Kansas, for that matter, that have been in the same family for 150 years.

From the looks of the crowd, I'd say that at least five hundred people showed up for the occasion, some from as far away as Massachusetts and California. There was a huge tent with dozens of tables for the afternoon's barbecue, music, and storytelling. Even the weather cooperated. The day was windy, but the tree-covered bluffs of the Cedar Creek valley, where the attractive stone ranch buildings are set, let in just enough of the wind to keep the temperature warm, not hot.

Besides visiting with many people, some of whom I had not seen for a long time, I was particularly interested in the museum that the Sauble family had arranged in the lower part of the barn, the upper part of which was set up for a dance that evening. The displays included photographs of family members, artifacts of various kinds, and clippings of newspaper stories about the ranch. Most interesting of all was a video of Pat Sauble telling the story of his grandfather and the founding of the ranch, a videotape that Pat's own grandchildren had filmed just for this occasion.

One article in the display was from a 1956 issue of the *Kansas Stockman* about the centennial of the ranch. Also on display were a couple of old saddles and a pair of David Sauble's chaps with his DS brand on them. Especially poignant were the remnants of a black felt hat, the very hat that David was wearing when he was struck by lightning and killed in 1894. He was only fifty-seven years old at the time, but he had done a lot in those years.

Born in Maryland, David headed west in his late teens and ended up in Kansas Territory. Near what is now Wichita, then an Indian trading post, he and a friend, Pete Hoover, got jobs with a cattleman named Wilcox, who had left (or been run out of) Texas because of his antislavery politics. Wilcox ran cattle in both the Gypsum Hills of Barber County and the Flint Hills of Chase County.

One of the family anecdotes is about the time that the two young cowboys delivered cattle at Newton in 1871, the one year it was a rip-roaring cow town. Bloody Newton, it was called back then. They feared getting robbed, even killed, if they stayed in town that night, so they camped out on the prairie. Hoover would eventually settle in Barber County on rangeland he had become familiar with while working for Wilcox, just as Sauble would do in the Flint Hills.

The two maintained a working relationship, and David would travel, usually by horseback, to the Gypsum Hills to help Hoover with cattle. On the occasion of his death, however, he had taken the train to Medicine Lodge where he was met by Pete in a buggy and leading a saddled horse. Just as they were crossing the railroad tracks, lightning struck and knocked down the team of horses pulling the buggy. After getting them untangled, Pete looked for David and found that he had been struck directly by the bolt.

David's son John took over the ranching operation, and he has since been succeeded by his son, Pat, David's grandson. The history of the Sauble ranch is a fascinating one, and I'm happy that Pat and Mary Sauble and their family chose to share the ranch's birthday celebration with the community. Maude Sauble, incidentally, married Henry Rogler, thus creating a tie between these two historic Flint Hills ranches.

Postscript

As I write this, it is 2019 and Pat is now in his late nineties. Pat's daughter Susan and her husband, Denny Hague, now handle the day-to-day operations of the ranch, but Pat was living by himself in the 163-year-old ranch house until last spring, when he moved into Presbyterian Manor, a retirement home in Newton. Susan and Denny's granddaughter, Piper Hayes, is planning to take over management of the ranch that her great-great-great-grandfather founded in 1856, thus keeping it the same family for six generations.

Post-postscript

Pat died on December 7, 2019, the last of the old-timers in this part of the Flint Hills. He was ninety-eight years old. His voice will not be lost, however, because his death coincided with the publication of a book, *Sauble: Stories from the Flint Hills*, issued by Mennonite Press and coauthored with Bonnie Lynn-Sherow.

Spring Hill Ranch and the Tallgrass Prairie National Preserve

On August 18 in the summer of 1878 an interesting man detrained at Cottonwood Station, as Strong City was known in those days. His name was Stephen F. Jones, a wealthy rancher from Colorado by way of Texas. Most likely he had in previous years accompanied some of his cattle when he shipped them on the Atchison, Topeka and Santa Fe Railway to the Kansas City stockyards and had noticed the lush grasses of the Flint Hills as he passed through.

Whatever it was that caught his attention about the area, he decided to start a ranch in Chase County. Ten days after his arrival he bought a quarter section farm on Fox Creek, and he continued to buy adjoining property to the east and west until he had amassed some seven thousand acres. Some of the plots he bought were only forty acres in size, some up to a thousand acres. Some he bought from individuals, and some was railroad land he bought from the Katy and the Santa Fe.

Although Jones did not move his wife and four children with him to Kansas on August 18, he did bring with him eighty-two carloads of "fine Colorado cattle," unloading some two thousand head that very day. Two days later he unloaded 1,500 more, grazing them on open range in Chase and Morris Counties.

Jones was a southerner, born in 1826 and reared in Tennessee. In 1849 he married Louisa Barber and left for Texas, settling on a stock ranch in Van Zandt County. There he was joined by his two younger brothers, Peyton and Jim. The Jones brothers prospered and in 1869 decided, as had another Texas rancher, Charles Goodnight, to establish holdings in the good cow country of eastern Colorado. By 1871 the JJ Ranch was flourishing south of Las Animas.

In his first few months in Kansas Jones continued to bring in cattle from Colorado, and he also built a small house on his original quarter section. Even though the herd law was not in effect at the time, he nevertheless began immediately to have fences built. Within five years his seven thousand acres were surrounded by over thirty miles of stone wall, some of which is still visible today. Jones was a pioneer in enclosed, as opposed to open-range, ranching in the Flint Hills, and he soon became well known around the state for his efforts to improve the quality of his cattle.

By 1887 Jones's ranch was valued at $200,000, this at a time when a single dollar was considered a good day's wages. In addition to his fine herd of Hereford, Durham (Shorthorn), and Galloway cattle, the ranch also raised purebred Hambletonian horses and Berkshire hogs. Besides the four hundred acres of bottomland used for raising grain, the ranch also had three hundred acres of tame and prairie hay; an acre of sweet and Irish potatoes; an orchard of over four hundred apple, peach, plum, cherry, and pear trees; and a quarter acre each of raspberry bushes, blackberry bushes, and grape vines.

Jones named his spread the Spring Hill Ranch, for the flowing springs on the site. In 1880 he began construction of the impressive limestone buildings overlooking Fox Creek that catch your eye today—especially a three-story house and a three-story barn. Limestone quarried nearby was used in their construction, and also in the springhouse/smokehouse, workshop, chicken house, and outhouse. The total cost of the project was some $40,000, over half of which went into the house, built in the Second Empire style that was popular in France at the time. The work crew comprised twenty men, whose bustling activity amid the sprawl of ranch buildings caused some travelers coming down from Council Grove to think that they had arrived at Strong City itself, which was three miles to the southeast.

Under the house to the northwest is a root cellar, while to the north a tunnel leads to a springhouse, where fresh-flowing spring water kept milk, eggs, and vegetables cool. Outside at ground level to the north in an unusual combination, a smokehouse was built on top of the spring house. Just to the northwest is an elaborate limestone three-holer outhouse, one with lace curtains. (One of the holes, by the way, was for children, only half as high as the other two.) The barrel-vaulted chicken house with a sod-covered roof lies southwest of the house and just north of the barn. It is built into the side of a slope and is larger than some of some of the dugouts that served as homes for pioneer families in Chase County.

Just as eye-catching as the house is the three-story barn on the south side of the grounds. Built into the side of a south-sloping hill, the barn at 6,480 square feet was the second largest in Kansas at time of its completion. The bottom floor was used for stabling horses, while the upper two floors served to store hay, grain, and implements. The second floor can be entered at ground level from the north, while the two ramps leading to the third floor allowed a grain wagon to enter on one side and exit from the other after being unloaded into a granary. Gravity could then dispense grain down chutes to feed boxes for livestock on the bottom floor.

It took two and a half tons of tin to cover the barn when it was roofed in December 1881. Originally a large windmill with thirty-foot blades was built into the roof on the north side of the barn. It was intended for use in shelling and grinding corn, but the extreme vibrations threatened the stability of the barn so the windmill was removed.

Jones was eminently successful in his desire to impress visitors and passersby with the appearance of his ranch. In 1887 a local newspaper reported:

> Our return home was down the west side of the creek, passing a number of good looking farm houses and a fine farming country, along the road, until we arrive at the palatial residence of the wealthiest man in the county, S. F. Jones. It stands on a very prominent hill and can be seen for miles, either way. At a distance it could be readily taken for an old Scotch castle, with secret stairways and underground passages. It is a magnificent structure, and we would convey no possible idea of its beauty with less than a half column of descriptive writing of the highest order.

Seen from the front, the house is indeed magnificent, but if one stands at the side of the house, its relatively narrow width is not in proportion to its length and height, a bit of cost-cutting Jones employed while magnifying its visual effect.

On April 16, 1971, the Spring Hill Ranch buildings were placed on the National Register of Historic Places, one of the first such designations in Kansas. Twenty-six years later the entire ranch was named a National Historic Landmark. One year earlier, in 1996, the ranch, then known as the Z Bar and expanded by interim owners to nearly eleven thousand acres, was named the Tallgrass Prairie National Preserve (TPNP), part of the national park system.

A quarter of a mile north of the Spring Hill house is Lower Fox Creek schoolhouse, a one-room, native-stone school built in 1882 on land donated by Jones. The district was organized in 1879, a year after Jones's arrival in Chase County, and the first classes, taught by Dora Peer, began on September 1, 1884. Average enrollment for all eight grades over the years was around twenty students. In 1947 the district disbanded and the building and the land it sat on reverted to then-owner George Davis.

In 1968 the Mid-East District of Kansas Garden Clubs began restoration of the school, and six years later it too was placed on the National Register of Historic Places. Today, as part of the TPNP, the school building has been opened to the public and is often used by teachers who bring their students there to experience what education was like decades ago. I never attended a one-room school (there were three rooms for eight grades at Cassoday), but the desks, wall maps, blackboards, and other furnishings bring back memories.

An interesting bit of folklore associated with the Spring Hill Ranch is the legend of the tunnel that is said to connect the barn to the house, some sixty or seventy yards to the northeast. The existence of this tunnel is sworn to by some area residents who claim to remember playing in it as children. The reasons given for the construction of the tunnel range from the prosaic (providing a way to get from one building to the other during blizzards) to the fantastic (the tunnel was built to provide a stop on the Underground Railroad, a network of people and places that helped runaway slaves reach safety). The fact that slavery had ended fifteen years before the house and barn were built would tend to negate the Underground Railroad theory. Perhaps the fact that when Jones moved his wife and four children to Kansas, they were accompanied by black servants, the Williams family, might have had something to do with it. Before emancipation they had been slaves for the Jones family back in Tennessee. G. H. Williams (born in Tennessee) and his wife Isabel and their seven children are listed as residents in the Jones household in the census of 1880.

For whatever reasons the belief in a tunnel on the Spring Hill Ranch persists, despite the fact that no evidence, including sonar soundings, supports its existence. Perhaps the tunnel from the house proper to the springhouse has been confused with a tunnel from the house to the barn. Nothing wrong with a good legend, however, and I hope that stories about the tunnel continue to be told.

Ten years after starting the Spring Hill Ranch in 1878, Jones sold it to Bernard Lantry for $95,000. He and his family then moved to Kansas City and had David Rettiger, who had constructed the buildings on the ranch, build them a house in Kansas City with stone cut from Chase County quarries. Captain Barney Lantry, a stonecutter from New York who had gotten his title from having piloted steamboats in Wisconsin, had come to Chase County in 1877. Not having much call for piloting boats in Kansas, Lantry returned to stone work, contracting with the Atchison, Topeka and Santa Fe to provide ballast for tracks, build bridges, and construct station buildings. Among many other projects (from Michigan to California and into Mexico) Lantry and his sons built the cog railway that runs up Pike's Peak near Colorado Springs.

The house that Lantry built for himself on the northwestern edge of Strong City, although not as spectacular as Jones's, was nonetheless a showpiece. His multifaceted operation, which he called Deer Park Place after the small herd of deer he kept around the house, included raising wheat, oats, and corn, as well as cattle, sheep, and hogs. Like Jones, he was interested in improving the quality of his breeding stock, which consisted of Hereford, Shorthorn, and Angus cattle. He amassed over twice as much ranch and farmland as had Jones, eventually owning some fifteen thousand acres. After adding the Spring Hill Ranch to his other holdings, Lantry's operation was interchangeably referred to by either that name or Deer Park Place.

Upon Lantry's death in 1895 (at which time he was a millionaire and reputedly the largest contractor in the country), his sons continued the construction business, but within a decade they had begun to dispose of some of the land. In 1904 over 9,500 acres, including the Spring Hill Ranch, was sold to Charles and Nannie Patten of Reading in Lyon County. Five years later the Pattens sold 1,080 acres, which included the Spring Hill headquarters, to Otto and Flora Benninghoven.

In 1935 George H. Davis, president of the Davis-Noland-Merrill Grain Company of Kansas City, bought the Benninghoven property, along with ten thousand adjoining acres that included the remaining six thousand acres of Jones's original holdings as well as much of Lantry's Deer Park Place. The ranch was called the Davis-Noland-Merrill Grain Company Ranch until 1975, when the company changed its name to the Z Bar Cattle Company and the ranch became the Z Bar Ranch.

In 1986 the ranch was bought by Boatmen's First National Bank of Kansas City, but it retained the Z Bar name. In 1988, with thoughts of a potential national park in mind, the National Audubon Society took an option to buy the ranch but did not do so. In 1994 the National Park Trust, formed some eleven years earlier by the National Parks and Conservation Association, bought the 10,894-acre Z Bar from Boatmen's, and two years later ownership of thirty-two acres, including the ranch buildings and the one-room school, was transferred to the National Park Service (NPS), the balance owned privately by first the National Park Trust, then the Kansas Park Trust, and now by The Nature Conservancy.

Establishing the Tallgrass Prairie National Preserve

Efforts to establish some sort of national prairie park go back to the 1920s. In 1930 Victor E. Shelford of the University of Illinois proposed that a large area of grassland on the Nebraska–South Dakota border be taken into the national park system. His suggestion went unheeded, and it was not until the later 1950s that interest again began to grow. In 1958, as a result of a nine-state study by G. W. Tomanek and F. W. Albertson of Fort Hays State University, the NPS proposed to establish a 34,000-acre national prairie park east of Tuttle Creek Reservoir near Manhattan, Kansas. Two years later the NPS added 23,000 acres to the proposal to assist in flood control plans after the severe flood of 1951. Opposition from Kansas farmers and ranchers was strong, however, crystallizing in a confrontation that drew national attention when Secretary of the Interior Stewart Udall and NPS director Conrad Wirth, arriving by helicopter to meet a tour guide at the proposed site, were met instead by rancher Carl Bellinger, who ordered them off his leased property at gunpoint.

In 1971 interest in a park grew when Sen. James Pearson and Rep. Larry Winn, both of Kansas, each introduced legislation to establish a sixty-thousand-acre prairie national park with an unspecified Flint Hills location. Initial opposition was led by the Kansas Livestock Association (KLA), supplemented two years later with the organization of the Kansas Grassroots Association (KGA). Pro-park support was coordinated by Save the Tallgrass Prairie, Inc. From 1973 through 1980 Congressman Winn continued to introduce legislation to establish a park, each time facing opposition from KLA, KGA, Kansas Farm Bureau, and the Kansas Association of Conservation Districts. Among the chief arguments of the anti-park faction was the loss of revenue once a sizable chunk of land had been taken off the tax rolls and the belief that ranchers were good stewards of the land. Pro-park adherents, including environmental groups associated with the Sierra Club and the Audubon Society, argued along with Stewart Udall that a tallgrass park would "fill the last gap in the nation's park system."

With the election of Ronald Reagan in 1980 and a concomitant moratorium on NPS acquisitions, Winn dropped his legislative attempts. In June 1988 the National Audubon Society optioned a purchase of the Z Bar Ranch from Boatmen's First National Bank of Kansas City, which had acquired the ranch two years earlier. The core of the Z Bar had been the Spring Hill Ranch, founded, as noted above, by Colorado cattleman Stephen F. Jones in 1878. Two years later, Jones spent $40,000 to construct the striking native limestone house and barn, which have become landmarks. In 1888 Jones sold his ranch to Barney Lantry, a stone cutter who had arrived in Chase County a year before Jones. Subsequently the property changed hands several times before being purchased in 1935 by the Davis-Noland-Merrill Grain Company.

Ron Klataske, west central regional vice president of the Audubon Society, working with Congressman Dan Glickman, set out three possibilities for the Z Bar: (1) purchase and operation of the ranch by the NPS, (2) purchase and operation by the National Audubon Society, or (3) purchase and operation by the State of Kansas. He further suggested that local leaders, ranchers, landowners, and environmentalists get together to work out a plan.

Anti-park groups, recalling that earlier proposals had specified parks many times larger than the Z Bar's ten-thousand-plus acres and fearing the imposition of eminent domain on neighboring properties, along with loss of tax revenue, again mounted heavy opposition. Many factors came into play in this debate, but in essence it boiled down to a controversy between ranchers versus environmentalists, each side believing that it would do a better job of caring for the land. Others outside these two core groups could see positive and negative arguments on both sides, and sentiment leaned toward setting aside some sort of prairie preserve open to the public. In 1991 the House of Representatives passed Congressman Glickman's bill to establish the Tallgrass Prairie National Preserve, but the two Kansas senators (Robert Dole and Nancy Landon Kassebaum) took no comparable action.

Early the following year, however, Senator Kassebaum convened a meeting at the Z Bar, bringing together a group that included interested parties both for and against the park. At her urging the conferees agreed to an outline of a plan that would keep some 99 percent of the land in private ownership, while allowing the NPS to own the buildings and operate the facility for the benefit of the public. Although Boatmen's Bank and the private foundation created to purchase the ranch (Spring Hill Z Bar Ranch, Inc.) were not able to agree to terms of sale, the principle established by what became known as the Kassebaum Commission had created the conditions that made it possible for the National Park Trust, a nonprofit land trust established in 1983 by the National Parks and Conservation Association, to buy the land with the intent of having the National Park Service administer the ranch as a part of the national park system.

Soon after the National Park Trust had obtained ownership of the Z Bar Ranch in June 1994, legislation was introduced by Senators Dole and Kassebaum and by Representatives Glickman, Pat Roberts, Jan Meyers, and Jim Slattery that would allow the NPS to own up to 180 acres containing the ranch buildings and the one-room school. The remainder, owned by the National Park Trust, would remain on the tax rolls. The purchase was assisted by Texas rancher Ed Bass, who contributed $1 million toward the purchase price and also negotiated a long-term lease on grazing rights for an additional $2 million.

Final passage of the bill occurred in October 1996, and the legislation was signed into law by President Bill Clinton a month later. But the seventy-five-year odyssey to establish the prairie park had not yet come to an end. In 2004 the National Park Trust agreed to sell the private portion of the preserve to the Kansas Park Trust (KPT), an agency that had been initially established for that purpose. In March 2005 the Kansas Chapter of The Nature Conservancy purchased the property from the Kansas Park Trust, thus adding nearly eleven thousand acres to its holdings in the Flint Hills, which also include the 8,600-acre Konza Prairie Research Natural Area (now called the Konza Prairie

Biological Station) south of Manhattan and the 2,200-acre Flint Hills Tallgrass Preserve east of Cassoday, in addition to the 38,000-acre Tallgrass Prairie Preserve in Osage County, Oklahoma.

Once the Kansas Park Trust had transferred ownership to The Nature Conservancy, its remaining mission was to initiate construction of a visitor center. That accomplished in 2012, KPT disbanded, and today the Tallgrass Prairie National Preserve is maintained and operated by a dual public/private partnership, the first such arrangement in the nation: the National Park Service as operator and manager and The Nature Conservancy as the primary landowner.

ON THE ROAD

Transportation and Status

An important measure of status in our society is how we get from one place to another. Used to be that airline travel was pretty much the province of the well-to-do, but nowadays airplanes, airports, and airport parking lots are as crowded with the hoi polloi as a rush-hour subway in New York or Tokyo. With ordinary folks flying the friendly skies, the rich now flaunt their affluence by getting to board the plane before the rest of us and then sitting in comfortable plush seats sipping champagne in first class as we peons file past to our shoulder-cramping, knee-squeezing seats in coach.

On the highways, and even on city streets, the sport utility vehicle has joined the Porsche, the Lincoln, and the Cadillac as the automobile of status, particularly if that SUV is a Mercedes, a BMW, or some other luxury model. The SUV has certainly come a long way since the rough-riding, dust-leaking blue Chevy Blazer our family drove back in the 1970s. Even the lowly Jeep has long since become the conveyance of the rich and famous, although Willie and Joe would hardly recognize the vehicle they bounced around in during World War II in today's top-of-the-line Cherokee.

The mode of seeking status in vehicles undoubtedly goes back to the earliest times when humans found some means other than their own legs to move from here to there. Except for those tropical or desert regions where elephants or camels were pressed into service, that has generally meant horsepower. I don't know whether using a horse to pull a chariot or riding astraddle sans stirrups came first. No question, however, that the wheel had to be invented before chariots or wagons could come into existence. I do know that the warriors of the ancient civilizations, the Greeks and Persians, for instance, used chariots, not mounted cavalry. It took the Scythians and their invention of the stirrup to make riding a viable military option, one that Genghis Khan fully utilized.

Oxen were also used to pull vehicles, but the horse was the beast of status. Serfs hauled their hay and grain with oxen during the Middle Ages while their noble masters rode by them horseback. Wealthy families were transported in fancy carriages while the poor continued to walk, ride in ox carts, or be pulled by horses in open wagons. Pragmatically, ox power was preferred to horsepower on the Santa Fe and Oregon Trails. There, status was not as important as keeping wagons operative, and it was well known that Indians didn't give a darn about oxen but loved horses and mules. The same principle holds today when you look at statistics on auto theft—a fancy new Corvette is much more attractive to a car thief than an '86 Ford Taurus. Horsemen have always been as concerned with status as automobile owners. Spanish noblemen, for instance, always rode stallions, relegating geldings to the merchant class. Women rode mares and servants rode mules while poor parish priests, perhaps reflecting the humility of their Master, rode burros.

In Chaucer's *Canterbury Tales* the pilgrims are often characterized by their mounts. The wealthy, well-traveled, and full-figured Wife of Bath rides an easygoing ambler, while the Reeve, who manages a large farming operation, is quite proud of his fancy gray horse. Both horses, I'm sure, would be comparable to registered, prizewinning show horses today. The Knight, on the other hand, who has fought horseback from Russia to Jerusalem, rides a solid horse that Chaucer describes as "good but not gay." Like today's working cowboy, the Knight cares more about a good solid using horse that can get the job done than he does a pedigree or fancy looks.

Cowboys, in the Flint Hills and elsewhere, are as status conscious as car owners. Many don't like to ride mares, considering them temperamental and not as dependable as geldings. Also, having a mare in a string of geldings often results in the horses fighting among themselves for her attention. I remember hearing a horse trainer at a clinic a few years back remark disparagingly when someone brought in a flighty mare to be schooled: "I like a mare. Especially if she's got a good horse colt following her."

Actually, I've always been partial to mares, and I know a number of good cowboys who feel the same. Two of the best cow horses my father owned were mares, and Raymond Prewitt swore by Betty Jo, his little bay calf-roping horse. Dusty Anderson told me that he used over a hundred horses during the summer when he was looking after cattle in nine Flint Hills counties. His favorites, he said, were mares because they have more spirit and heart than many geldings. They might be temperamental, but they can be more fun to ride.

If I'm honest, the best all-around horse I ever had was a big dun gelding (Buck), but nearly all the other horses I've really liked have been mares, including my calf-roping horse (Kitty) and my bulldogging horse (Jan), who was out of Star, one of the mares I rode in my grade school years; Dusty was the other. We raised colts with the latter two. From the 1990s up to a little after 2000 my favorite horse was Molly, a little sorrel mare that was an excellent cow horse. She would often pitch when you first got on her in the morning, could almost duck out from under you when turning a steer, and was always edgy, ready to go. She was a catty little mare.

We were doing something at the Flying W one day a little after the turn of the century, and Cathy's horse (I think she was riding Smoky) started acting up. We swapped horses, putting her on Molly, which I had always been a little leery of doing up until then. They say a horse can tell who is on its back, and Molly sure did. As soon as Cathy mounted, Molly became calm and dependable, losing her edginess, and she never again offered to pitch. From then on she became Cathy's horse, and a few years later a kid horse for the grandchildren. I would never have thought it possible.

In 1947, when I was seven years old, Dusty came close to killing me. Not intentionally; she didn't have a mean bone in her body. We (Dad Hoy, Dad, Rita, and I) were getting some cows out of the Mosteller to take back home. One got into the railroad right-of-way, and I went running after it. About that time a train came by heading north (as we were) and, I think, blew its whistle. Whatever it was, something startled Dusty and she bucked, for the first and last time in her life. I was thrown, and even today as I'm writing this, in my mind's eye I can see her belly as she walked over me, stepping on my right ribcage as she did. I do not, however, remember her actually stepping on me, nor any pain or much of anything else, just a dim impression later on of a hospital room.

I'm told that Dad or Dad Hoy flagged a motorist down. I was taken to Cassoday, where Dad and Mother and my uncle, Marion Reed, took me to Wesley Hospital in Wichita in his new Mercury. There the doctors cut open my stomach to reveal a crushed liver that "looked like a piece of hamburger," they told my parents. The reason I'm here today writing this some seventy-three years later is that only a few months earlier someone had devised some sort of membrane that the doctors wrapped around my liver, then sewed me up. My liver healed, the membrane dissolved, and I have a long scar all the way across my stomach as a souvenir. Thanks to those doctors, and many other people as well, I have lived a long and generally happy life.

To get back to the theme of this essay, the ungelded male horse has always been considered the mount of highest status. Most of the world's great generals have ridden stallions. The mythic aura associated with a conquering hero riding a stallion is so pervasive that sculptors have insisted on the male horse even in the face of history. Gen. Winfield Scott's favorite mount was a mare, but his statue in Washington, D.C., had him astride a stallion until his family protested and forced the sculptor to neuter the bronze beast. The family of Gen. John Morgan was apparently not so effective with his statue, for the plaque at the hooves of an obvious stallion reads "Morgan on His Bess."

Another area of status among horsemen is color. Paint horses, for instance, are popular now, but in an earlier era they were considered inferior mounts. Andy Adams, in his classic novel of the Trail Drive Era, *The Log of a Cowboy*, says that pintos were all right for kids to ride, but "practical cattlemen" know that the color is a result of inbreeding "with consequent physical and mental deterioration." Today, however, as a result of crossing with Quarter Horses, many paints are solid, dependable mounts.

The appaloosa is more popular with pleasure riders than with working or rodeo cowboys. As a couple of jokes have it: Why did Indians ride appaloosas? Because that was the only horse they could catch on foot. And: Why did Indians like to ride appaloosas to battle? Because by the time they got there, they were so frustrated and mad they would fight anything. As with paints, there are some good appaloosas. My dad had a well-made appy gelding out of Wilber Countryman's appy stud that was pretty good with cows. Then again, he named him Psycho, which tells you something.

Back to Andy Adams. When the members of the trail crew are selecting horses for the drive, the foreman, who gets first choice, picks a dozen horses, all of them bays or browns. Solid colors were considered indicative of stamina and endurance.

Me? I've owned all colors, but I'm partial to buckskins and red duns, neither of which I own right now, but I'm real happy with my gray mare (now turned almost white, as is the wont of grays), Pudge.

Farm Trucks and Stock Trailers

In early August 2018, Cathy and I rode along with Josh and Gwen when they hauled a cow and a bull to the livestock sale barn in Paola. It was a nice day and a pleasant trip, the only excitement occurring when Josh opened the interior gate of the stock trailer to let the cow out. Whether she was by nature feisty or had instead gotten stirred up by the ride I don't know, but she charged out snorting and looking for something to headbutt, causing both Josh and the yardman to get out of the way in a hurry.

I'd never been to the Paola livestock sale before. It's located a mile or so southwest of town in an appropriately bucolic setting, but what really caught my eye was an unusual vehicle in the parking lot. There among cars, pickup trucks, and stock trailers of various sizes was a throwback to fifty years ago—a one-ton, dual-wheeled Ford truck with stock racks.

When I was growing up, the parking lot of the El Dorado livestock auction would have contained pickups and trucks of various sizes, all outfitted with stock racks. One set of loading (and unloading) docks would have been low for the pickups, another higher for the trucks. There might have been a bumper-hitch horse trailer or two there too, but none of the gooseneck stock trailers that are ubiquitous today.

We had a one-ton dark green GMC truck, bought new in 1951, that had a set of Omaha Standard stock racks, the lower half solid for hauling grain and the upper half spaced for livestock. Before that we had a smaller, dark-colored truck, which I can still see in my mind's eye but can't recall the make. (It might have been a three-quarter-ton flatbed Dodge or a Ford.) During World War II we had the use of Charles Bates's one-ton Diamond T while he served in the army. That was the first vehicle I ever drove, and that when I was four and five years old. Dad would put it in compound gear, I would stand on the seat behind the steering wheel, he would jump out and onto the back and pitch off

Rita and Kenneth and our 1951 GMC truck.

the alfalfa hay, I would steer down the pasture in a straight line, then he would jump back in and relieve me of my driving duties. I'm proud to say I had a perfect driving record—no wrecks, no flat tires, no speeding tickets, and no bumps big enough to throw Dad off the back.

In addition to hauling oats to the bin at home or wheat to the elevator in Cassoday, we mainly used our GMC to haul our horses to pastures to help ship cattle or to haul some of our own cattle to the sale at El Dorado or to the stockyards in Wichita. In 1957 we bought a new green Chevy half-ton pickup and built some stock racks for it, but we didn't have a horse trailer until sometime around the early or mid-1960s. My sister and I hauled our rodeo horses in the Chevy or the GMC.

I'm not sure when Dad bought a bumper-hitch stock trailer, probably in the mid- to later 1970s. He never did own a gooseneck. It was that gooseneck stock trailer that revolutionized farming and ranching in the Flint Hills, throughout Kansas, and beyond. That was probably in the later 1960s, about the same time that the potbelly cattle-hauling truck replaced single-bed semitrailers, which in turn was about the time that railroads stopped hauling cattle.

Until the gooseneck came along, a farmer or small rancher would have to hire a professional trucker to take his cattle or hogs or sheep to a sale barn or stockyards. The smaller operators often couldn't afford the capital investment required for a truck big enough to do the job. Thus the stock trailer forced some of the truckers who had been hauling livestock to shift their focus.

The gooseneck also spelled the death knell to the trader, the man who made a living by traveling the countryside and buying a cow here, a couple of pigs there, and hauling them to a sale barn. He would buy them a little below market price, but the farmer was spared the expense of hiring a trucker. Lamar Jones was a trader based out of El Dorado who we often saw at the community sale east of town.

Marley Berger was also a trader who lived north of Halstead. In my later teens and early twenties I spent quite a bit of time at the Berger place because Marley was the father of my friends Kenny, Don, and Bobby. Kenny put me on my first saddle bronc, and Bob and I traveled together some before he went pro and later won a world championship in saddle bronc riding.

Those were a few of my thoughts triggered by the sight of that one-ton stock truck at Paola.

Cattle Country Road Etiquette

The late Phill Pinkston used to remark that he thought it not unlikely that his photograph might be found in every state in the union. He based that unegotistical observation on the number of drivers who would stop and get out of their cars with cameras when the Pinkstons were driving cattle to the Bazaar cattle pens alongside the Kansas Turnpike, halfway between Emporia and Cassoday. (A scenic overlook has been made on both sides of the road there with a great view of the Hills to both the north and the south. Stop sometime to admire the view—and read the plaque that Cathy and I wrote.)

Just like those turnpike travelers, I agree that a livestock drive out in the wide-open spaces is a colorful sight. I remember one Fourth of July when the kids were little and we were camping on Panther Creek in Idaho, we saw two Basque shepherds with their dogs, a sheep wagon, and a big flock of sheep in the Sawtooth Mountains. Unlike the cattle being driven in the pastures bordering the Kansas Turnpike, these Idaho sheep were on a public road. Remote, but public nevertheless. Traffic was brought to a complete standstill for ten or fifteen minutes until the sheep had all passed. We happened to be the only traffic, but we didn't mind the delay because we were seeing a vanishing bit of Americana in action, just like those drivers on the turnpike.

These thoughts came to mind a while back when we were moving some cattle along a Chase County road. Just as we were getting the yearlings started across a bridge, an impatient driver pulled up fast, tooted the car horn, and scattered steers everywhere. Unfortunately, this was not an isolated incident. Several times in the past couple of years drivers have driven through (or attempted to drive through) the cattle we were moving down a gravel road, instead of waiting until we had passed or waiting for a rider to lead them through the herd.

Basque shepherd with his flock near Panther Creek, Idaho, 1975.

You might be thinking, what can you expect from city slickers? I hate to say it, but the impatient drivers were not city slickers, but local residents who should have known better. And actually did. Nowadays it seems that people are in such a hurry that they either ignore, or have never learned, proper driving etiquette when you're out in the middle of cattle country.

I know that when I was young and helping drive cattle into the railroad pens at Cassoday, we often had a herd of several hundred two-year-old steers strung out for well over half a mile on the township roads or Highway 13 (now K-177). I don't recall ever having cattle spilled by an impatient driver. Occasionally an outsider would get a little nervous and maybe honk his horn, but if he did he usually got a quick visit from one of the older hands. I was never close enough to hear the (one-sided) conversation, but when it was over the driver would invariably lag back or even shut off his motor and wait until we had cleared the road.

A knowledgeable driver meeting the herd would pull to the side of the road and slowly ease forward as the cattle parted and went on either side. If he had come up from the rear, he would wait until one of the cowboys rode over to him and let him know how much farther we had to go. If it was quite a distance and the driver had to get through, the cowboy would ride ahead of the car, parting the cattle and leading him through.

It was always my understanding that cattle had the right-of-way, and in fact the official rules of the road state that the occupant of the roadway has the right-of-way over any other person or vehicle approaching. Recklessly driving through the herd, honking and yelling is not only bad range country manners—it's also illegal. So if you happen to get stuck behind a herd of cattle going down a rural Flint Hills road (or even a state highway), just relax and enjoy the rare sight of cowboys at work. They'll soon be out of your way.

LIFE AROUND CASSODAY

Bruce Behymer

School mornings came early for a kid back home on the ranch, but Dad didn't always have to holler at my sister or me to wake us up. Not that we were naturally early risers, but Dad usually turned the kitchen radio on to KFH when he got up, and if we hadn't been awakened by the sound of his putting wood into the stove, we would darn sure lose hope of any further sleep at 6:05.

What happened on KFH at 6:05 a.m.? Ask that question of almost anyone reared on a farm or ranch in the central Flint Hills at mid-twentieth century and you'll get this answer: Bruce Behymer made his initial farm broadcast of the day. First there was a clanging cowbell that could beat any alarm clock for noise, followed by one of the most distinctive and (if you're still trying to hold onto sleep) the most irksome nasal twangs you can imagine: "Wichita's hog market today. . . ." It seemed that the only variation in the routine of his several daily broadcasts were the numbers and selling prices of animals at the Wichita stockyards. The morning market reports were always followed by Bruce's personalized weather report: "When I walked out onto the back stoop this morning . . ."

For years I didn't even know what a stoop was (it sounded vaguely scatological, like my grandfather's euphemism, "daily constitutional," for his morning trip to the outhouse), but maybe that term came from Behymer's boyhood in Illinois, where he was born in 1895, his family moving to Sedgwick, Kansas, when he was nine. After college in Wichita he started writing a farm column for the *Wichita Eagle* in 1917, returning to the paper after service in World War I. His radio reporting began by chance. The regular farm reporter for KFH (owned at the time by the *Eagle*) got sick and Bruce was asked to substitute. This was in 1931, and for six days a week for the next forty-three years Bruce Behymer was the voice of the Wichita stockyards.

Like many others throughout the Plains, these particular stockyards are no long operating and have been torn down (a great loss to history, in my opinion), but over the years when I was at home we hauled many a load of cattle to Wichita in our one-ton GMC. I remember the first time that Dad pointed out Bruce (as we called him at home—the radio had put us on a first-name basis with someone we'd never met in person). He was walking among the stock pens, getting a feel for the closing market he would report at noon. Bruce was a kindly looking man with a quiet demeanor, but I was expecting someone much older and rougher looking, an appearance to match the twangy voice that was always talking about canners and cutters, baloney bulls, and rough-bellied sows.

As I grew older, I no longer held Bruce responsible for ruining my sleep—I realized that I would not have been allowed to stay in bed much longer anyway. In fact, during the summer we often listened to his opening broadcast at breakfast, having already milked the cows and fed the calves. And when Bruce would occasionally report at noon on some cattle that had been shipped to Wichita from "Cassoday, the Cow Capital of Kansas," I would feel a swelling of hometown pride—and a touch of affection for the reporter.

May Memories

May is usually a pretty good month in the Flint Hills. The pastures are all green (assuming we've had some April showers), the wheat is heading out in the bottomlands, and the weather is usually temperate—warm but not yet hot. May this year (2003) has been particularly nice—the ponds are full, the nights cool, the days warm, which helps keep the flowers in full bloom, and we've been getting rain.

May, however, can be a bad month, especially for tornadoes—over three hundred nationally in one week earlier in the month, which set a new record. And I was reminded by my son that last May (2002) we had something like nine or ten days of ninety-degree-plus weather. That was the year we had a visitor in May, a horse trainer from Perth in southwestern Australia. I took him with me to help a rancher work calves down in Butler County. The temperature was in the mid-nineties and the humidity almost that high. After every half dozen or so calves, we'd all feel like taking a break to catch our breath, but not Glen; that heat was normal for him. In fact, he thinks that anything below fifty degrees is extremely cold.

Enough about the bad weather in May; this piece is about the good things that happen in this month. Indians in the Central Plains called late May and early June the Moon of Making Fat. It never ceases to amaze me to see how quickly the rough-haired, bony yearlings that are dumped into Flint Hills pastures in mid-April can become so sleek-haired and fleshy by the end of May. That fresh bluestem grass is like a tonic. When I was a kid, we usually wintered our horses in a section pasture near home. We'd bring them home in March, rib bones showing, but by mid-May they'd be fat and sassy from eating wild oats and new bluestem—Makes Fat Moon.

One reason my sister and I looked forward to May was because that was the end of the school year. I do feel sorry for the kids today whose school starts

The Arch Bridge over the Walnut River southwest of Cassoday.

in mid-August and doesn't end until early June. We started in September and were out by the middle of May. The year always culminated with a last-day-of-school picnic.

Our all-school picnic, which included all eight grades plus teachers, as well as any parents or townspeople who wanted to come along, was usually held at the Arch Bridge southwest of Cassoday, the traditional picnic site for our community. The bridge spanned the Walnut River, which had a couple of fishing holes at that spot, in addition to a big grove of oaks, cottonwoods, hickories, hackberries, ash, and other shade trees. We each brought our own sack lunches, although there may have been a time or two when we roasted hot dogs. We ran races and played games, from hide-and-seek to pasture softball, dodging rocks, cow piles, and the occasional prickly pear.

One year we held the last-day-of-school picnic in one of Grover Prewitt's pastures south of Cassoday along the Rosalia Road. There was a pool in a draw deep enough for swimming, but not many trees around for shade. The other place for the picnics was on the Sunbarger farm just northwest of town. This was long before the Kansas Turnpike split that eighty acres in two.

The Sunbarger was a good site. The Walnut ran through the place so there was plenty of shade, water for wading, a good stretch of flat bottomland for races and games, and there were also a couple of cavelike sinkholes that captured the attention of the more adventurous kids. My most vivid memory of a Sunbarger picnic is the time a careless badger made the mistake of emerging, very briefly, from his den, which caused my classmate Doris Robinson to yell excitedly and repeatedly, whether from delight or fear I am not sure, "A banjer, a banjer!"

I wonder if any schools still have last-day-of-school picnics? If so, I'll bet they don't let the kids swim in a creek, explore sinkholes, or chase "banjers."

Central

In the later 1990s I read a newspaper article about the end of party line telephones at Panther Creek, Idaho, which were said to be the last in the country. When our children were young, our family, along with Cathy's sister Carolyn's family, used to camp along Panther Creek for summer vacations. It was definitely a remote area, pristine enough at the time that you could drink the water from the stream without fear. So I could well imagine that these indeed were the last party lines. In December 2002, however, the *New Yorker* magazine had a short article about one of the last party line telephone systems in the country, this one in Michigan (I assume in the Upper Peninsula), and the article implied that there might be another one or two in the far West.

It was an interesting article, and I recognized many of the details of party line communication, as I'm sure many early Flint Hills residents did too. It wasn't all that long ago (or so it seems) that a majority of phone lines, and almost all those in rural areas, were party lines. In fact, back in 1976 when our family first moved into the country a couple of miles south of Emporia, we were on a party line. There must not have been many other households on our line, and undoubtedly no teenagers, because rarely if ever do I recall the line being busy when I wanted to make a call. I was actually rather sorry when a few years later everyone in our area was given a private line because the rates went up rather noticeably.

The major difference between our Emporia party line and the one from my childhood days was that the Emporia phone only rang when it was for us, but at Cassoday we heard the ring of everyone else on our line. Our number (funny how some numbers will stick in your mind) was 303—two long rings. Others on our line would have a short and a long, or maybe two longs and a short, etc. You were supposed to pick up the phone (wall mounted at Cassoday, a desk phone at Emporia) only on your ring, of course, but in those

Stella Hinde at the Cassoday telephone office, 1958.

pretelevision days many people seem to have derived their at-home entertainment from "listening in."

A Topeka teacher I know told me that once many years ago when she had called her parents in central Kansas to invite them to Topeka for Thanksgiving dinner, she asked her mother to bring a certain favorite food. "Oh, I'm sorry," her mother said, "so-and-so borrowed the dish that I usually bake that in." At which point the neighbor woman's voice broke into the conversation: "I gave that back to you last summer!"

There was one situation, however, when you were supposed to listen in. A whole series of longs signaled a "line ring," which could mean either an announcement (a play at the high school or the Christmas program at church) or an emergency (a prairie fire or a burning house).

Stella Hinde was the central (and only) operator at Cassoday, and I remember as a kid thinking she was kind of nosy. From the perspective of hindsight I realize now that what appeared to be undue inquisitiveness was actually proof that she was doing a good job. One of the functions of an effective small-town telephone operator was to know what was going on in the community. You could always call Central to find out what was happening at the schools or the church or to find out if the Doodlebug (officially the Little Ranger, a single-car locomotive that used to run up and down the line each day on the Santa Fe) was late. You didn't need an answering service back then or a neighborhood watch, either. Central would often notice a strange person in town, especially one who was acting a little suspiciously. And if your family had gone to El Dorado or Cottonwood Falls for the day, you might just get a call from Central when you got home telling you who had tried to phone while you were away.

And those services were free. No monthly add-ons to your phone bill for an answering service, call-waiting, caller ID, caller ID block, or a block for blocking caller ID block. The biggest advantage, though, was that we were not addicted to a cell phone.

Opal's Café

In the summer of 2007 we pulled into the Gas Kan (by then renamed the Cassoday Country Store and now called Rick and Jenny's but still referred to by locals as the Gas Kan) on our way to ship cattle out east of town and received some shocking news—the café downtown was closed! Shocking because there had been a café there for well over a hundred years. The news was so nearly unbelievable that we had to drive by to check it out for ourselves. Sure enough, there was a closed sign in the window. Two reasons were given for the closure, the first one minor—a small fire in the kitchen. The second was much more troubling. Diana Carlson, the tireless, cheerful, energetic, personable, fun-loving, outgoing (I'm running out of adjectives) owner/cook, was ill.

Diana took over the Cassoday Café in 1995, and in doing so she took over a piece of history. My mother wrote a piece about cafés in Cassoday for the centennial history book, *Cassoday: Cow Capital of Kansas*, published in 1984. According to her reckoning there had been at least twenty different eating establishments in Cassoday, beginning with one at Sycamore Springs built in 1870 by Frank Donaldson. One of the more memorable cafés was operated in the early twentieth century by John Warren and his wife. It was called the Maggie and Jiggs Café, nicknames based on the newspaper cartoon characters that suited them well, so said early residents of the town. In 1927 Myrna Diller and Leah Parsons opened the Saunter Inn, famous for Myrna's chocolate pie. Somehow or other our family acquired and passed down the recipe, and I can attest that it is indeed an unequaled delicacy, the best chocolate pie ever. Nay, the best pie period.

One of the more amusing dining incidents took place in a café run by a Mrs. Gangwer, where one evening some men were enjoying a Saturday night meal. At one point an adventuresome mouse came out of one farm hand's collar (the man had been working in a kaffir corn field earlier in the day), played around a bit, then returned to the warmth of his hiding place. None of the other patrons said a word, leaving the mouse to a few more hours of undiscovered peace. I don't remember the café run by Carrie and Bon Lines, but I do remember Mother and Dad talking about it.

I also remember when Bill (Wilma's nickname) Young added a café to her beer parlor while the Kansas Turnpike was under construction in the mid-1950s. The building had previously housed the Cassoday Bank, which went under during the Depression. There was also a concrete slab in back where outdoor Saturday night dances were held. That's where my career as a professional musician began. One Fourth of July after Countryman's Rodeo in the late 1950s or early 1960s, Richard Young, my cousin Gary Reed from Bartlesville, and I played the dance. The songs were all country/western or rockabilly, and there was no drummer—just three guitars. This was about the time that Bobby Helms had a hit with "Fraulein," and several of the older guys there who had been stationed in Germany had us play that song several times. Brought back some good memories for them, I guess.

About three weeks later my second and last gig as a professional musician took place at the 54 Club, a honkytonk on Highway 54 south of El Dorado. Richard had gone to a rodeo, but Gary, a real guitar player he brought up with him from Oklahoma, and I played for the drunks and dancers. No fights, no beer bottles thrown at us, and we were paid thirty dollars, which I gave to the Okies so they would have gas money to get home. After that I figured it would be more fun to ride broncs and rope calves and dance to somebody else's music. But I digress.

Opal's Café is the earliest eating house I recall. Opal Hart Green and her husband Holt lived northeast of town in Fred Burk's old two-story house just across the Santa Fe tracks on the north side of the road that runs to Teterville. Just south of the road was the Cassoday pasture where early in the twentieth century Billy Mercer, in the English tradition of the commons, let those townspeople who had them keep their milk cows and buggy horses free of charge.

Opal opened the café in 1945 in what had once been Rich's produce store. The building was only half as big then as it is today, the east dining room having been added when Harold and Jane Roberts bought it sometime after I had left home in the mid-1960s. There was a lunch counter on the east side of the original café and a few tables along the west wall, a sink for washing hands in the southwest corner, and the kitchen in back. There was no indoor restroom. But there was one out back. Opal cooked and served meals (I don't remember any waitresses, though there might have been some), and Holt would sit

An earlier incarnation of Opal's Café, probably 1920s.

behind the cash register collecting money and eating navy beans covered with sugar, cheese sandwiches, and ice cream.

I remember Opal saying more than once that if she could just get Holt to quit the cattle business, she could retire. He always had big ideas. I remember in the late 1950s that he built a big set of working pens just east of his house that he didn't really need because less than a quarter of a mile away, just across the tracks, were the Santa Fe stockyards that he, or anyone else in Cassoday, could use for working cattle.

I don't know how she did it, but Opal could feed all those cowboys quickly and efficiently, and you never felt rushed. Ranchers would call her up a day or two before they shipped and tell her how many cowboys would be in their crew, and she'd cook accordingly. She would open early or stay late on whatever day of the week she needed to in order to accommodate the cowboys. Besides getting that advance warning from the rancher, she kept things simple. I don't remember a printed menu to order from; you ate what Opal cooked, usually roast beef, mashed potatoes, gravy, and green beans or corn. You'd never founder on one of Opal's meals, as my dad said, but you felt satisfied, and it always tasted great.

Best of all was the pie. Opal's pies had very thin crusts and were always baked the morning of the day they were served. I doubt if there was ever any leftover pie at the end of a shipping day. She made all the standard varieties—apple, cherry, cherry cream, banana, coconut, lemon, and chocolate, all with the flakiest of crusts. She also made a great raisin cream pie. My favorite was pineapple cream, the likes of which I have never had anywhere else. Cathy has tried to make me one, but pineapple is acidic and causes the vanilla filling to turn watery. Somehow, Opal's never did.

When Diana bought the café in 1995 (Opal was gone by then, and I don't remember who was operating it at that time; maybe a dozen different people had run it after Opal retired), she soon instituted a first-Sunday-of-the-month outdoor breakfast buffet for motorcyclists, which caught on fast. Often there were three to four thousand bikers in town for the event. Even though Diana has been dead for many years now, the event is still going strong with other vendors coming in just for the day, even though the café itself is closed. I've learned to avoid town on the first Sunday, both for the congestion and especially the noise.

Diana also catered, all while operating the café itself. As I said, she was energetic. Several years ago a CBS movie, *Stolen Women, Captured Hearts*, was filmed east of town. A photo of the star, Janine Turner, hung on the wall of the café, alongside scenes of shipping and other cattle work. Other celebrities who have eaten there over the years include Dennis Weaver of *Gunsmoke* fame and Kevin Costner. Diners have come from as far away as Australia, Germany, Africa, and England, according to Debbie Hoy (no relation), who worked alongside Diana beginning in 1997. These diners did not make the trip to the United States, or even Kansas, just for the experience, but once in the area they enjoyed the well-stocked buffet (two or three choices of everything—salads, main dishes, vegetables, desserts), Diana's trademark.

We all had our fingers crossed for Diana's recovery, but unfortunately that didn't happen. After her death, someone from El Dorado bought the café and, I'm told, did some extensive remodeling, but then never opened it. In the ensuing years both locals and travelers have gotten good food and friendly service at Rick and Jenny's, the filling station and convenience store just north of town. But it's just not quite the same as Opal's.

Conway Springs

Some of my fondest childhood memories are the visits we made to my maternal grandparents, Ben and Fern Rice, who lived in Conway Springs, in the wheat country of Sumner County (Sumner and Thomas consistently vie for the title of largest wheat producer in the state). Grandpa's house was only a couple of blocks east of the city park where the band shell and the springs for which the town was named were located; I don't know if it's still on the market, but Conway Springs water used to be sold in grocery stores.

Times do change. I remember once when some sort of celebration was going on in the park and Grandpa was in charge of the food booth operated by the Odd Fellows Lodge. They were going to serve hamburgers: "Not those little ones but the big fifteen-cent kind," Grandpa said. And they were big.

Christmas we always spent with Dad Hoy and Grandmother at Cassoday and the Fourth of July was always celebrated at Countryman's Rodeo a few miles south of town, but Thanksgiving was always spent with Grandpa and Grandma Rice, as often were Memorial Day and Easter. Thanksgiving was fun because all the aunts, uncles, and cousins were there, and they were a lively bunch. A favorite for us kids was when our uncles (Mother had four brothers) would put on "a play in five acts." The uncle playing the announcer would say, "Act One," and the uncle playing a prospector would lead an uncle on his hands and knees playing a donkey across the stage (this was in the basement community room of the First Christian Church, where we often had our Thanksgiving dinner). The donkey would cry out, "Water, Master, water!" and the prospector would respond, "Silence, Jackass, silence!" Then the announcer would say, "Act Two," and the prospector and donkey crossed the stage from the opposite direction with the same dialogue. Act Three was a repeat of the first two, but then the announcer would say "Act Five," and we kids would all cry out "What about Act Four?" or "You skipped Act Four!"

Jim's maternal grandparents, Fern and Ben Rice, c. 1960.

and the announcer would turn to us and cry, "Silence, Jackass, silence!" Pretty dumb, but we loved it.

I especially enjoyed Memorial Day (Decoration Day, as we called it then), not only for the fresh strawberries we picked from Grandma's garden, but also because of the veterans' ceremony at the cemetery. After a few forgettable speeches, the local honor guard would fire a salute and the other boys and I would scramble for the empty cartridge cases. I probably have a couple of those yet if I would dig around in the basement.

The movie theater was a block north of Grandpa's house where my sister and I first saw *Dumbo* and *Pinocchio* and *Bambi*. That was right next door to the newspaper office, which had a window full of Indian artifacts. On the other side of the street was the Odd Fellows Hall where Grandpa played dominoes. He was also a fisherman, so there were numerous trips with him to Slate Creek and the Ninnescah River.

Grandma Rice was a Gooch and would proudly tell us that there was a Gooch castle in England somewhere (she knew, but I forget), and that one of our ancestors had been governor or lieutenant governor of colonial Virginia. Aunt Myrtle, her sister, liked to play cards, but could apparently go on and on shuffling the deck until one of her brothers would lose patience and cry out, "Deal, Myrt, deal!" At home if one of us became distracted or would mindlessly continue at something or other, "Deal, Myrt, deal!" would always bring us back to the moment.

One of my favorite Conway Springs memories is of the racetrack just northwest of town. Originally, back around the turn of the twentieth century, Grandpa said, the locals raced trotters and pacers on a track east of town, but at the end of World War II a consortium of local horsemen built a half-mile track for jockey races on twenty acres at the location I remember. There they held races for a number of years, and Grandpa took me to several of them when I was around eight or ten years old. Sometime in the later 1940s Grandpa bought a bay filly from Dad with the intention of racing her. Our horses were plenty fast enough for roping cows or steers in a Flint Hills pasture, but they weren't racing stock. I don't think Grandpa ever made much on his investment, unless he sold the filly at a good price, but he enjoyed messing with her.

And she did win him some money at the track. The one time I saw her run, Grandpa had bet one of his domino-playing cronies a quarter that she wouldn't come in last. She didn't, but only by half a length. A quarter isn't that much of a pot, but remember that at the Odd Fellows food booth it would have bought you a big hamburger and a bottle of Coke or Grapette.

The racetrack closed down after a dozen or so years and was planted to wheat until a saddle club leased the ground for a rodeo arena in the 1960s. Still, horse racing is part of the Conway Springs culture. Since 1977 the H. C. Murphy Memorial Saddle Horse Race has been held on the old racetrack. And in that same year Mr. and Mrs. Harold Burford had a two-year-old Quarter Horse stallion, My Easy Credit, on the track at Ruidosa Downs in New Mexico. There he won the Triple Crown of Quarter Horse racing: the Kansas, Rainbow, and All-American futurities. Impressive as those wins are, I get more pleasure remembering the quarter Grandpa won at the Conway Springs track.

Basketball at Cassoday High

Cassoday Rural High School was too small (never more than three dozen students in all four grades during my time there, nine of them in my class) to field a football team, so we had baseball in the fall, basketball in winter, and track in the spring. The home baseball games were played in the afternoons on an open field with no grandstand, so rarely were there more than a dozen spectators, and because our excuse for a track was just an oval dirt path around the baseball diamond, all our meets were away.

Basketball, however, was another story. For a school so small that even I could make the starting lineup (although it took until my senior year to do so and even then I was almost always the first player to be substituted for, usually before the first quarter ended), Cassoday fielded competitive teams. I think my all-time high in a game was ten points, or maybe it was just seven; that was over sixty years ago.

Now the home court/field advantage is a given in any athletic contest, from Little League to the pros, but the Cassoday High School gym was a snake pit for visitors. Our basketball court was so short that the center circle touched the circles containing the free-throw lines. Heavy pads, something like thin mattresses without innersprings, were hung under each basket so that players who crashed into the wall after a layup had at least a fighting chance of escaping a concussion or a bruised shoulder. Visiting players would sometimes get to thinking about the crash and miss a layup.

According to basketball regulations, you have to be out of bounds when throwing the ball inbounds. On most courts that is no problem, but at Cassoday the line marking the playing court was only about a foot away from each wall, so it was pretty easy in the excitement of a game for an opposing player to forget and accidently have his feet crossing the line as he threw the ball inbounds, which meant that we got the ball back.

We, on the other hand, were conditioned to turn our feet sideways so they wouldn't touch the line. The only Cassoday player I remember having much trouble in this regard was Ed Smith who was, for the times, exceptionally tall (something like six-four, which today would be guard height, but back then made him one of the tallest centers in the county; he also had a wicked hook shot). Ed's feet were proportionate to his height, so he had more trouble than the rest of us in turning them sideways far enough to stay legal.

Our biggest home court advantage, however, was the balcony that circled the court on the west, south, and north sides. On the north and south walls, where the baskets were, the balcony went straight up from the playing floor, but on the west side it extended over the court a good couple of feet. Not only that, but it was so low that even I could jump up and touch it. If the ball hit the balcony, it was whistled out of bounds. Seldom did a Cassoday player throw or shoot the ball so that it hit the overhang, but visiting players throwing the ball inbounds, distracted by making sure their feet were behind the line, often hit the underside of the balcony with an inbounds pass, so we got the ball back.

Besides the balcony overhang, the west side of the court gave the home team another advantage. At court level that side was open with a row of chairs lining the pipe rail that separated spectators from players, each easily within arm's reach of the other, and that's where the most vocal, aggressive fans always placed themselves.

On the east wall was a stage where the timekeeper and scorekeepers sat, some four feet above the action on the court, with the coaches and substitutes of each team on either side of them. During time-outs the coaches and subs had to jump down from the stage to huddle with the players, then jump back up when play resumed. Ed Johnson, our bus driver, was usually the timekeeper, but instead of an electronic buzzer to signal the start or end of a period, he used a homemade contraption that was freestanding, like a floor lamp, with a handle that when jerked down would slam a hammerlike object onto a round piece of clanging metal (an old car wheel, I think) with a gonglike effect.

Add a competent, competitive coach (Ted Pankratz), some good players, and a crowd of raucous, intense, highly partisan fans to the tiny court and narrow out-of-bounds lines, along with a balcony that usually gave us at least three or four turnovers a game, and it was little wonder that Cassoday High had a winning basketball team.

Hometown Stories

One writing assignment I used to give students back when I was teaching composition classes was to write about a local character, someone with a touch of eccentricity who made life interesting and amusing, or sometimes more irritating, for the more normal (or perhaps I should say, less colorful) citizens. Many of my students were from small towns in Kansas, but no town was so small that it didn't have someone who fit that description, and I got some very interesting papers.

I suppose the genesis of that writing assignment came from some of the characters and some of the amusing incidents that occurred in my hometown. Cassoday, in fact, seems to have had an abundance of both. I was born well after many of the following incidents took place and the people who perpetrated them were long dead, but the stories live on.

George Ellis, for instance, was one of the very first settlers in Sycamore Township. Old Number One School, in fact, was called Ellis School. Ellis believed in preparing for his ultimate demise, so he made his own casket out of walnut lumber from a tree he had cut on his own farm. Unlike some people I have heard of, he didn't sleep in his casket at night, but he would often lie in it during the daytime, much to the chagrin of his wife. He was laid in his casket for the last time in 1911.

Around the time that George Ellis was buried, a man named Herzig (there was no one of that name left in Cassoday in my memory) was living on the old DeGarmo place, about three miles from town. One day Herzig sold a horse for $100, but that night lost it all in a poker game. When he got home his wife asked about the horse money. He told her that he had lost it on the way home, which was technically the truth. She spent the rest of the night with two lanterns retracing the route from their house to town looking for the money. She never found it.

Halloween pranks, especially those that involved tipping over outhouses, were common in the small towns of Kansas, and Cassoday was no exception. One resident had the habit of visiting his outhouse at the same time each night, so one year the pranksters, instead of upsetting it, simply moved it back about four feet. I remember my father and uncle talking about how one man (they said who it was, but I can't remember his name), after having to set his outhouse up after every Halloween, decided that he had suffered enough. So he took his shotgun and took up watch sitting in his outhouse, waiting for the tricksters to come by. But they, having learned of his armed vigil, took another approach. Two young men on horseback stretched a lariat rope between their saddle horns and at full gallop hit the outhouse from behind and tipped it over, door side to the ground, with the man inside. Who the guys on thc horses were, they didn't say, but I always had my suspicions.

Another Halloween prank that occurred year after year at Cassoday was a little less noisome. It involved taking Gus Larson's goat out of its pen and turning it loose in the high school study hall. This story is helped if you knew Gus Larson. He was either a widower or more likely an old bachelor, and he lived by himself at the edge of town where he kept a few chickens to go along with his goat. He might have worked on the railroad at one time, but if so he was retired by the time I was growing up. There was no doubt about his ethnicity, however. I don't know if he came over from the Old Country or was born here, but he spoke with a strong Swedish accent and his English was liberally sprinkled with Swedish words. Gus didn't seem to mind having his goat stolen every Halloween. In fact, as he proudly boasted: "My goat iss der only von in der town mit a high school education."

Here are a few more episodes of life at Cassoday in an earlier day.

Kids in any time period would rather have fun than work, and Ross and Dwight Harsh were no exception. When their father sent them out every day in the summer to hoe corn, they would work for a while, then slip off down to the Walnut River that ran through their farm and go swimming. Rather than chew them out, their dad, Len Harsh, decided to take a different approach.

There was a longhorn steer running with their cows, a cantankerous critter that would take you if you weren't horseback. So Len slipped down near the swimming hole and started making noises like a steer on the prod rushing through the corn. The boys were so scared, they jumped out of the creek and ran to the house as fast as they could, where they told their mother that they barely escaped from the angry steer. But they had a little more trouble explaining how they lost their clothes when they were supposed to be hoeing corn.

A few miles southwest of the Harsh place was Oakdale School. One night after some sort of gathering at the school, Len Diller and Ace Lanning decided they were hungry for watermelon and raided Mr. Hahn's nearby watermelon patch. They grabbed a couple of melons, then hopped into their buggy when they heard someone coming at them, shouting angrily. They didn't know if Mr. Hahn had a shotgun or not, but they weren't taking any chances and started whipping up their buggy horse. The other buggy gave chase, and after a few turns around the adjoining hay meadow, Ace and Len were cut off. In the other buggy were Frank Rohmeyer and a friend who had also come out for some free melons, but they couldn't resist giving Len and Ace a scare.

Fourth of July has always been a time of celebration with fireworks in the small towns of Kansas. My dad told me about the time that some of the older kids decided to tin can a dog with fireworks tied to his tail. (Not a nice thing to do, but amusements were a little rougher then.) As the dog went running down the road scattering sparks, the young ruffians chasing him horseback and whooping and hollering, the procession went whizzing past my grandfather. His amusement (or bemusement, whichever it was) quickly turned to panic, however, when the dog turned north at the corner of the cemetery west of town. "My God, I've got to get home," he cried. "That's my dog, and he sleeps in the barn!"

Besides watermelons, chickens were also a target for swiping. One time Turk Harsh and an oilfield worker east of town got hungry late at night and decided to pay a visit to Mr. Deaver's henhouse at the edge of town. But as they slipped inside and grabbed a hen, the wind blew the door shut, the latch fell into place, Deaver's dog started barking, a light came on in the house, and, peering through a crack, the two young men saw Deaver armed with a shotgun and heading to the chicken coop ready to kill the possum or weasel that was bothering his flock.

"What are we going to do?" the oilfield man asked in a panic. "Just be ready to run like hell when I holler," said Turk. As Deaver opened the henhouse door, Turk slammed the chicken in his face and yelled, "Run!" And they did.

This next story is one of my favorites, and I'll tell it just as Turk told it to me. (Well, almost; I'm leaving out his colorful adjectives. Turk couldn't say three words without cussing.) Jess Spence, Bill Wallace, and Lee Smith were throwing firecrackers at Bill Childers and wouldn't stop when he told them to. So he went inside his house and came out with a shotgun, blazing away with both barrels. As the boys took off running as fast as they could, Jess yelled out that he was hit in the leg and was bleeding bad. They ran to the livery stable, all of them out of breath and Jess limping. When Bill and Lee were able to calm Jess down long enough to take down his pants and look at his wound, however, they discovered that the blood was yellow, not red.

Turk was one of the great old time cowboys and storytellers in Cassoday. His wife, Marie Baird Harsh, was one of my teachers at Cassoday Grade School way back when. A good one, too; third and fourth grades. In 1978 she printed a little book of fourteen pages (*Tales of Turk*) recounting some of his life and stories.

Turk's given name was Ray, but nobody ever called him that. Most Cassodayites probably never even knew that was his real name until his funeral. Everybody called him Turk. He got the nickname, according to my father (eleven years Turk's junior), because he was "as speckled as a turkey egg," an opinion confirmed in Marie's book.

Dr. Welty of Matfield Green ushered Turk into the home of Milton and Lola Harsh on Thanksgiving Day 1893 in their house about a mile northwest of Cassoday. To give the newborn a bath, the midwife, Aunt Lizzie Harsh, carried him over to a pot of hot water where the baby's waving arms came into contact with the hot woodstove, giving him a scar on his left little finger that he carried the rest of his life.

It wasn't the only scar Turk ever got. He lost the thumb on his right hand when he was attempting to tie up the hind leg of an ornery mule he was shoeing. The rope pinched off the first joint of the thumb, and the doctor amputated the rest. Turk said, "I still remember the sound of that bone that they chipped off when it hit the ceiling." He also claimed to have cured his grandchildren from sucking their thumbs by showing them his missing one.

Another time, coming home from the Strong City rodeo, a tire blew out, sending the car onto its side into the ditch. Neither Marie nor Turk's brother Phil was hurt, but Turk had a sore neck that caused a lot of pain. Every trip (of many) to the chiropractor made it worse, so he quit the treatments. He then discovered that the problem was a broken collarbone, not a sprained neck.

None of his accidents slowed him down, however. Turk lived a busy and strenuous life doing about everything there was to do in a small Flint Hills town in the first half of the twentieth century—farming, cowboying, raising livestock, shoeing horses, mowing right-of-way on the Santa Fe railroad, and freighting, among other things. He claimed to have hauled all forty-eight thousand bricks for the high school building in Cassoday, and he also hauled many loads of pipe to the Teterville oilfield east of town. All this with a team of workhorses.

I have a couple of photographs from around 1930 showing Turk riding a bucking horse. It seems that Cassoday didn't have anything planned for the Fourth of July, so Turk and Andy Torrance, a friend from Matfield Green, decided to put on a bronc-riding exhibition for the town. They rounded up

Cassoday blacksmith shoeing a horse and Turk Harsh (middle) helping to hold rope, c. 1920s.

fifteen or twenty bucking horses for the show, but then Andy decided to go off to a rodeo, so Turk rode them all. The only one he didn't stay on, he told me, was one that lost the saddle in the middle of the ride.

In 1932 Turk was one of several local cowboys who responded positively to Ruth Meyer's suggestion that they put on a rodeo at Cassoday. So they built some pens in Jick Reed's pasture southwest of town and gathered up some roping and bucking stock. In spite of a big rain the night before, the rodeo was a success, so for the next two years Turk, Buss Young, and Frank Cannon produced the rodeo. Turk dropped out in 1935, and the Young brothers (Deak, Frank, and Buss) put it on. In 1938 Wilber Countryman took over, moving it to his ranch south of town where it became a Fourth of July institution, running for thirty years.

Marie didn't include this story in her book, and it may well be apocryphal, but it captures Turk's spirit. As I heard the tale, someone was walking past Turk's barn one morning (the Harshes lived east of the tracks a block or so) and saw him looking at the ground and kicking around in the corral dirt. "What are you doing?" he asked. "Looking for my teeth," Turk replied. It seems he had come home inebriated the night before and had vomited in the corral. In a little while, Turk reached down, picked up his dentures, wiped them on his Levi's, stuck them in his mouth, got on his horse, and rode off for a day's work.

Turk Harsh riding a bronc, c. 1930s.

Turk had many accidents, but if he ever had a disease, I don't know of it; old age finally got him in his nineties.

When Turk and Marie were first married they would ride horseback across pastures twenty-five miles to Cedar Point for a barn dance, then ride home just in time for Marie to go teach school and Turk to swap horses and head to the pasture. I went to visit him once when he was well into his eighties. He showed me a photo of a group of riders from half a century ago, then named the horse each was riding and who owned it before identifying the rider.

Now that I've become one myself, I miss the old-timers like Turk. He was a great storyteller, and his life had given him great stories to tell. I'm glad that Marie collected a few of them in *Tales of Turk*, even if she did censor most of his colorful cuss words.

NATURE

Coon Hunting

Cool October nights often get me to thinking about the years of my youth when I used to hunt raccoons with hounds. I was never a really serious practitioner of the sport, but I did keep some dogs for a few years, and I did enjoy it.

I was probably about twelve or fourteen when I went on my first hunt. Benny Thompson, a good calf roper and bulldogger from Wichita, was also a coon hunter, and he called Dad one autumn to see if he could hunt on our place outside of Cassoday. When he and a couple of other guys showed up, they took me along with them. We jumped a coon at the edge of the timber, but soon the hounds were running fast across pastures and the hunters were cussing because it was a prairie coon, a variety, according to them, that was difficult to tree. True enough, we did not tree that one.

A few years later, when I was riding broncs and bulldogging steers, I would often stay a few days at a time at Marlin Berger's farm near Halstead. Marley was a coyote hunter, but his youngest son, Bobby (later a world champion saddle bronc rider), liked to hunt coons. I remember one time when Bob and his friend George Toews brought their hounds over to our place and we treed the first coon about a hundred feet from where we turned the hounds out. Kind of impressive, but not as satisfying as a decent chase before treeing.

I later traded Bob a cheap electric guitar for two coon dogs, a bluetick and a redbone. The former was old and past his prime, and the other was young and not well trained, but Bob never learned to play the guitar, so we came out about even on that trade. At the time I had another dog, a black-and-white Treeing Walker named Bullet that had wandered in down at my friend Jay Young's east of Cassoday. When no one claimed the dog, Jay gave it to me. Or maybe we traded something, or maybe his mother told him to get rid of the dog; I don't know.

Jim and his Treeing Walker coonhound Bullet, c. 1963.

Jay and I later figured that the hound was not lost but had most likely been intentionally abandoned because he was great at jumping and running coons but wouldn't stay on a tree. However, until the old bluetick died (a few years after I got him), I did pretty well. Bullet would jump a coon, run him up a tree, and Blue and the redbone would tell me which tree while Bullet was off looking for the next one. I never penned him, so he was free to run day and night. Neighbors told me that they were able to raise sweet corn for the first time in years while I owned that dog. He would run the creeks at night, keeping the coons in the trees and out of their gardens.

The best payoff I got from my dogs was from an unexpected source. It came during the first year of my first teaching job, eighth-grade English at El Dorado Junior High. In my homeroom there were three boys—Randy Maddox, Curtis Nickel, and Dick Sturdivant—who hung out together. Basically good kids, as it turned out, but ornery. Their classroom behavior wasn't always the best, to put it mildly, and they were well on the way to making my first year in the profession miserable. About the end of the second month of school, however, I got the idea to invite them to go coon hunting with me on a Friday night. We went out toward Chelsea on the Walnut River, about where the north end of the big federal reservoir is today, and it didn't take long to jump a coon.

After a long chase, the dogs finally treed him and the fur flew after I knocked him out of the tree. By that time we were a long way from where we'd started, and those city kids had no idea where they were or how we'd ever get back to the pickup. It was a little after midnight when I dropped them off at their homes. Next Monday morning there was a marked difference in their attitudes, and from then on they were my buddies and unofficial keepers of classroom discipline.

I have nothing but admiration for those teachers who can handle eighth graders; I couldn't. During my second (and last) year of being driven crazy by them, I didn't take any of my more rambunctious students coon hunting, but several of them happened to see me win second place in the saddle bronc riding at the El Dorado Saddle Club rodeo, which made them a little more respectful in the classroom.

I got rid of my hounds about a year after the hunt with Randy, Curtis, and Dick. Blue died during the winter, and I gave away the other two. I've only been out a couple of times since then, and that was years ago. I had a good time with my coon-hunting experience, but I don't really have any desire to take it up again. For one thing, it's too high-tech to suit me nowadays. Coon hunters now outfit their dogs with GPS tracking collars so that they can pinpoint their whereabouts at all times. What would Davy Crockett think of that?

Bumblebees

Putting up hay is not the fondest memory of my youth, but as time passes so the hard edges of those haying memories soften. The season for making hay is always the hottest, driest, dustiest part of the summer, just as feeding it is always the coldest, stormiest, snowiest part of winter (both versions exaggerated).

My earliest haymaking memory goes back to when I was probably around five years old, and it was in what we called the Big Pasture, which wasn't all that big, 120 acres, but it was the biggest pasture close to our house. For some reason either my father or my grandfather (probably both) had decided we needed some square bales instead of our usual stacks of loose hay. In my mind's eye I can see a tractor powering a stationary baler, a pile of loose hay, a man with a pitchfork, and two men sitting on the baler to thread the wires for the bales. Whether the baler was powered by a belt (as was the corn grinder at Dad Hoy's barn) or by a power-take-off shaft, I don't know. The baler was owned and operated by John and Clarence Morgan, who lived with their younger brother, Arthur, southwest of Cassoday. All three were bachelors, and their farm was just south of the half-section Mosteller pasture, which we leased for summer grazing. It was about two and a half miles south of our house.

Any way you look at it, haying, whether alfalfa or prairie, was hot, dirty, tedious work, but it could be exciting if you happened to stir up a nest of bumblebees. Back in the days of horsepower haying, bumblebees were a real danger; a bee-stung runaway team hitched to a mowing machine could wreak destruction to life and limb. I talked to a man one time who was driving a dump rake when bumblebees hit. He was thrown in front of the rake, but just as he was about to get speared by the teeth, the rake wheels hit a bump that tripped the teeth and left him safe in a roll of hay.

I've only been bumblebee-stung once, but that was enough. Since then I've given them plenty of room—a bumblebee sting hits like a hammer. I was in high school at the time and cutting prairie hay with an old-model mowing machine that was side-mounted on an Allis-Chalmers WC. When I cut over the nest, the bees boiled up and swarmed around my hat. When one hit me in the back of the neck, I knocked my hat off and jumped off the back of the tractor, the pitman stick still pumping away and the sickle still cutting bluestem as the bees followed the tractor, which was wending toward a draw while I ran off in the other direction. Fortunately, I had without thinking jerked the throttle down before I jumped (or maybe did it accidentally as I jumped), and the tractor choked down and died before it had a chance to hit a tree or run over the edge of the draw.

After the bees had cooled off and gone back to their nest, I started the tractor up again and went back to mowing, but I left a little island of grass where the nest was; I wasn't about to drive over it again. When Dad came out to get me that afternoon, I pointed the spot out to him and he gave the nest his usual treatment—a good splash from the gasoline can. Kills them dead and kills them quick. Probably not too good for prairie ecology, but a little revenge can make you feel better.

Other people feel the same way. I recently read an interview with Willie Nelson in which he said this about his favorite childhood memory: "All the kids used to fight bumblebees on Sunday afternoon with paddles we made from apple boxes. We wouldn't quit until all the bees were gone, although we'd often go home with swollen eyes."

When I was growing up we never did anything that foolhardy (or masochistic), and Dad said that he and his friends didn't either, but not too long back I had a chance to see the unpublished memoirs of the late Russell Behmer, who was born in 1902 and grew up in the little Flint Hills town of Hamilton. Behmer and his pals thought it was great sport to organize bumblebee fights in the hay meadows near town. Local farmers would often stick a marker near a nest when they found one, knowing that the boys would find it and get rid of the bees for them.

The Hamilton boys made their fighting equipment from the soft pine packing-case boards they found in the alleys back of the stores in town. They would whittle a board into a paddle, then bore several holes in it to cut down on air resistance. Wielding a paddle in one hand and a leafy tree branch in the other for self-protection, they were ready for battle.

Here is Behmer's account of battling bumblebees:

> The fighters surround a bumblebee nest and when all are ready, someone makes a few jabs at the entrance with a stick. All heck breaks out as the bees boil forth, mad as the dickens and afraid of nothing. Country dogs are smart

enough to keep their distance. Show-offs would stand over the nest, trying to exterminate each bee as it came out. This is risky, even foolhardy, but when dared, some boys will try anything. If there is a stiff wind and the fighters have stationed themselves upwind of the nest, the advantage is all with them. They can swat the bees with ease and little danger.

The bees seem to concentrate on two or three of their enemies, so the rest of the attackers can enjoy watching the battle. It is wise to stay alert, however, as sometimes a stray will surprise you with a sneak attack on the ear or back of the neck. Some of the sports carried baking soda to put on their wounds. Others might use a mud pack if any was handy. The losers became grotesque characters with one eye, or both, swollen shut, blubber lips, legs or arms puffed out of shape. These were battle wounds, paraded before the more timid boys with a devil-may-care manner.

Once I was stung on the calf by a sneaky bee. My leg doubled in size, and I had to sit in one chair with it propped up on another. I couldn't walk for several days. My mother was angry and didn't show me much sympathy.

One fight I'll never forget. It began just south of town in a sloping hay field with no obstructions and plenty of room for action. One of the gang brought along his cousin, visiting from the city. He didn't know what a bumblebee was. Neither did his Boston pug. The country cousin had warned him that he should tie his dog up and leave him behind but the city cousin thought he knew best. Boy and dog had a lot to learn.

We gathered around the nest site, and some wise guy suggested that the visitor be given the honor of stirring up the bees. He stepped forward and was given the stick and shown where to poke. Just as he hit, his dog made a lunge and stuck his nose into the nest. The bees swarmed over him en masse. The poor beast slobbered and yelped as he rolled in the grass and fought his head with both fore paws.

We thought we'd help with our paddles and began whacking the bees on the dog, but he only howled more. His unlucky owner was in the midst of the swarm without a paddle, struck dumb and motionless. He tried to pick up his dog and run, but there were too many bees. The rest of us were fighting like mad, bees coming from all directions. Someone finally pulled the poor city cousin away from the nest and he ran crying after his dog, who by this time was far ahead, howling and running with all his might.

It was a dirty trick to play, but we enjoyed every minute of it. There is a natural animosity between the country boy and the city sissy. The country cousin was worried: "I'm going to get killed when I go home."

"Blame everything on your no-good friends," someone told him. The visiting relatives left the following day, the boy bandaged all over his head and hands. We watched from behind some packing crates on the depot platform.

The episode couldn't have done much for family relations, but it was the most exciting bumblebee fight we ever had.

Bumblebee fighting was a sport unknown in Cassoday when I was growing up, and I'm glad of it.

Badgers

Back in the late summer of 1989 Cathy and I took a drive down into the Flint Hills. We had a picnic at Camp Creek (where Zebulon Pike is reputed to have crossed the Verdigris River), then drove up to the Bazaar cattle pens on the Kansas Turnpike, and from there onto the cattle trail across the hills to Sharpes Creek. We must have gone through ten miles or so of nothing but cattle, tall-grass, wildflowers, and wildlife, including a coyote, two jackrabbits (an unusual sight these days), and a badger.

Badgers are not an endangered species in the Flint Hills, but you don't see one out in the daylight all that often, either. This happened to be the first one I had seen in the wild for some time, but by chance we had had one visiting our house just a little while earlier. Actually he was in the garage. As I drove in from a night class about 10:30 p.m., I saw our two dogs in the headlights and heard them barking at what I first thought was an opossum (they sometimes come in to raid the dog food), then a raccoon. But when I heard the visitor's growling and hissing, I knew it was no possum or coon.

For those who think badgers are nice creatures, like the ones children read about in *The Wind in the Willows* or *Frances the Badger*, let me assure you that they are fierce. This wasn't the biggest badger I had ever seen, but it was full grown with bearlike claws that can dig faster than a tractor-powered posthole augur, and I have never before heard hissing as loud as that coming from the corner where he huddled under a ladder away from the dogs.

Not that our dogs are ever in imminent danger of getting close enough to be bitten by anything, but they do like to bark. So after I had called Cathy out to see the badger, I shut the dogs in the shop, turned out the garage light, and went to bed. Along about 4:30 I woke up and thought I'd better let the dogs out. Darned if the badger wasn't still in the corner under the ladder. I poked him with a broom handle to make him leave, but he just hissed and growled and looked mean. So I hit him with a stream of water from the garden hose and he waddle-ran right off into the graying morning. What he was sticking around for in the garage I don't know. Maybe he liked to hear our dogs bark.

Badger "fights" were a staple of rural recreation in earlier days. For instance, I remember reading in a 1914 Wichita newspaper about some men at the Livestock Exchange Building who learned that a tenderfoot visiting there had never seen a fight between a badger and a dog. So while somebody rustled up a likely canine opponent, a couple of others brought out a "badger" in a barrel, a gunnysack hanging loosely over the open end. Betting was spirited, with some of the perpetrators talking up the fierceness of the dog and others touting the invincibility of the badger.

In the meantime, however, some tender soul had reported the impending animal cruelty to the local humane society, and before the "fight" could commence a number of policemen showed up. The most officious of the officers, refusing all explanations, pulled on the rope attached to the "badger" and jerked out a bundle of rags, to the great amusement of the spectators.

The policemen didn't take the embarrassment at all well. Three cattlemen leaving the stockyards on a streetcar, laughing loudly over the incident, were arrested for disturbing the peace. One of the cattlemen, an Oklahoman, wasn't overly pleased by the strict interpretation of Kansas law: "This is the first time I've ever been arrested for laughing," he groused as he paid his fine.

Another badger fight at the Wichita stockyards featured a real badger, also in a barrel. I think it was the late John Hogoboom who told me about it. All good storytellers can make a good story even better, and John was a great storyteller. I have no doubt, however, that this story was founded on reality, as most of the others I heard him tell over the years were also. John was an old-time teamster in the El Dorado oilfield (which opened in 1915) back when horses did most of the transporting of equipment. He'd seen many things in his day, and he had a good way of talking about them. Anyway, the man who had brought the badger into the Exchange Building was making money by betting that no one had a dog good enough to pull that badger out of the barrel. Staghounds, bulldogs, cow dogs—the badger took them all on in turn and defeated all comers. There was a lot of biting, growling, and barking as dog after dog stuck his head into the barrel to engage in combat. One or two got hold of the badger and managed to get him off the back side of the barrel, but no dog was good enough to get him all the way out.

Then a man came in with a little feist dog, some sort of terrier mix that wouldn't have weighed more than fifteen pounds, John said. After some preliminary talking, he bet the badger man a hundred dollars that his feist could bring that badger clear out of the barrel. You're on, said the badger man. So the dog man picked up his little dog and threw him, rump first, hard into the barrel. The yipping and squealing was intense as the terrier came running out of the barrel as fast as he could manage while simultaneously dragging a badger whose teeth were firmly embedded in his rump. When he cleared daylight, the badger blinked his eyes, looked around, let go, and scurried back into his wooden den. Amid great laughter from the onlookers, the badger man paid up, packed up, and left the building.

Flies and Screwworms

Winter might be cold and miserable in many ways, but at least you don't have flies to contend with. In mid-July, however, fly season is in full swing in the Flint Hills.

Having houseflies buzzing around the kitchen is outweighed in repulsiveness only by seeing mice scurrying across the floor. I consider both animals dirty, disease-carrying pests with no redeeming qualities. Ecological biologists see them differently, of course.

Some people will use a pesticide spray against houseflies, but I hate to have poison floating in the atmosphere inside the house, so I employ a flyswatter against them. The flyswatter seems the sort of device that would have been in use forever, but it is actually only a little over a hundred years old. Dr. Samuel Crumbine, the official health officer of Kansas early in the twentieth century, was a medical pioneer who recognized the danger to public health from several different sources—among them flies, rats, and the common drinking cup. He encouraged the use of disposable paper cups at public drinking fountains by publishing a cartoon showing a schoolteacher standing at a pail of water handing schoolchildren a drink from a single dipper—but look more closely at the teacher's face and you see it is actually a death's head. Crumbine did not invent the flyswatter, but, by capitalizing on the national popularity of baseball, he popularized its use by organizing a "Swat the Fly and Bat the Rat" campaign to raise public awareness of the health problems associated with this vermin. He also changed the name from "fly bat" to "flyswatter."

One of my childhood memories is visiting relatives in Iowa at age twelve, where an outdoor family picnic was held on Cousin Forrest's farm near Buck Grove. My mother's cousin was a flamboyant, outspoken man, and my sister and I (who had heard little cussing and no profanity around home, unless the mules were giving Dad a hard time) thought it hilarious when Forrest waved away a fly from his plate with a hearty "Goddam bastard! Get a plate of your own!" (Equally funny to my ears was the comment made by a couple of women that Grandpa Rice and Uncle Myron had paid to clean the fish they had proudly caught: "Damn. Little sons-of-bitches.")

Houseflies aren't the only ones that bother me. The deerflies are out in full force in summer, and they can sure make a horse toss its head when they settle on its ears. And the horseflies can drive a horse crazy. One lit on the rump of one of our gray mares in the corral eating oats the other night, and if she bucked in a rodeo like she did trying to get rid of that fly, she could make the National Finals.

When I was a kid, we used several different means of combating horn flies, which are a major cattle pest in the Flint Hills. Dad believed that horn flies were not native but seasonal, carried up from Texas on the backs of the steers that were shipped up on trains each spring, but now I think they are permanent residents. Maybe they were back then too, and their emergence in the spring just happened to occur at about the same time that the Santa Fe brought up the Texas cattle. I remember that we would help various neighbors round up their cattle a couple of times each summer and spray them with DDT (a not unpleasant odor that I can still smell in my memory). Black clouds of flies would hover over the backs of the bunched steers as the spray hit them, just as they hover now over a loading chute at shipping time.

Cattle rubs became popular about that same time, some of them commercially produced and some, like those we used, homemade. Dad would set a couple of posts, loop down a chain or some twisted barbed wire between them, then wrap the chain or wire with burlap. He would either pour DDT powder on the gunnysacks as he wrapped them, or else he would soak them with used motor oil. He would also sometimes wrap treated sacks around the posts. The cattle would walk under the wrapped wire, which would rub against their backs leaving traces of the DDT or oil, or they would rub against the posts with the same effect. Either way, the insect repellent would get applied without the hassle of penning the cattle and spraying them.

Today little spraying is done, and I don't see many rubs. Instead, ranchers will sometimes throw handfuls of insecticide powder (no longer DDT) onto the backs of cattle when they are crowded into a pen. Or they will fasten a plastic tag permeated with insecticide (like a dog's flea collar) into the steer's ear.

Despite all our efforts, however, flies are still ubiquitous. And, biologists tell me, without them (and mosquitos) we would lose many species of birds that consider flies not pests, but food. Those songbirds are a pretty good silver lining to those black clouds of flies.

Whenever I hear a rancher complaining about welfare and what a waste of money government programs are, how none of them ever work like they are supposed to, I just ask him how many calves he has lost to screwworms in the past half century. If I'm talking to someone my age or older, you can almost see his mind hearkening back to the days when you wanted all your calves worked and your yearlings dehorned before the last frost in spring. Otherwise you had to wait for cold weather to return in the fall. If he is younger, then I tell him about screwworms and the government program that has saved cattle raisers from Panama to the United States a billion dollars a year.

Up until my mid-twenties the major reason for pasture-roping cattle in the summer was to doctor for screwworms; today it is foot rot. A yearling afflicted with the latter will lose weight, but the death rate is much, much lower than it was from screwworms. Today we can castrate and dehorn at any time of year without a second thought, but up until the mid-1960s a minor wire cut on a cow or the untreated navel on a newborn calf was likely to become infested with screwworms.

In my mind's eye I can still see the swollen navel of a calf filled with a writhing mass of whitish worms, looking like maggots but much smaller, as my father would take a can of foul-smelling KRS and squirt it into the infected area, knocking worms loose with the nozzle as he squirted. Like DDT spray, in my memory I can still smell the putrid wound and the KRS, the former nauseating, the latter, again like DDT, not too unpleasant if just a whiff. Some people would use turpentine or diesel fuel to kill them, while others would pick them out with tweezers, but the KRS did the trick easier and better. Occasionally a second or third application would be needed if the worms had gotten a good head start. Get a little KRS on your hands or your clothes, however, and it took repeated scrubbings to get the smell out—if it would come out at all.

All this began to change in 1933 when Dr. Emory Cushing discovered that the screwworm was a separate species from the blowfly, whence come maggots. Screwworms were costing ranchers hundreds of millions of dollars a year until a couple of USDA-funded entomologists, Edward Knipling and Raymond Bushland, came up with the novel idea of castrating male screwworm flies. Well, something like that. They hypothesized correctly that the males could be sterilized by radiation so that any eggs laid by females they had mated with would not hatch. Their experiments continued through World War II, culminating in the SIT program: sterile insect technique. The theory behind SIT was that if enough sterilized male screwworm flies could be released, they would mate with females whose eggs would then not hatch. The problem of how to sterilize sufficient numbers of males was solved by using cobalt-60 gamma rays from the atomic laboratories at Oak Ridge, Tennessee. As an added benefit the radiation had a viagric effect on the sterilized males, who aggressively outcompeted their unzapped counterparts for the affections of female flies.

Early experiments in Florida and the Caribbean island of Curaçao proved the efficacy of SIT, and by 1959 Florida was screwworm free. Efforts then moved to the Southern and Central Plains, where each spring screwworm flies would work their way from Texas to as far north as South Dakota. By releasing literally tens of millions of sterilized (and horny) male flies a week over the next few years, Texas and the entire United States were screwworm free by 1966, although an occasional outbreak would occur in Texas as late as 1982.

The United States and Mexico began cooperating in the screwworm battle in 1972, and within ten years (thanks in no small part to a lab in Chiapas that produced 500 million sterile males each week) screwworms were essentially wiped out in Mexico, where the last small outbreak occurred in 1990. Since then the battle has moved to Central American countries (Belize, El Salvador, Honduras, Nicaragua, Costa Rica, and Panama). In 2004 a 210-acre plant for producing sterile flies was completed in Panama. I haven't heard if the effort will then move into South America, but that would seem a logical progression. According to a report released in 2007, U.S. cattle producers alone have benefited to the tune of some $900 million a year from the SIT program against screwworms.

And I haven't heard any cattlemen complaining about that government welfare program.

The upshot of all this anti-screwworm activity was that by the mid-1960s cattlemen in the Flint Hills (and the rest of Kansas and the Southwest) were free to work their calves any time of year they wanted to. The dearth of screwworms meant a loss of pasture roping for young cowboys, as I was back then, but nowadays there is always foot rot or pinkeye to provide an excuse.

As if a young cowboy needs an excuse.

Coyotes

One of my favorite animals is the coyote, the beast that Mark Twain reviled as the "living, breathing allegory of Want." That same animal, however, was a deity in every tribe of Plains Indians, albeit a fallible one. To many he was a trickster, much like Shakespeare's Puck or the Scandinavian Loki; in others he was Promethean, the inventor of fire. Coyote's most important gift was in introducing death into the world in order to save Earth from overpopulation. (A gift that, unfortunately, isn't working.)

Unlike almost all of the other native animals of the Great Plains—bison, elk, pronghorn, grizzly bears, wolves, mountain lions—that succumbed to the invasion of the white man, the coyote thrived in the face of massive efforts to destroy him. Many were killed by the poison that eliminated the wolf and the government programs that during the 1930s killed over a million coyotes a year. The wolf, however, wasn't flexible, whereas the coyote was adaptable. Coyotes could hunt individually, by pairs, or in packs, whereas the wolf was a pack animal. In order to greatly diminish, but not eliminate, the coyote population, we would have to kill 75 percent of their numbers each year for fifty years. As an experiment on one large West Texas ranch, fish and game agents were able to eliminate every single coyote; the following year some 80 percent of the original number were back on that ranch.

In fact, coyotes somehow regulate their litter sizes to accommodate their food supply, increasing pup numbers when prey numbers increase. Although omnivorous (an aside: for several years we have had a coyote that visits our backyard pear tree, picks up a windfall, takes it back to the edge of the timber to eat it, then comes to the tree for another), that prey is largely made up of rabbits, prairie dogs, mice, rats, and insects. The seventeen-year cicada is a delicacy apparently anticipated, for in the sixteenth year of the seventeen-year cycle, litter sizes dramatically increase.

Every few years the coyote population will be ravished by mange. Not only does it take off their hair, but it weakens the coyote. I've never hunted coyotes with guns (although many years ago I liked going coyote hunting with Marley Berger, who had a pack of greyhounds). The only coyote I ever shot was a mangy, hairless one that was in our barn one winter, just to put him out of his misery. A bushy-tailed, heavily furred coyote is an attractive animal, but one devastated with mange is one of the ugliest things I've ever seen.

The coyote was unknown to eighteenth-century Americans east of the Mississippi (although not to French trappers farther west), and was first reported by Lewis and Clark, who thought at first it must be a species of fox or jackal. Today coyotes are found in every state except Hawaii, every Canadian province, every Mexican state, every Central American country, and at least one Caribbean island (although how they got there is a mystery).

Whether or not coyotes kill baby calves is a controversial topic. Most cattlemen think they do, while many wildlife professionals think they don't. They believe that coyotes eat stillborn calves, but cattle raisers counter that coyotes will distract a cow away from her newborn calf, which will, especially in cold weather, die if it's not immediately licked off.

There is no doubt, however, that coyotes are the bane of sheepmen. Not only lambs but full-grown sheep are a mainstay of a coyote's diet in sheep country. Some years ago I spent a summer teaching at Idaho State University. While there I met an old-time cowboy, Frank Kiefer, who carried on the old frontier rivalry between cattle ranchers and sheepherders: "Sheep meat don't hurt a coyote," he said. He didn't tell me the following joke, but he would have appreciated it: A particular two-toed coyote played continual havoc with a flock of Colorado sheep, despite the many efforts to kill him. One morning the owner arrives in his pasture greeted by a sight of sickening devastation, dead and mangled sheep everywhere. But there is a bright spot—Old Two-Toes is caught in one of the traps the sheepman has set for him. Looking at the mayhem the coyote has created, the sheepman decides that a bullet is too good for this monster. He drives back to his ranch, picks up half a dozen sticks of dynamite from his tool shed, speeds back to the coyote, wraps the dynamite around its body, lights the fuse, and turns his nemesis loose. But instead of running across the prairie, the coyote runs directly to, and under, the sheepman's brand-new $40,000 pickup.

When I was a senior in college, a couple of my sister's friends found a coyote den, twisted some barbed wire into it, and pulled out the pups, their eyes still closed. They gave one of the dog pups to my sister, which my father immediately and wisely castrated. Rita bottle-fed the pup, which she named Spooky. He got along fine with our shepherd dog and got along well with

Spooky, the pet coyote, relaxing on Jim's bed, c. 1962.

us humans, too. In fact, he would come when called and liked to be petted. When my sister got married, the coyote became my pet. He even slept on my bed at night. He didn't shed like a lot of dogs do, and he didn't have that distinctive doggy odor, either.

In fact, in almost every way our coyote acted just like a dog. But not all. If I was out hunting with our dog, for instance, and jumped a rabbit, Jackie would chase after it at full speed. But if I jumped a rabbit with Spooky, he would only lope after it, and a slow lope at that. Obviously, with that lackadaisical attitude he would have soon starved to death in the wild. More likely, however, is that he would have teamed up with another coyote or two, and they would have relayed the rabbit as it ran in a big circle until it tired and slowed down enough to be caught.

Even more puzzling was Spooky's behavior with the neighbor's chickens. Coyotes have a reputation, along with foxes, raccoons, and weasels, of relishing a chicken for dinner. Spooky would occasionally make a foray to the neighbor's house, catch a chicken, then bring it back to our place and bury it in the loose hay we stacked in the corral feed rack. When I would be pitching hay to the horses and milk cows, I would occasionally come across one of the chickens the coyote had purloined and hidden. The unusual thing was that the chicken was alive and unharmed. So I would carry it back home. Fortunately, the neighbors thought it was amusing.

I think we had that coyote for two or three years before my father gave him to an acquaintance who lived near Eureka. Unfortunately, someone mistook him for a wild coyote and shot him.

I wouldn't mind having another coyote as a pet, but the laws have changed and it is now illegal, without a special permit, to own and keep wild animals like raccoons, skunks, and coyotes. So I'm stuck with dogs.

A Bit about Birds

I know that I don't have the patience, or the inclination, to be a serious bird-watcher, but there are times I wish I had spent more time learning about birds. It would be nice to be able to identify the birds, especially the little ones, that fly up from the prairie grass as I ride through it, or the many varieties that gather around the bird blocks we put in the backyard every winter.

In case you're not familiar with bird blocks, they are a lazy man's bird feeder. Instead of having to keep a traditional bird feeder full, you can just put one of these out in the yard, in essence giving birds access to a self-service buffet. The only place I've ever found them is at the Bluestem Farm and Ranch Supply store here in Emporia. They are composed of seeds, grains, and molasses pressed into the shape and size of a salt block.

I have no trouble at all identifying the cardinals, flickers, woodpeckers, and blue jays, but most of the small ones clustered around the bird block are just birds to me. I also wish I was better at identifying birds by their songs. Meadowlarks (both the eastern and western varieties), crows, hoot owls, and quail are no problem, but the others? I don't know. Many pretty melodies float down from the trees in our yard during the summer, but the leaves obscure the singers.

I like seeing and hearing the birds that frequent our yard and the little hay meadow just south of the house, but I particularly like to see the birds that live in the pastures of the Flint Hills. The song of the meadowlark is beautiful, and it's fun to ride after a mother killdeer or plover (although I think what I call a plover ornithologists call an upland sandpiper) flopping as if injured in order to lead me away from her nest, then flying off once she has me past the danger zone. Or to see hawks, falcons, and an occasional bald eagle, or even more occasionally a golden, sailing smoothly through the sky. Or to ride close to a nighthawk (bullbats, Dad called them) sitting on top of a fence post, then watching it fly off zigging and zagging as you get near. Often a flock of turkey vultures, circling with their jerky, wavering motion, can alert you to a possible lightning-killed heifer, although thankfully, it's usually the carcass of a raccoon or possum. But I'm most happy because the sight is rare and becoming rarer when I jump a prairie chicken out in an expanse of bluestem, even though that unexpected explosion nearly under his hooves might spook the colt I'm riding.

When I was growing up back in the 1940s and '50s, prairie chickens were relatively abundant. We would see big flocks, often as many as fifty, sixty, or even more birds nearly every winter morning as they flew off the shocks of kaffir corn when we pulled into the field in our mule-drawn hayrack to load bundles to feed the cows. Dad didn't mind feeding the prairie chickens because he liked the birds, both to look at and to eat. A couple of times each winter he would carry the .22 along on the hayrack, and he would leave me with the mules while he sneaked up to the flock, keeping a shock between him and the chickens until he was close enough for a shot.

I say "relatively abundant" because back in pioneer times there were many millions of greater prairie chickens, not only in the Flint Hills but in all the midwestern states, from Oklahoma to the Dakotas and as far east as Wisconsin and Indiana. Like the bison, much of that population was decimated by hunters. Prairie chicken graced the tables of fine restaurants in New York and Boston, shipped back east on trains in barrels by the thousands. As of 2010 Missouri had only an estimated five hundred birds left. Kansas, again relatively speaking, isn't much better. As recently as 1980, wildlife biologists estimated that the greater prairie chicken population in the Flint Hills was nearly 900,000; twenty years later that number had dropped to about 160,000. As of 2010 it is somewhere below 100,000.

Prairie chickens are a type of grouse, and there are three species. The greater prairie chicken, the largest variety, is a tallgrass-prairie bird. The lesser prairie chicken, three-fourths the size of its larger cousin, likes the shortgrass country of southwestern Kansas, southeastern Colorado, northeastern New Mexico, and the panhandles of Texas and Oklahoma. About the same size as the lesser, the Attwater's prairie chicken has suffered the greatest decline in numbers. In 1900 a million of these birds could be found in the coastal prairies along the Gulf of Mexico in east Texas and Louisiana. Today, however, less than 1 percent of the coastal prairie is left, and the Attwater's prairie chicken is dangerously close to extinction.

Although hunters have shot millions of these birds since the later nineteenth century, the biggest threat to the greater and lesser prairie chicken, like that of the Attwater's, has been loss of habitat. Primarily ground birds, prairie chickens like to avoid trees where predatory hawks often perch. They also avoid buildings, and recent studies have shown that the massive wind generator towers that are beginning to dot the landscape are detrimental to prairie chicken populations, and to those of other prairie birds as well.

Other studies show that greater prairie chickens need at least ten thousand acres of contiguous prairie for a healthy population. Within this expanse of prairie, chickens do best when the grass exists in three conditions. In early spring (March through April) prairie chickens need short grass, or burned pastures, for breeding. For the nesting season that follows (eggs hatch in about four weeks), hens need tall dead grass from the previous season that has not been burned. For feeding, the birds need the mid-level grass that springs up after burning.

In recent years pasture management in the Flint Hills has been directed toward intensive early-season grazing of yearlings: double-stocking, in the cowman's parlance. Double-stocking means that twice as many cattle are put in a pasture, but for only the first half of the traditional six-month grazing season. That means that yearlings are on grass when it is its most nutritious, packed with protein, in its greatest growth spurt, and when rainfall (and thus grass) is most abundant. But to make this work efficiently, pastures have to be burned every year. Thus that tall dead grass needed for nesting is in short supply.

You know when it's prairie chicken mating season because that's when you hear the distinctive booming of the male birds, a sound that can carry a long distance out on the prairie. I have heard that sound all my life, but I had never seen the mating ritual until the spring of 2010 when Cathy and I drove out to the Homestead Ranch east of Matfield Green. That's where Jane Koger used to offer excursions out to a lek each March and April. *Lek* is the term for the booming ground where male birds come to strut their stuff, trying to attract a female.

We arose about 3:30 a.m. and made the hour-long drive to the ranch, where Jane then transported us and another viewer out to a blind positioned on a flat area with short grass. It was still pitch dark on a cloudy, drizzly day when we took our seats inside the blind and waited. And waited. Jane nervously wondered if the birds had chosen that day not to show, but as it grew a bit lighter she pointed out some small dark splotches moving over the ground in quick, start-and-stop motions. As the light improved, the splotches became prairie chicken roosters, a dozen of them (which was twice as many as she had seen on that lek previously that spring). Some got as close as ten feet from where we sat.

They would strut, occasionally run at each other and leap straight up three feet into the air, wings aflutter. Or they would stamp their feet rapidly, holding their spread wings low to the ground. As they boomed, the bright orange air sacs on each side of their necks inflated colorfully. Each of the cocks seemed to have a particular area, and if another encroached, that's when the leaping and wing flapping occurred.

This went on for three or more hours, during which time about three hens strolled through the strutting males, checking them out for a potential mate, rather like a trio of young women strolling through a bar to check out the guys. Jane said that the hens would visit numerous leks before making a choice, and that something like 90 percent of the hens are bred by one dominant male. That seems to me a lot of energy needlessly expended by a lot of disappointed males who spend three or four hours booming each morning for six or seven weeks each spring for no reward.

As a native of the Flint Hills who had often heard but never before seen prairie chickens booming, I am really glad I made the effort. The experience was almost surreal and totally magical.

The Green Glacier

Back in the 1950s my father would dig up every little cedar tree he found in the pastures and roadsides near Cassoday. He would bring them home and plant them on the north and west sides of our house. Once he got enough there, he started planting a windbreak north of the house about sixty yards long by ten yards wide. It took him about a decade to get enough trees, but they are big now and really slow down that cold north wind.

Today, however, he could plant that windbreak in a day and still have scores if not hundreds of little cedars left growing in those same roadsides and pastures. We (and by that I mean the whole Midwest) are being crushed by the Green Glacier, a not-so-slow invasion of *junipurus virginiana*, the eastern red cedar.

Back in 1960 cedars were counted by the tens of thousands in Kansas; in 2017 there were 100 million of them. Between 2005 and 2015, we went from 55 million to 85 million. In the five years between 2007 and 2012, some fifty thousand acres became filled in with cedars.

It's even worse in Oklahoma, where 780 acres, almost a section and a quarter, of prairie is lost to red cedars—every day! It's so bad in the Sooner State that they are thinking of using convicts to aid in clearing the trees. (Better that than sitting in a cell all day, every day, if I had that choice.)

I was visiting about the Green Glacier with a Kansas state senator a while back, and he mentioned rather casually about getting the cedar declared a noxious weed. Not a bad idea, in my opinion. I'm not sure, though, that a noninvasive plant can be considered a noxious weed. The red cedar is native to Kansas, as town names such as Cedar, Cedar Bluffs, Cedar Point, and Cedar Vale attest. No, *junipurus virginiana* is not an invasive plant, like *sericea lespedeza*, but it is pernicious and just as persistent an invader. Just look at the Flint Hills on the south edge of Manhattan. When I was attending KSU in the early

1960s, those hills were covered with bluestem, but today they are covered with a rank evergreen forest.

Plant succession suggests that much of the Central Plains today could, maybe even should, be cedar forest. Why isn't it? The answer is clear: fire. As Julie Courtright shows in *Prairie Fire*, Great Plains Indians burned the prairies, seemingly constantly. When Washington Irving made the trip from which he wrote *A Tour of the Prairies*, he saw clouds of smoke all the way from Guthrie to Stillwater in today's Oklahoma. Europeans are pyrophobes. No matter where they settled and colonized—Africa, Australia, North America—they suppressed the burning practiced by the aboriginal peoples. Those fires kept the underbrush cleared away, thus depriving fuel that today has built up for decades, thus further resulting in the massive forest fires that plague our western states.

There is no question that cedars can be a tremendous fire hazard. A prolonged dry spell, low humidity, hot temperatures, and high south winds and the town of Manhattan could be devastated. Such were the conditions that created the then largest-ever wildfire in Kansas, the Anderson Creek fire in Barber County in March 2016 that burned over 400,000 acres. Just one year later the Starbuck fire in Clark County set a new record, a wildfire half again as large, 600,000 acres. Wind-blown burning chunks of cedar from the Anderson Creek fire at Medicine Lodge would start new fires three-quarters of a mile in front of the head fire. The one good thing about that fire was that it wiped out hundreds of thousands of acres of the cedars that had blanketed the Red Hills in only a few decades. I have read that it would have taken $55 million and many months to mechanically clear the cedars that the fire did in just a few days.

A digression. Brian Obermeyer, who heads The Nature Conservancy's Flint Hills Initiative, was on Ted Turner's ranch in the Gypsum Hills as the Anderson Creek fire was raging. Turner, on all his many properties in the West, raises bison instead of cattle. The people on Turner's ranch managed to get a few of the bison into corrals at the headquarters, but they were unable to pen the majority of the herd. The bison in the pens died from smoke inhalation, but those unpenned all survived unscathed by gathering on a prairie dog town where the grass was too short to burn. It's been well over a century and a half since free-roaming bison on the Plains survived prairie fires in just the same way. That is one strong instinct.

Fire is eastern red cedar's worst enemy, but it can't work as just a one-time fix, and it is more effective on immature trees. In an article for *This Land* Kyle Walker tells of driving across the thirty-thousand-acre Black Kettle National Grassland from Cheyenne, Oklahoma, to the Texas border, accompanied by cowboy-manager Chuck Milner. Cedar trees were everywhere, but when they reached an area that had had a heavy fire fewer than five years earlier, the cedars were gone. Dead trunks and branches, like stark white skeletons, had replaced the grass-smothering live ones. Walker was struck by the sight: "It looks morbid." "No," said Milner, "it's beautiful. Nero fiddled while Rome burned. We're fiddling around by not burning." (Walker also reported seeing a couple of bumper stickers: "Be a leader; kill a cedar," and a cartoon match saying, "Take me to your cedar.)

Cedars are devastating to a prairie. No grass grows under a cedar tree, which means that if the Green Glacier completes its insidious work in the Flint Hills, the ranching industry here is dead. Experts say that if we don't burn the Flint Hills, the way ranchers have done for a century and a half, Indians did for hundreds of years before them, and Mother Nature (lightning) did for thousands of years before that, then we will have a scrub forest of cedars, hedge, and locust, rather than the tallgrass prairie of the Flint Hills that is the largest one on the continent—and the last of its size in the entire world. The tallgrass prairie is the most threatened ecosystem on earth.

A few years ago Cathy attended a docent training session at the Konza Prairie Biological Station, a Nature Conservancy property managed by Kansas State University's Biology Department. Scientists at Konza have been conducting controlled burning experiments since its founding in 1971. Some watersheds are burned at different times of the year, some every year, some every other year, some at five- or ten-year intervals, and some have never been burned. On these latter plots trees have completely taken over. That scrub forest of cedar trees, hedge, and locust could happen in under two generations.

It is a common misconception that to do something good for the environment, you should plant a tree. On Earth Day 2018 the Symphony in the Flint Hills did something just the opposite; they coordinated a cedar tree cutting at Rock Springs 4-H Center. I recall from attending camp there decades ago some hardwood trees but no cedars. As we drove into the center for the event, there were cedars everywhere. According to SFH director Christy Davis, volunteers cut little trees off seventy acres. That sounds like a lot, but it's literally just a drop in the bucket.

A couple of years back Cathy and I spent a weekend at the Lied Center Lodge in Nebraska City, the home of Arbor Day. Tree promotion was all over the place. I was particularly struck by a photograph of a large tree with a caption stating that this tree would consume up to a hundred gallons of water a day, which will in turn respire into the clouds and result in rain. Didn't we learn anything from that old disproven nineteenth-century bromide of "rain follows the plow"? My reaction to the photograph was that it's much better to leave the water in the ground for the grass. After the Anderson Creek fire, Barber County springs that had been dry for decades started flowing again.

Like the Dust Bowl, the Green Glacier is the product of misguided human action, but the land survived and has at least partially recovered from the Dust Bowl. But will—and can—it recover from the Green Glacier? To paraphrase an extremely influential large furry animal, "Only you can prevent a forest!"

Konza Prairie Biological Station

So what does the Great Chicago Fire of 1871 have to do with the premier tallgrass prairie research facility in the world? Here's what. Chauncey Dewey bought up as much ruined property as he could in the aftermath of the fire at bargain (I resisted saying "fire sale") prices, then, as property values quickly rebounded, sold it and made a fortune. In 1872 he started buying up ranchland in Kansas, both in the Flint Hills near Manhattan and in the far northwestern corner of the state. The Oak ranch in Rawlins and Cheyenne Counties reached 200,000 acres in size at its largest, while the Dewey ranch, just south of Manhattan, was 8,000 acres. A rancher-farmer range war in 1903 resulted in the deaths of three members of the western Kansas farming Berry family and a folk song, "The Dewey-Berry Feud." Chauncey died in 1904 and his son, Chauncey, Jr., took over the properties (and was also acquitted of murder) that same year.

Financial problems, perhaps related to the beginning of the Great Depression, forced Dewey to sell off his Flint Hills ranch in 1930, with the Geary County portion going to the Providential Institute for Savings and the Riley County holdings eventually split among four different buyers.

In 1956 the Kansas State University Biology Department started looking for some pasture land that could be used for research purposes. Among the various faculty involved, the efforts and vision of Lloyd Hulbert and Ted Barkley were particularly important. In 1971 a site then owned by Elizabeth Cobb Landon was identified and, with financial backing from Katherine Ordway, The Nature Conservancy bought the Geary County portion of the Dewey ranch. Two years later TNC bought the Riley County part of the Dewey ranch, bringing the total acreage to 8,616. When K-177 was widened to four lanes, Konza was reduced to its present 8,600 acres.

The mission of Konza Prairie is to provide ecological research facilities for, promote the conservation of, and provide education about the tallgrass prairie. The Konza Prairie Biological Station is the umbrella organization under which the KSU Biology Department operates the facility, which includes the Konza Environmental Education Program (KEEP) and the Long-Term Ecological Research (LTER) program.

KEEP, under the direction of Jill Haukos, brings school classes to Konza where students learn about scientific research and conservation, do hands-on projects that teach the importance of the grasslands, and find out just how special the tallgrass prairie is and how fortunate they are to live in the Flint Hills.

A few years back Cathy attended several days of docent training at Konza, with the intent of helping to establish something like that at the Tallgrass Prairie National Preserve in Chase County. It was an extremely informative experience, she said, especially the fifty small demonstration plots of native grass near Konza headquarters (the stone house that was part of the Dewey ranch) that schoolchildren see. Some of these plots are burned every year and some on a schedule of every other year, every third year, etc. The growth of trees and denseness of brush varies accordingly. From 2,500 to 3,500 students each year come out to see real science at work at Konza, along with some 1,500 adults at various times. There is also a public hiking trail at Konza and some three hundred bison, introduced in 1987.

The tallgrass research on which education ultimately depends is carried on at Konza through the LTER program, underwritten by the National Science Foundation. Studies range from various types of prairie plants and animals (from microscopic to large herbivores), but the three major areas of research at Konza are fire, grazing, and climatic variability.

From the beginning one of the major types of research carried on at Konza has been fire and its effect on the prairie environment, which is of particular interest to me. From the late nineteenth through the mid-twentieth centuries fire was considered detrimental to the grass, but the long-term experiments at Konza have proven just the opposite. Fire, in fact, is essential to a healthy tallgrass prairie.

Konza has been divided into fifty different watersheds, each of which is burned on different schedules in order to study the effects of prescribed burning. Some are burned every year, others at varying numbers of years or different seasons of the year, and some not at all. Those never burned since 1971 are now completely covered with trees and brush.

Smoke from the prescribed burns that occur each spring by ranchers in the Flint and Osage Hills (i.e., southern Flint Hills) sometimes cause pollution levels in cities such as Kansas City, Wichita, and Omaha to rise a little above EPA standards during a few weeks in April, which stirs up some denizens in those places (particularly Nebraskans, it seems) to protest, claiming that these prairie fires are causing climate change. What they don't realize is that grass sequesters carbon much more effectively than do trees. (And also that automobiles and factories cause much more pollution that the annual spring burn.) Moreover, Konza studies show that the carbon released into the atmosphere from a pasture burn (and maybe even more) is fully returned to the earth during the growing season. Moreover, if not burned, the Flint Hills would be covered with scrub forest in just a couple of generations, destroying the last major stand of tallgrass prairie in North America and the world.

Back when I was teaching my Flint Hills Folklife class, we would often make a field trip to the Konza, where personnel would take the class out into the watersheds and past the bison pasture. My students were impressed by the scientific studies and the beauty of the landscape, but the thing that seemed to stick in their minds was the ten-foot-tall electrified fence that kept the bison from straying.

Water and Water Witches

In the summer of 2015 we went to see the premiere of *When the Well Runs Dry*, a documentary film about water in Kansas. The event was well attended (standing room only) and was held at the Masonic Center in Florence. Ranchers, farmers, well drillers, and other Kansans from the Flint Hills to Dodge City were interviewed in the film, which was produced by Reuben Aaronson and Steve Lerner.

In the spring and summer of 2015 we had abundant rain: ponds full, springs running, grass tall, and cattle fat. But filming for the documentary had been done a couple of years earlier when the state was experiencing a prolonged dry spell. Still, the lessons of the film, as was made abundantly clear in the excellent panel discussion following the showing, are fully relevant, for here in Kansas we can go from flood to drouth, from drouth to flood in a matter of weeks.

Considering what is happening in light of California's growing water crisis, Kansans had better not take water for granted. In the Flint Hills, for instance, with no underlying aquifer, finding underground water is a chancy thing. One of the panelists owned a ranch near Council Grove, where one of the ranch worker's houses ran out of water a couple of years ago. After fruitlessly drilling five dry holes looking for water, they fortunately found a reliable supply in an old abandoned hand-dug well. They were lucky.

Another of the panelists, Bonnie Lynn-Sherow, who teaches history at Kansas State University, was told by one of her students from Garden City that there was no water problem out there. "What do you mean?" she asked him. "I just turn on the tap and the water comes out," he replied. Sitting in the audience, I was stunned by this naivete. Had this student no conception of the declining water level in the Ogallala Aquifer? Some 170,000 center-pivot irrigation pumps are operating out there on the High Plains. One man from central Kansas was shown in the film standing by one of his center pivots, but he said that his well takes only what is replenished annually. Fossil water, on the other hand, takes centuries to replenish.

I don't really know much about irrigation farming, but I do remember being shocked a few decades ago when I drove out to Colby and saw field after field of corn and soybeans on the High Plains, crops I associate with the wetter climate of eastern Kansas. Back in the early 1960s when I was rodeoing in western Kansas, the crops were wheat and milo, which don't require center-pivots.

Back to the tallgrass prairie, something I do know more about. Or thought I did. I learned that a cow drinks some twenty-five gallons of water a day. I also learned that a mature cottonwood, the Kansas state tree, drinks up to a thousand gallons a day. Or so the geologist on the panel said. A tree, as he put it, is like a straw that is constantly sucking up water from the ground. Like a windmill that pumps constantly, he said.

I have sometimes shocked some of my urban friends when I have called trees weeds, but that's what they are out in a bluestem pasture. (A weed, a botanist once told me, is any plant growing where you don't want it. Even a rose, he said, can be a weed.) It disheartens me to see so many more trees—particularly hedge, locust, and cedar trees—growing in the Flint Hills than when I was younger. I remember someone telling me about a flowing spring in Greenwood County that had been reduced to a trickle. The pasture owner cut down the big oak trees overshadowing the spring, and the full flow returned.

Anyway, like the student from Garden City, we all tend to take water for granted. But what will we do when the well runs dry? The film got me to thinking about the severe drouth of the 1950s, the trouble we had with water on the ranch, and water witches.

At home we drank, cooked with, bathed in, and washed clothes with well water. Our well was hooked up to an electric pump, thanks to the Rural Electrification Administration. The water had a good taste, unlike that at my grandparents' house a quarter of a mile north, which was hard as could be with a strong mineral taste. We had a pit in our front yard for dishwater and the bathtub to drain into. One of my chores, once I got big enough, was to dip water out of the pit and pour it on the trees and flowers that my parents had planted in the yard. We didn't waste water because there was little to waste: our well wasn't very strong.

Sometime in the mid-1950s Dad decided to have another well drilled at the house and some in nearby pastures. By the time it was all over, drillers had put down five holes for us, including three in nearby pastures. The trouble is that here in the Flint Hills, unlike areas underlain by an aquifer, veins of groundwater are unpredictable. Some produce plenty of water, others only a trickle.

In order to try to find a good vein, Dad called on Chester "Doc" Danby to witch a well. Doc ran a filling station in Cassoday and was also the local water witch.

A diversion into water witching: water witch, water staker, diviner, dowser, finder, locater—water witches have answered to various names throughout history. Water witch, a uniquely American usage, derives not from a link to demons but to the colonial practice of using branches from witch hazel for divining rods. Various types of trees are favored by diviners. Some specify apple or peach branches of just the right thickness, about twice the circumference of a pencil. Others swear by willow, hazel, ash, oak, myrtle, or other deciduous trees; conifers are not used.

Employing instruments ranging from the familiar forked stick to welding rods to coat hangers to pieces of number nine wire to pendulums to a pair of pliers to bobbers (a weight dangling from the end of a single stick), dowsers have over the centuries located not just water but also tin, copper, gold and other ores, petroleum, buried pipes, dead bodies, unmarked graves, and even criminals.

In the late seventeenth century a Frenchman named Jacques Aymar claimed that his divining stick jerked down over the grave of a murdered woman, then immediately jerked up to point at her husband, who took off running. Aymar received a royal permit to hunt down murderers, which he did avidly. He was even recruited by Catholic officials to locate Protestants. In 1701, however, the Inquisition outlawed divining as a tool in identifying heretics and the dowsing stick soon reverted to finding water.

In the later 1200s Marco Polo witnessed divination in China with cane stalks. The earliest surviving detailed written account of divining is a 1556 document published by Georgius de Agricola that describes how illiterate German miners used forked sticks to seek out ore deposits. The Roman historian Tacitus (died c. AD 120) described how the Frisians used cuttings from fruit trees to find out murderers, while the Greek historian Herodotus (died c. 425 BC) tells of the Scythians using willow sticks to detect perjurers. And in northwest Africa there are eight-thousand-year-old petroglyphs in the Atlas Mountains that appear to show dowsers plying their trade.

When most people think of a water witch, a Y-shaped, forked stick that looks like a wishbone most often comes to mind. Think of a kid's slingshot, only the "arms" are much longer than the "foot" of the Y. The dowser grips the forks firmly at chest level with his up-facing hands, then walks over the ground until the water underneath his feet causes the tip to dip sharply down.

(Or, with some dowsers, up.) The pull of the water can be so strong that it can rub the skin off the hands of the dowser. If the water witch is using metal rods instead of a forked stick, he or she holds them chest high and they will cross over each other in an X to indicate the water below. Or the gas pipes, the minerals, the corpses, or whatever it is that the diviner is searching for.

Whereas the forked stick is gripped tightly, if metal rods are used they are held loosely. Rods are first bent into an L-shape, with the handheld part much shorter than the part extending out from the dowser's chest. In fact, many dowsers place the rods into short pieces of pipe and hold the pipe in order to let the rods move freely. Some diviners claim to be able to tell the depth of the water they have located, and some will specify the strength of the well. Some just look at a piece of land from the roadside and point out the spots where water can be found. Some even claim they can hold their forked stick over a map of the world and tell wildcatters where to dig for oil.

Does dowsing really work? Scientists scoff, but satisfied landowners who have successfully had a well witched say it does. If so, how does it work? Back in the seventeenth century, European explanations tended toward either heavenly or demonic forces behind the phenomenon. But colonial Americans were more practical and ruled out magic as an influence. The amount of water that comprises the makeup of the human body, after all, ranges from 50 to 75 percent, with the average adult being made up of around 60 percent water. Some dowsers think that might be a factor. Other members of the craft, however, credit electromagnetism or radioactivity. And some think any attempt to explain it is pointless: if one has the gift, don't question how it works, just use it (the ultimate expression of American pragmatism).

I personally don't have the gift, but when those who do have placed their hands lightly on the backs of mine as I held a divining rod, it dipped.

When the first well drilled by our house was a disappointment, Dad imported a water witch/well driller from Sumner County, one recommended by my maternal grandfather, who lived at Conway Springs, to dig another. I don't remember this fellow's name, but I do remember that he chewed Beechnut tobacco, lots of it. He guaranteed that there was a lot of good water over the spot he had witched, which was just east of our house, an excellent location for a well. If not, he said he wouldn't charge a dime. The problem was depth. Once he had drilled seventy-five dry feet, Dad told him he might as well stop because if he went deeper he would hit salt water. The Sumner Countian insisted on going ahead, however. At somewhere around 115 feet he hit water, lots of water, salt water. He left without a check, and we were left with our old well that we had to nurse along until the drouth finally ended. And a yard full of slowly deteriorating wads of chewing tobacco.

So how did the other wells that we drilled back in the mid-1950s turn out? All of them produced water, a couple of them enough to merit putting up windmills, but not enough to forestall our need to haul water from Fox Lake east of Cassoday in order to keep the livestock from going thirsty.

As I said earlier, water veins in the Flint Hills are not easy to find. One female water witch from the Wichita area, who usually charged about twenty-five dollars if her services were successful, turned down a thousand-dollar offer from a Flint Hills rancher to witch a well because she didn't think she could find one for him: "Water is as scarce as hen's teeth out there."

With the advent of farm ponds, rural water districts, and Corps of Engineers watershed dams, fewer water wells are being drilled in the Flint Hills than in past decades, but given the slim odds of hitting that odd vein of water underneath all that rock, I doubt the water witch will completely disappear from these bluestem pastures.

Some Thoughts on Drouth

I know that the usual spelling (and pronunciation) for a prolonged dry spell is "drought," but I've always preferred "drouth," the older (or, as my dictionary says, the uneducated) version of the word. That's probably because that's how I heard it pronounced when I was growing up back in the 1950s.

The middle years of that decade were dry. I remember riding across the Funk pasture just north of our place the first year the bad dry weather hit in 1953. It was the middle of July, and there wasn't a clump of grass tall enough to hide a jackrabbit in that whole pasture. In fact, the ashes from the spring burn still crunched under a horse's hoof—there hadn't been enough rain either to wash away the ash or to grow the grass tall enough to cover it.

It didn't take long to make hay in the '50s, both because there wasn't much hay to make and because what there was didn't take long to dry. My father-in-law used to tell about a time in the 1930s when they followed the mowing machine directly with the rake and the rake directly with the baler. I remember in the 1950s that the hay was so short in our hay meadow that we had to rake several windrows together just to get enough to run up the ramp of our Allis Roto Baler.

None of the wells on the home place was very strong, so it didn't take much to pump them dry. Then it was wait a few hours before you could pump a little more. We didn't waste a drop of water. We shared bathwater, and Mother used it and the dishwater to keep some little trees around the house and her flowers alive.

Dad had several wells witched, but none of them produced enough to keep the livestock watered. So we hauled water from Fox Lake, the lake east of Cassoday that had been built by the Santa Fe in 1923 to provide water for its steam locomotives. For quite a while there was a spigot near the railroad tracks that we (and many others in the community) could back under to fill the metal tank on the back of our truck. Then the lake got so low that we had to go to the dam, a mile east of the tracks, and use a gasoline-powered pump to fill our tank. And then the lake went dry. I don't recall just what we did then, but we managed to keep our stock alive.

The Great Plains can be described as either subhumid or semiarid, both terms meaning that precipitation (from either rain or snow) is scarce. Worse, it is also erratic. Average rainfall means one thing if it falls predictably at certain times of the year, but something else again when you can get your entire average rainfall in just a day or two. A few years ago I was out in Elkhart in the far southwestern corner of the state (the town borders Oklahoma on the south and is about five miles from Colorado). It was dry, as usual, there, and I asked one of the locals what the average rainfall was. "Seventeen inches a year," he said, then paused and added, "And you should be here the night we get it."

It's not quite that bad here in the Flint Hills, where our average runs about thirty-five inches per year, but our dry spell in the summer of 2003, when we went from early June through July and August with only an inch and a half of precipitation, was broken over Labor Day weekend with nearly a dozen inches of rain in less than twenty-four hours. The storm resulted in some unfortunate deaths when several vehicles were swept off the Kansas Turnpike in the Flint Hills southwest of Emporia.

What we in the Flint Hills call a drouth, however, is often just a dry spell compared to the dry cycles that occur on the High Plains. Texas novelist Elmer Kelton once told me that he was talking to a man from eastern Kansas who complained that they'd had three drouths that summer. Elmer just laughed—a drouth in West Texas can last four years, not four weeks, he said.

Was Emporia's dearth of rain in the summer of 2003 a drouth? Well, just an inch and a half of rain in over ten weeks can make things pretty dry. The ground was as powdery and the grass as brown and brittle as I ever recall seeing it that time of year, even in the 1950s. (Of course I was in my teens back then, so my memory might have lost a little clarity in half a century and more.) But so far (knock on wood) we haven't had the string of several dry years in a row that gave us the drouth of the '50s. Or, worse yet, the Dirty Thirties.

In addition to death and taxes, I suppose we should add drouth to the certainties of life here in Kansas.

Let There Be Night

In the fall of 2017, when the Philadelphia Eagles were playing the Kansas City Chiefs in Arrowhead Stadium, the ground crew for the Eagles went to the Flying W Ranch to ride horses and otherwise enjoy the countryside. Josh said the men had a good time riding and liked the scenery, but what most impressed a number of them was that it was the first time in their lives that they had ever seen the Milky Way.

About ten years ago *National Geographic* ran a story about the Flint Hills, illustrated by the photographs of Jim Richardson. Probably the most spectacular of those photos was one of the Milky Way. Noted in the text was the fact that, because of light pollution, 80 percent of the world's population had never seen the Milky Way, and that percentage is constantly increasing.

Having been reared in the country near the town of Cassoday, and having lived in the country a few miles south of Emporia, the Milky Way is something I've always taken for granted. Admittedly the galaxy is noticeably brighter at the former town (population maybe a hundred) than it is at the latter (population around twenty-five thousand with a multitude of street and business lights shining all night). I don't remember if Cassoday even has street lights, but the overly tall, overly bright lights at the Kansas Turnpike exit just north of town, and at the Matfield Green Service Area five miles northeast, can be seen from at least fifteen miles away.

Then there are the lights at the federal prison east of El Dorado, twenty miles to the south, that are visible from our ranch at Cassoday, not to mention the glow in the sky from El Dorado, Emporia, and Wichita. Here at our house south of Emporia we often can see the Wichita and the Topeka glows, in addition to the constant glow from Emporia.

In our neighborhood our house is one of the few places, I think actually the only one, that doesn't have a space light that automatically comes on at dusk and goes off at dawn. What's the point of living in the country with one of those? If you want an electric light burning in the yard all night long, why not just live in town? We had a yard light at home when I was growing up, but it was one we could turn on and off as needed. It was off most of the time.

Maybe people think a space light deters theft, but I think it just lets the thief see more easily what he wants to steal. A better idea, it seems to me, would be a motion sensor that turns the light on automatically if someone is prowling around the yard.

Several years ago I left Garden City for home at midnight, and to help pass the 250-mile drive, I decided to see how many miles it would be before I could no longer see a light of some kind—from a town, from a feed lot, from a farmyard, from a radio tower. In all that way the only time there was not an artificial light visible, either in front or in back or on either side of me, was for a couple of miles in the Flint Hills on Highway 150 between Marion and Elmdale. That's not possible today because the road was leveled out some a few years back.

Up until the middle of the twentieth century, cowboy wisdom held that you never wanted to take a job on a ranch with electricity. It's one thing to work from can see to can't see, from sunup to sundown, from saddling in the dark to unsaddling by moonlight. But with lights in the barn and corrals, when would the day end?

Nighttime satellite photographs of the earth show either vast blankets or large spots of light all over the world, except for North Korea and the centers of the Australian outback, South America, Africa, and the steppes of Asia. I recently read that in 2020 Chinese scientists are going to place an artificial moon in the sky above Chengdu, a moon that will shine every night at eight times the luminosity of the real moon when it's full. If successful, how long will it be before New York, Chicago, Tokyo—all the big cities in the world—will each have its own moon?

I can't help but wonder, though, if all this artificial (i.e., unnatural) light is necessary, or even healthful. When the sun goes down, it's supposed to get dark. We need a Voice from Above to declare: "Let There Be Night!"

LEGENDS AND TALES

Preston Plumb

A very large granite boulder rests atop the grave of Preston Plumb in the Maplewood Cemetery of Emporia, Kansas. Plumb, born in Ohio in 1837 and a staunch free-state activist, came to Kansas Territory in 1856 and was one of the founders of Emporia one year later. He was, among other things, a newspaperman, establishing Emporia's first newspaper, the *Kanzas News*. He rose to the rank of lieutenant colonel during the Civil War, practiced law, and was president of Emporia National Bank.

Plumb was also an able legislator, serving in the Kansas House of Representatives both before and after the war and was three times elected to the U.S. Senate, the last time unanimously, the only Kansas senator thus honored. (This was back when senators were elected by state legislatures, not by popular vote.) He was a hardworking senator, highly valued by his colleagues, and was credited especially for his work in conserving natural resources. He died in office. His reputation was such that the lead character in the 1890 Broadway play *The Senator* was based on Plumb. Back in Emporia the main building on the Emporia State University campus is named after him. In fact, my forty-five-year teaching career at ESU was spent in an office in Plumb Hall.

You would think with a résumé like this that local legend would have treated Plumb kindly, but you would be wrong. Thus the story of the granite boulder:

It seems that Plumb's wife Caroline suspected that Preston was not adhering to his marriage vows. So when he told her he was taking the train to Colorado Springs on yet another business trip, she quietly took the next train west. It further seems that Preston rendezvoused with a young lady at the swank Broadmoor Hotel. Caroline took rooms nearby where she could watch Preston's comings and goings.

One afternoon Preston and his paramour took a walk in the Garden of the Gods. Caroline followed at a discreet distance and observed her husband with his lady friend supine atop a large granite boulder, enjoying much more than just the scenery. Mrs. Plumb quietly retreated to her room and the next day hired a contractor to remove that very boulder and ship it back to Emporia.

When Preston returned home he was greeted by the sight of that boulder resting on the front lawn. Neither he nor Caroline ever mentioned the rock, but his trips to Colorado ceased. At her husband's death in 1891 Caroline had the boulder removed to the cemetery and placed atop his grave, where, at the end of the burial service, she reportedly was heard to mutter, "That should hold the son-of-a-bitch down."

Some legends contain a grain, sometimes many grains, of truth. This legend? Not a single one.

In fact, there was no boulder on Plumb's grave until many years after his death. If you walk through Maplewood Cemetery today, however, you will see a three-by-six-foot pink granite boulder with a nameplate reading "Plumb." Caroline Plumb spent the next seventeen years after Preston's death looking for just the right stone with which to mark his grave. She finally found it, not in Colorado's Garden of the Gods, but in Montpelier, Vermont.

Not as colorful as the legend, but then real life rarely is.

French Frank

In 2013 the Cottonwood Hole segment of the Santa Fe Trail in northwest Marion County was placed on the National Register of Historic Places. The quarter section of grass that contains Cottonwood Hole, along with at least half a dozen well-defined wagon ruts made a century and a half ago by Santa Fe traders, is owned by Steve and Glenda Schmidt of McPherson, who gave me a tour of the property a few months before the National Register nomination was approved. This particular piece of ground is of even greater historical importance because, as a sign on the south side of the section says, the Chisholm Trail also crossed here, longhorn cattle moving from south to north across the east-west wagon ruts.

Cottonwood Hole is about a half day's travel by ox team (i.e., five or six miles) southwest of Cottonwood Crossing. There is good spring water at the location, but no trees for a fire, so it was a good spot for lunch, not for overnight camping. Susan Shelby Magoffin, in *Down the Santa Fe Trail and into Mexico*, her classic 1846 account of accompanying her husband on the trail, tells of stopping there.

Somewhere near the Cottonwood Hole spring a French immigrant named Claude Francis Laloge established what was called a road ranch. These road ranches were, in essence, the convenience stores of the Santa Fe Trail where a traveler could buy food, drink (i.e., whiskey), and other essentials. Laloge had a partner, Peter Martin, who usually stayed at the store while Laloge traveled east into Chase County to buy supplies or west out onto the High Plains to trade with Indians or settlers. The Laloge road ranch was known as French Frank's.

Frank Laloge was born in Lyons, France, in 1831. At age twenty-six he arrived in New Orleans where he and Peter Martin, who had probably come over on the same ship, worked for a few months in a bakery. After a stint of hunting and trapping on the Plains, Laloge tried prospecting, unsuccessfully, for gold at Pike's Peak in 1859. A year later, flat broke, he walked to Kansas City and hired on as a cook with a Santa Fe trader. Then, in 1861, he started his road ranch, which he operated for a few years before selling it.

He didn't actually sell the store but traded it in 1864 to a Santa Fe teamster, George Russell, for the man's two oxen teams, wagons, and contents. A year earlier Frank had married a young French woman, Mary Eugenia Hallotte. They had met on one of Frank's trips to Chase County to buy produce—eggs, buttermilk, vegetables, etc.—from farmers in the Cedar Point area. A few months later the couple was married by a justice of the peace, J. L. Crawford, in the town of Crawfordsville, a village later renamed Clements.

After disposing of his store, in no small part because of Indian troubles (more about which below), Frank took up farming two and a half miles southeast of Cedar Point in western Chase County, a region that was home to many French immigrants. The early years were lean, what with periodic floods, drouths, and the terrible 1874 grasshopper invasion. Here, as in other places, the hoppers not only cleared the foliage in the Laloge garden but ate the root vegetables into the ground, leaving only a hole where the turnips and beets had grown. Frank Laloge was well respected by his neighbors, serving several terms as township treasurer and being elected, along with David Sauble, as a constable. For many years Laloge organized an annual French picnic on Bastille Day, but the custom died with him, in 1899.

French Frank's was a little less than twenty miles east of McPherson and about the same distance west of Marion. The exact location of the store isn't known, but it was probably close to the freshwater spring for which Cottonwood Hole is named. Why hasn't the site been pinned down? That's an interesting question with an even more interesting possible answer.

During the Civil War, when the nation's attention was largely diverted from the Great Plains, many of the Indian tribes that did not want their homeland taken from them found it a good time to resist the white incursion. The Texas frontier, for instance, was pushed back significantly during this time period.

In September of 1864 the Kiowa, Comanche, and Cheyenne raided well into the eastern half of Kansas. On one occasion Satanta, the most prominent of the Kiowa war leaders, and eleven of his men entered the store, where they confronted Frank and his wife Mary. Satanta, according to the story passed down in the family, picked up a butcher knife from among the items for sale and threatened Frank. Frank was not armed, but he was near a can of gunpowder on the store counter. He grabbed a handful and threw it into the stove. The resulting explosion and smoke frightened the intruders, who immediately left, but Frank assumed that they would soon come back. And they did.

In the meantime Frank had placed a full keg of gunpowder in the middle of the store. He drilled a hole in the wooden lid of the keg, and he placed an iron poker in the stove, in which he kept a good fire going. He also sent Mary back to her parents' farm near Clements in Chase County.

Two days later Satanta returned with twice as many braves. When the Kiowa entered the store intent on dispatching Frank, the storekeeper grabbed the red-hot poker, held it above the hole in the powder keg, and said, "We are all going to die bravely." But no one did. Seeing that Frank was ready to kill himself along with all of them, Satanta and his men again skedaddled.

The following day was when George Russell offered to swap his outfit for French Frank's store, and Frank, realizing the precariousness of his situation vis-à-vis the Kiowa, gladly took him up. He and his partner, Peter Martin, packed up and left for Chase County that very evening, traveling all through the night.

About sunrise next morning Frank and Peter were overtaken by a rider who told them that his store was on fire and that about a hundred Indians were milling around it. Although no one knew for sure, the new owner was apparently killed in the attack. All that was left of the store was ashes, which disintegrated with the rains, so that today we do not know just where French Frank's road ranch stood.

Or perhaps the Satanta story is a bit of family folklore. Steve Schmidt, an ardent pursuer of Santa Fe Trail history, has located records that show Laloge still living in Marion County in 1865. Schmidt believes that Laloge sold his road ranch to Russell in 1866, about the time that Santa Fe traders were beginning to meet railroad trains in Junction City, then heading their wagons west to Ellsworth and southwest to a point west of Great Bend. Sensing that business for his and other road ranches east of Great Bend would dry up, Frank unloaded it. As further evidence Schmidt points to a dram license being granted to Laloge and Parker in 1865, then a year later a similar license being granted to Russell.

This version certainly isn't as colorful as the Satanta raid, but whichever is true no physical evidence of the road ranch at Cottonwood Hole has yet been found. Still, one can always hope that some future archaeologist will locate the spot where the store stood, along with the rusted remains of the butcher knife that Satanta waved in French Frank's face.

Yeager's Raid

The Civil War, like railroads or genealogy, seems to inspire amateur history buffs to the point of obsession. I'm not one of the obsessed, although I have taken a more than casual interest in one particular Civil War incident because it took place in the Flint Hills, with whose history I will admit obsession. Also because part of that incident, an 1863 raid led by Dick Yeager (or Yager—I've seen it spelled both ways) took place on the Flying W Ranch south of Clements.

I first became aware of Yeager's Raid while editing Elisha Mardin's 1863 diary.* At the time of the raid Mardin owned and operated the second-largest ranch in Chase County. His home was east of Strong City a few miles, about where the Palenske feed yard is now located. In his diary spelling was whimsical and punctuation unknown. Here is his entry for May 8:

> I went up to the falls [i.e., Cottonwood Falls] & over to Bazaar after a band of garillas got back about two oclock in the after noon Jo Randolph and Charles Bundren came with me

The guerrillas that Mardin was helping track were Missouri bushwhackers led by Richard Francis Yeager, one of William Clark Quantrill's captains. Dick Yeager was born in Kentucky in 1839, and soon thereafter the family moved to Missouri, where his father became the presiding judge of the Jackson County

*In 2009 I edited both Mardin's diary and the 1862 diary of his wife for the Center for Great Plains Studies at Emporia State University: *A Window on Flint Hills Folklife: The Mardin Ranch Diaries, 1862–1863*.

court. The elder Yeager also had a freighting business, and his son led wagon trains on the Santa Fe Trail.

Soon after the Civil War broke out in 1861, Yeager returned from Santa Fe to find that his father's house had been burned to the ground by antislavery Jayhawkers. Yeager immediately joined up with Quantrill. Yeager's first raid into Kansas occurred in late October 1861, when he and thirteen others, including Cole Younger, invaded the Johnson County town of Gardner brandishing double-barreled shotguns. No one was injured, nor were the bushwhackers successful in their attempt to rob a store.

Two years later Yeager led a couple of dozen border ruffians (terrorists, in today's parlance) on a raid into Kansas, this time much deeper. His plan was to pillage his way up the South Fork River valley and then go on to burn Council Grove. Fortunately for the settlers who lived along South Fork, Yeager didn't recognize the stream and the gang ended up on Coyne Creek where it runs into the Cottonwood River near the ghost town of Clements.

Local lore has it that when Yeager reached the Cottonwood, there were not enough trees to supply firewood, so the group headed back up Coyne Creek (also called Coyne Branch). After about three miles they spotted some cottonwood trees growing by a spring about half a mile south of the creek. There they found enough dead branches for a fire, so they made camp.

Volume 1 of the *Chase County Historical Sketches* (1940) states that Coyne Creek was named for an M. Coyne, "a squatter located near mouth of creek." (Actually, his dwelling was near the head of the creek; the mouth would be close to Clements.) This is the only printed reference I have found for Coyne, so everything else I know about him comes from stories (some of which have him named Michael, others Arthur) passed down locally.

According to this lore, Coyne immigrated to Mexico from Germany sometime before the mid-nineteenth century. From Mexico he worked his way north to Santa Fe, then followed the Santa Fe Trail east into the Flint Hills. This was well before Kansas Territory opened for legal settlement in 1854, so he truly was a squatter in the dugout he built and lived in.

Coyne had no visible means of support; he didn't farm or have a job. Sometime in the 1850s he is said to have built a road paved with cottonwood logs, planning on charging a toll for its use by travelers. They, however, simply drove their wagons over the open prairie on either side of his road, paying no toll.

Before he died (I don't know the date), some fifteen or twenty families were living between him and the Cottonwood River at Clements, about four miles to the northwest. With his Black Forest muzzle-loading rifle he would shoot prairie chickens off shocks of feed his neighbors had made, giving the landowners half. Whether he sold his half or subsisted on them, I don't know.

Coyne lived the rest of his life in his dugout. He died a bachelor and is said to be buried in a local cemetery, but which one, again I don't know. Obviously, there is much about Coyne I don't know, and how much of what I have written about him is literally true? Facts get bent around as stories are passed down, and in this case the stories go back to events some 175 years ago. In my opinion the important thing is that something really interesting happened on this little patch of Flint Hills landscape, and that it was not unique. Something interesting has undoubtedly happened on every acre of land in the world, if we only knew what it was.

But back to Yeager and his bushwhackers. If they had continued on up Coyne Creek another half mile, they might have run into Michael Coyne and killed him as a Union sympathizer. The next day they rode on up to Diamond Springs, where they robbed the store, killed the storekeeper, and wounded his wife. From there they planned to ride on to Council Grove and burn the town, just as Quantrill would do to Lawrence three months later.

If you've never heard of the Sack of Council Grove, however, it's because it never happened. By the time the cutthroats neared town, Yeager had a raging toothache. Leaving his men camped outside town, Yeager and one of his gang rode into Council Grove and to the office of Dr. J. H. Bradford, a native Missourian. Yeager knew Bradford, either from Missouri or from his Santa Fe Trail freighting days, and once inside the office he asked for relief from his aching tooth. The dentist said he would treat Yeager if the raider would spare the town. He then pulled the tooth and gave Yeager a bottle of laudanum for the pain. (Laudanum, incidentally, is made from opium and was a popular nostrum for ladies in the nineteenth century. Wyatt Earp's wife is said to have been addicted. It could be bought without a prescription until early in the twentieth century.)

True to his word, Yeager spared Council Grove from the torch. The gang then split up and headed back to Missouri, plundering houses and stores, robbing stagecoaches, stealing horses, and killing two more men on their way.

This is the way I heard the story from residents in the vicinity of Coyne Creek, but there are other versions.

Volume 14 of the *Collections of the Kansas State Historical Society*, published in 1918, contains some recollections of the episode by longtime residents of the Council Grove area. According to this source it was on May 4 that the raiders camped along Elm Creek near Council Grove on land owned by Col. George Armstrong Custer. On May 5 Yeager and a companion rode into town and straight to the office of Dr. J. H. Bradford where he got his tooth pulled and his bottle of laudanum.

The day after the visit to the dentist (not the day before) the guerrillas rode west from Elm Creek, not north from Coyne Creek, to Diamond Springs, where they robbed Augustus Howell's stage station and general store. When he attempted to stop them, they shot and killed him and severely wounded his wife, Sarah, when she tried to defend him.

A posse of several dozen men, led by James McDowell, a U.S. marshal from Leavenworth, caught up with the raiders where the Santa Fe Trail crossed the Cottonwood River west of Diamond Springs, capturing about a dozen of the guerrillas. Another half dozen were caught by an Emporia posse when they forded the Neosho on their way back to Missouri. These raiders, being taken to the jail at Fort Riley, made a break for freedom (or so said their captors) and were all shot to death in the attempt. What was left of the gang headed back to Missouri, plundering houses and stores, robbing stagecoaches, stealing horses, and killing two more men, including a Union soldier at the Rock Springs stage station.

It is not surprising that details of Yeager's raid vary in the retelling, as is true in general for traumatic incidents. Some think that Yeager raided Diamond Springs the day before going into Council Grove to get his tooth pulled, some the day after. Malcolm Conn, a prominent early resident of and storekeeper in Council Grove, thinks it was his intervention, not the tooth-pulling dentist, that saved the town. Conn, a Missourian who had become friends with Yeager when the latter was a Santa Fe trader, claims to have gone into Yeager's camp on the evening of May 4, when the raiders were just outside Council Grove, and persuaded him to spare the town, not only because of their friendship but also because of the many southern sympathizers who lived there. (But, I wonder, why would Yeager have been bent on destroying Council Grove if it were leaning toward the Confederacy?)

I like the first version, the folk history, of the story best because Coyne Springs is located on the Flying W Ranch, which is owned and operated by my son Josh and his family. I had earlier wondered whether the late George Yeager, a rancher who lived near Rock Creek west of Bazaar, was kin to the leader of the raiders, but I checked and I'm glad to say that he wasn't, his name untainted.

Knute Rockne

I am writing this chapter on the last day of March 2019, which marks exactly eighty-eight years since a Transcontinental and Western Air passenger plane, a Fokker F-10 Trimotor, crashed in a Flint Hills pasture southwest of Bazaar in Chase County killing everyone on board—a total of eight people. There had been other wrecks of commercial air flights resulting in deaths, although this was one of the largest numbers of casualties. But what brought this particular crash both national and international attention was the passenger list.

As headline after headline proclaimed: KNUTE ROCKNE AND SEVEN OTHERS KILLED. Although today there are many people, particularly younger sports fans, who would not recognize that name, in 1931 he was a living legend. In thirteen years his Notre Dame football teams had recorded five undefeated seasons and three national championships. His total record as head coach was 105 wins, 12 losses, and 5 ties, a winning percentage that has never been equaled. His fame was such that at the time of the crash he was on his way to Hollywood to participate in the filming of *The Spirit of Notre Dame*.

Rockne had stopped in Kansas City to visit his two sons, Billy and Knute, Jr., who were attending Pembroke Country Day School. Sadly, the boys were returning from a trip to Florida and got to Kansas City too late to see their father.

The response to Rockne's death was one of shock and grief, as if a great national leader had died. President Herbert Hoover sent a telegram of condolence to Mrs. Rockne, calling the death of her husband "a national loss" and saying, "I know that every American grieves with you." Rockne had come to America as an immigrant from Norway, and King Haakon VII sent a personal envoy to the funeral. He also posthumously knighted Rockne. Over a hundred thousand people gathered to watch the funeral procession in South Bend, which was broadcast live on the radio throughout the country and Europe and also to parts of Asia and South America.

At the time investigations of plane crashes were done by the Department of Commerce, and previously the findings were not made public, but because of the intense interest every detail of this wreck was published. Also a new agency, the Civil Aeronautics Board (later the National Transportation Safety Board), was created to conduct future investigations and report them to the public. Other changes in the airline industry that resulted from the crash included increased and more detailed safety inspections, greater attention to design and maintenance, and better regulation. As a result air travel is now one of the safest modes of transportation, not one of the most dangerous.

Because almost all the press coverage concentrated, naturally enough, on Rockne, the other men who were killed are almost always referred to as "and seven others," but the monument erected in the pasture where the plane crashed lists all of them: Knute K. Rockne, Waldo B. Miller, H. J. Christen, John Happer, Spencer Goldthwaite, C. A. Robrect, Robert Fry, and Herman J. Mathias. Fry was the pilot, Jess Mathias the copilot. I'm assuming that the names chiseled in this stone are correct, although the day of the crash the Associated Press listed Happer as Hooper, Christen as Christensen, and Robrect as Lobrech.

Three memorials to Rockne exist, one on the Notre Dame campus, one in the Matfield Green Service Area on the Kansas Turnpike, and a large stone marker in the Baker pasture, where the crash occurred. That pasture borders K-177 on the east, but the monument itself is not visible from the highway.

Back in 1961 when I was cowboying on the Rogler ranch, the Baker pasture was one that Wayne Rogler leased. Several times I had occasion to ride in that pasture, and I would sometimes ride by the monument, which had been rubbed down by cattle. A few years after that, some local people put it back in place and built a fence around it to keep the cattle away. I don't know who those people were, but chances are that Easter Heathman was one of them. Easter was a week shy of his fourteenth birthday when the crash occurred, and he was one of the first to arrive at the scene. Another was Edward "Tincum" Baker, whose father, Seward, owned the pasture.

Baker's mother heard the crash and thought the plane had exploded in midair. Early news reports quote her as saying, "My son watched it spin down in flames and bury itself in the soft pasture." As in many such news stories, it wasn't quite accurate. One report had the plane crashing in a wheat field, not a pasture. Also, a rocky Flint Hills pasture would not be soft, nor was there fire associated with the crash. According to investigators, pilot Robert Fry had apparently cut the engines before the crash, nor was there any evidence of fire at the scene.

Rather, it was the design of the plane that caused the wreck. The outer skin of the Fokker F-10 Trimotor was made of plywood, attached to the ribs with water-based glue. The weather that day was moist—foggy and rainy. The moisture caused the glue to soften, which caused a wing to separate and come off, falling half a mile from the plane.

Five of the passengers were found at varying distances from the wreckage. The other three—Fry, Mathias, and Rockne—were at the plane itself, or what was left of it. Jess Harper, a rancher at Sitka in southwest Kansas, came to Bazaar to identify Rockne's body. Harper had been the coach at Notre Dame and had hired Rockne as his replacement, then returned to coach at Notre Dame until a new coach was named.

By the time investigators arrived at the site, news that Rockne had been a passenger was widely known, and souvenir hunters had picked up many pieces of the wreckage. The plane was a regular carrier of mail, and eighteen intact mailbags were found in the area and sent on to Wichita by rail.

Among other early arrivals at the scene besides Heathman and Baker was Wally Evans, who later opened a successful wholesale restaurant supply company in Emporia. At one point I took students in my Flint Hills Folklore class to meet with Wally, who told them of his experiences that day. Easter Heathman, who continued to live near the site, became an unofficial caretaker of the monument and a guide to visitors who came in remembrance of Rockne.

It is estimated that Easter took a thousand or more visitors to the site and told them the story of the wreck. He organized anniversary commemorations at the Bazaar schoolhouse on the 60th, 65th, 70th, and 75th anniversaries of the wreck. In 2006, the 75th, he was awarded an honorary monogram from Notre Dame for his dedication to the memory of Rockne, and he also, at various times, had been given autographed footballs by Notre Dame coaches Ara Parshegan, Charlie Weiss, and Lou Holtz. Heathman died in 2008 and some of his ashes were scattered at the Rockne monument.

Maud Wagner

Although the Flint Hills are better known for producing beef than for producing celebrities, still there are a few famous people that have had a connection to this tallgrass prairie. As recounted in the previous chapter, probably the biggest name connected with the region was a Norwegian who became the winningest coach in football history. Knute Rockne's Notre Dame teams won 105 games, lost 12, and tied 5. I don't know how they figure ties into winning percentages, but his record has to be at least .850. His connection to the Hills was a sad one, killed in a plane crash on March 31, 1931. The entire nation went into mourning.

In terms of national prestige, undoubtedly the most famous person with Flint Hills roots was Jess Willard from Emmett up in Pottawatomie County. As a youth he had a big enough reputation as a fighter to challenge the entire town-team baseball team from Maple Hill, and they all backed down. A few years later he turned to professional boxing and won the Heavyweight Championship of the World. I tell his story in *Flint Hills Cowboys*, as I do the Roberts family in the next paragraph.

Rodeo doesn't have the same public following as boxing, not to mention football and baseball, but in the world of rodeo five world champions have lived in the Flint Hills. Foremost among this number are the Roberts family of Strong City, where Gerald was a two-time All-Around Cowboy (1942 and 1948), while older brother Ken won the bull riding title three years in a row (1943, 1944, and 1945). In 1940 their older sister Marge won the last women's saddle bronc riding contest ever held at the Cheyenne Frontier Days, the equivalent of a world championship in the days before there was a Women's Professional Rodeo Association.

This prologue of Flint Hills residents with national reputations is leading up to the story of Maud Wagner, the nation's first and most famous woman

Maud Wagner.

tattoo artist, whose final resting place is in Homestead Cemetery, located in the countryside south of Clements, a few miles away from the Flying W Ranch. Not being a tattoo aficionado, I had never heard of Maud until Brian Obermeyer told me about her in February of 2020. I'm always eager to learn about interesting people with a Flint Hills connection, even if the connection is, in this case, esoteric. Esoteric to me, maybe, but Maud is famous in the tattoo world. She was born in Emporia, on February 12, 1877, to David and Sarah Stevens. At some point Maud left home to become a circus performer, a contortionist, and a trapeze artist.

Maud was plying her aerialist profession at the 1904 St. Louis World's Fair (officially the Louisiana Purchase Exposition) when she first met tattooist Gus Wagner, the self-described "most artistically marked up man in America." Wagner, born in Ohio five years before Maud, had traveled the world as a merchant seaman from 1897 to 1901. That's where he became acquainted with tattooists in Borneo, Java, Japan, and Australia, who taught him the technique of hand-poke tattooing. By 1908 he is said to have covered his body with over eight hundred tattoos.

Gus, billed as the Tattooed Globetrotter, was attracted to Maud at the World's Fair, which ran from May through November, and asked her for a date, which she agreed to if he would give her a lesson in tattooing. After several more lessons and dates, they were married on October 3, 1904.

Like her husband, Maud also had a lot of tattoos. One upper-body-frontal photograph of Maud shows a young woman (Maud herself?) mounted on a lion with another lion behind her right shoulder. There are also palm trees with monkeys swinging on them and pythons crawling up them, birds of various kinds, butterflies, the head of a running horse on her left arm, an eagle with an American flag and her maiden name on her right arm, along with all sorts of flowers and leaves filling in the bare spots. How much ink is on the rest of her body, I don't know.

Gus and Maud had a daughter, Lovetta, who was also a tattoo artist, but with unmarked skin. Maud wouldn't let Gus put a tattoo on their daughter, and Lovetta herself, when she grew up, apparently decided against self-decoration. Gus and Maud never took up the newfangled electronic tattoo machines just coming into vogue, preferring to stay with the time-honored hand-poke method.

Just where, when, and how many years the Wagners lived in the Homestead neighborhood, I haven't learned, but long enough that they had a house there and became an accepted part of the community. Gus was struck and killed by lightning on June 10, 1941, just six days before his sixty-ninth birthday. He too is buried in the Homestead Cemetery.

Maud died at age eighty-four on January 10, 1961. She had spent the last few years of her life in Lawton, Oklahoma, with her daughter, Lovetta Davis, but her body was returned to Chase County for burial. I personally knew two of her pallbearers, ranchers David and Alfred Mercer, and had met another, Cecil Yoakem, when I was a boy. It was a morning service, mourners meeting afterward for lunch at Alfred Mercer's home.

I am adding Maud to the list of other nationally significant Flint Hills people. She might not rank up there in the mind of the general public with football coaches, heavyweight boxers, or rodeo champions, but in the world of tattoo artists Maud Stevens Wagner is a legend.

Three Flint Hills Cowgirls

Okay, so Caroline Lockhart doesn't have the same Flint Hills cred as the other two women in this chapter (Helen Olson and Bobbie Downs), but she was one of the most interesting and influential women in the American West, and she did spend her childhood on the Kansas tallgrass prairie, later on often visiting her father on his ranch in Wabaunsee County, so I'm including her story here. I want to thank Bruce Waugh for introducing me to her.

Caroline was born on February 24, 1871, in Illinois, where her father, Joseph Lockhart, had been an officer in the Civil War. When his daughter was two years old, Colonel Lockhart claimed a homestead near Wakarusa, and after proving up five years later, he moved the family to Burlingame, on the Santa Fe Trail. A few years after that he was living in Topeka, where he is listed in city directories as a cattle trader. Along the way he began acquiring land, and by 1889 he had established a ranch in the Flint Hills of Wabaunsee County, a ranch that is still in the family today. At one point the ranch, located west of Lake Wabaunsee, was larger than twelve thousand acres.

In 1888, while Caroline was attending Bethany, an Episcopal school in Topeka, her mother died. A year later Caroline, a rambunctious and hard-to-handle teenager, was sent back east to boarding school, the Moravian Seminary in Bethlehem, Pennsylvania. When she turned eighteen, she became the first female reporter for the *Boston Post*. Her adventurous spirit led her to take on some daring assignments, such as donning a deep-sea diving suit and spending over half an hour at the bottom of Boston Harbor and jumping out of a fourth-floor window to test the efficacy of a fire department safety net.

Her vicarious introduction to the West came from interviewing Buffalo Bill Cody when his Wild West and Congress of Rough Riders of the World was playing in Boston, while her literal introduction occurred when the *Philadelphia*

Bulletin sent her to Montana for a story on the Blackfoot Indian tribe. That trip led her through Cody, Wyoming. She loved the area and by 1904 she had moved to Cody and lived there until she started her own ranch in 1925, just across the border in Montana. Beginning with a 160-acre homestead, she was soon running a six-thousand-acre ranch, the L Slash Heart, before moving back to Cody twenty-seven years later.

In 1920 Caroline helped found and was the first president of the Cody Stampede rodeo. Four years later she bought the *Cody Enterprise*, the local newspaper that Buffalo Bill himself had started. When he died in 1917, Caroline organized an effort to honor him with a statue. She not only convinced famed sculptor Gertrude Vanderbilt Whitney to create the twelve-foot-tall monument but also convinced her to spearhead fundraising for the $50,000 cost. The efforts of these two women played a large role in establishing Buffalo Bill's legacy as an icon of the Old West.

Among other things, Caroline was a best-selling novelist who set her stories in the contemporary American West, unlike Owen Wister and Zane Grey, whose Westerns took place in a romanticized past. At least two of her seven books were made into motion pictures: *The Man from the Bitter Roots* and *The Fighting Shepherdess*. Some of the characters in *The Lady Doc* were modeled on people she knew in Cody, which caused similar hard feelings to those Willa Cather encountered with *My Ántonia*.

Caroline was a free spirit, a liberated woman long before the term was created. She never married but had many lovers. Her biographer, John Clayton, describes her as a "serial monogamist." She also opposed and argued for the repeal of Prohibition, which, along with the many "wet" parties she held, upset her more staid fellow Codyites, who had voted three to one in favor of the issue. Mike McAfee, who organized the effort for her successful 2018 induction into the National Cowgirl Hall of Fame in Fort Worth, was the grandson of Caroline's younger sister. He never met Caroline, but he remembers that when her name came up at family gatherings, people would say, "Oh, we better not talk about her in front of the kids."

Caroline loved horses. As a child she rode all over Burlingame, and when she lived in Cody, she would ride every day from her house to her newspaper office four blocks away. She also rode on her father's ranch in the Flint Hills, which she visited both while living in the East and later in Wyoming.

After moving back to Cody at age eighty-one, Caroline lived a quiet, obscure life. She would invite neighborhood children over to watch *Hopalong Cassidy* on her new television set, one of the first in town. She died ten years later, on July 25, 1962. Her ashes were scattered on the L/♥.

Helen Olson, Andy Olson's first wife, was the daughter of Bill Ebbutts, a legendary cowboy of the northern Flint Hills. I've heard that back in the 1930s and '40s kids around Junction City didn't just play cowboy, they played Bill Ebbutts. Helen was a skilled calf roper who competed successfully against men in many of the local Flint Hills rodeos. Once at a rodeo in Emporia she was riding a horse that, while good in the pasture, had never before been inside a rodeo arena. When Helen nodded for her calf and started her horse, he was leery of the barrier rope and leaped clear over it as he left the roping box. Helen roped her calf, and when some of the male ropers protested about the barrier jumping, the judges ruled that it was released as the horse was in the air and that he would not have broken it had he stayed on the ground. Despite the disadvantage of combining steeplechasing with calf roping, Helen won the event.

When asked about Helen, Andy often teared up, especially when telling of the funeral procession to the cemetery on a road that ran alongside one of Andy's Morris County pastures. The steers in the pasture, Andy said, lined up along the fence as the hearse drove by, as if in honor of the cowgirl who had been caring for them that summer.

Many years ago one of my students in a folklore class gave me some old rodeo photographs that had been passed down through her family. One of them, showing a woman bronc rider at a rodeo in Chase or Greenwood County in the mid-1930s, remains to this day one of my favorite old rodeo pictures. The photograph itself leaves a lot to be desired. There's a big washed-out patch in the lower part of the picture, and the action isn't all that exciting. A mounted pickup man or field judge is in the background, while the bronc, just lunging out of the chute, hasn't really started bucking yet. The reason I like the picture, however, is not because of the action, or rather the lack thereof, but because of the story behind it.

My student told me that when the whistle blew and the pickup man moved in, the rider, a woman named Mattie Downs, refused to get off until the bronc was standing perfectly still because, she said, she didn't want to get hurt. The reason she didn't want to get hurt was because she was over eight months pregnant. Why she got on a bucking horse in the first place I don't know.

According to the story I was told, and my student believed it to be true (which makes it a legend, whether or not it actually happened), Mattie had a full-term normal-birth baby seventeen days after the photograph was taken.

Mattie Downs, eight months pregnant, riding a bronc at a Flint Hills rodeo, c. 1935.

Now there are recorded instances of cowboys riding bucking horses backward and bulldogging (or at least attempting to bulldog) steers from low-flying airplanes, but Mattie Downs proved that rodeo cowgirls can be just as crazy as their male counterparts.

The only other thing I know about Mattie was that her husband's name was Bobbie. There was a Texas bronc rider, Booger Red Privett, who could ride a saddle bronc with both hands in the air or with both hands tied behind his back. He was not only skilled but extremely self-confident. On two separate, documented occasions he rode a bucking horse while holding his own baby in his free arm. I don't know where his wife was while he was doing this, but he should have been married to Mattie Downs. They were made for each other.

Rufe King

Since territorial days the Flint Hills have done their share of contributing to the lore of the Old West, not least in the area of violence. I know of at least half a dozen places in the Hills that local residents call Dead Man's Hollow, Dead Woman's Canyon, Dead Man's Gulch, or some variant thereof. Tales of mayhem—murders, bank robberies, fights, and brawls—abound.

Toward the end of 2006 Cathy and I stopped by the Wabaunsee County Historical Museum in Alma, where the curator at the time, Alan Winkler, told me about one of that county's notorious denizens from the early twentieth century, the livery stable owner at Maple Hill, Rufe King. The name seemed familiar, and sure enough when I checked Roderick Turnbull's entertaining reminiscences of a childhood in that Flint Hills town, *Maple Hill Stories*, there was a chapter on Rufe King, "The Town's Toughest Man."

Turnbull, as a native of Maple Hill, related many more incidents from King's life than came up in my brief conversation with Winkler, although the latter gave a nice succinct version of the story. The livery stable business was being threatened by the advent of the automobile during the early years of the century, so King and his wife moved to California in 1909. Ten years later a renter discovered human remains on King's former property, and King was arrested for murder and brought back for trial. According to Turnbull (who had King in Colorado, not California, in 1919), a renter was wanting to buy a house King had lived in and was having some repairs done. A workman found a sack of human bones in a shed.

In another version schoolteacher Georgia Perine recalled that three of her students were playing in the hayloft of the livery barn and found some sacks of bones. Whatever the case, the investigation turned up some jewelry in the house, and local residents recalled that a jewelry salesman had disappeared some ten years earlier. At just about that same time a man named Guschall from Rossville disappeared, as well as a local boy, Anderson Woody, who had been thought to have sold his team and wagon to King before going to Oklahoma and never being heard from again.

It seems that King ran poker games in the livery office, and Woody had won something like $150 (half the price of a new Model T at the time) just before leaving for Oklahoma. Only, of course, he never left. King killed him, took back his own poker losses, and kept the team and wagon as a bonus.

Although the evidence was circumstantial, King was convicted and sent to the state penitentiary at Lansing. Before leaving, he threatened the lives of those who had testified against him, including Turnbull's father. These threats were taken seriously, for King was a bully and feared by the locals. Turnbull, for instance, tells of rancher William Sells whose baled hay was being stolen a little at a time. One night he heard a wagon in the hay meadow and, afraid to confront the thief or thieves by himself, hurried into town to get King to help him. King wasn't home, and as Sells was returning to the ranch, he met King on the road driving a team and wagon loaded with hay. Sells nodded to King and kept right on riding.

King spent the rest of his life in the penitentiary, dying there in 1947. At the time of his death he was the longest-serving inmate. A few years before King's death, Maple Hill banker Howard Adams was in Lansing and decided to see his old town mate. Only family members were allowed to visit, but because Adams was at the time a state legislator, the warden admitted him. When Adams signed the log to go in, he discovered that he was the first visitor in the twenty-five years that King had been in prison. Presumably, Adams was his only visitor ever.

Turnbull reports that King knew Adams at once and asked how Adams's younger brother, who had recently been thrown from a horse, was getting along with his broken arm. "How did you know about Warner?" Howard asked in astonishment. "Oh, I have always taken the *Alma Enterprise*," King replied. "I like to keep up on the old hometown."

And there's the story of Rufe King, who, by the way, insisted to the end that he was innocent.

SCATTERINGS

The Flint Hills and Hollywood

Some major films have been shot in the Flint Hills region, including in 1977 a television dramatization of the story of *Mary White*, the sixteen-year-old daughter of famed editor of the *Emporia Gazette* William Allen White, who died in a horse-riding accident in 1921. Mary was played by Kathleen Beller, her father by Ed Flanders, her mother Sallie White by Fionnula Flanagan, and her brother William L. by Tim Matheson. Several years later a television series was made of each of Patricia MacLachlan's award-winning books: *Sarah, Plain and Tall* (1991), *Skylark* (1993), and *Sarah, Plain and Tall: Winter's End* (1999). All three were filmed near Osage City and starred Glenn Close and Christopher Walken. The skydiving scenes of *The Gypsy Moths* from 1969 (with Burt Lancaster, Deborah Kerr, and Gene Hackman) were filmed at Benton in Butler County, with some scenes shot in El Dorado and Cottonwood Falls.

In mid-1983 Sandy Bird, wife of Lutheran minister Tom Bird and secretary for the Math Department at Emporia State University, was found dead in the river at the bottom of Rocky Ford Bridge, which spans the Cottonwood south of Emporia, the victim of an apparent car wreck, although suspicions of foul play hovered around the incident. In November of that year Marty Anderson, also of Emporia, was shot and killed just off K-177 Highway in Geary County. It turned out that the common element in both deaths was Lorna Anderson, wife of Marty and church secretary for Messiah Lutheran where Tom Bird was pastor—and also the lover of Lorna. Both Bird and Anderson were eventually found guilty of the murders and sentenced to prison. Rocky Ford Bridge, by the way, has become the site of legend trips by students in the Emporia area, who call it Bird Bridge and claim it is haunted.

The case became the basis for a television film, *Murder Ordained*, starring Keith Carradine as a dogged highway patrolman, Terry Kinney as the errant preacher, and JoBeth Williams as the promiscuous church secretary. It was also the subject of a *New Yorker* article by Calvin Trillin, "Rumors around Town," published in the January 6, 1986, issue. It was in the spring of 1985, as I recall, about midway into my tenure as chair of the English Department at ESU, that Trillin came to Emporia to research the article. One day he called and offered to come speak to our students, something he often did, he told me, as a kind of thank-you to communities where he was working. I naturally said yes, and he gave a nice, understated talk about his work as a writer. He described his technique as the "vomit out" approach: do extensive research, then sit at your typewriter (this was before the days of word-processing computers) and just let the words pour out, and then go back and organize and refine those words into a coherent and interesting article. When he had finished, I, again naturally, thanked him and also asked about maybe coming again to speak should he happen to be visiting his hometown, Kansas City. Yes, he could do that, he responded, but his fee would be in the range of a year's tuition at an elite eastern school, which he planned for his daughters to attend.

Each of the above movies or miniseries was filmed in the Emporia region (except *The Gypsy Moths*), as was a scene from Truman Capote's *In Cold Blood*, but for films that actually show some Flint Hills countryside you would need to see *Stolen Women: Captured Hearts* and *Bad Company.* The former, a made-for-television film starring Janine Turner, is based on the actual abduction of Anna Morgan by Cheyenne Indians in 1868 (Lakota Sioux in the film). It was filmed on the Vestring Ranch south and east of Cassoday in Butler County.

"*Bad Company*," to quote from the Turner Classic Movies website, "was filmed in the Flint Hills region of Kansas near Emporia over an eight week period with individual scenes shot in Neosho Rapids and Elmdale." Town scenes were also filmed in Severy, which stands in for Saint Joseph, Missouri. While I didn't recognize any of those towns, I easily recognized the rolling hills where the outdoor scenes were shot. The film had a theatrical release in 1972 and starred Jeff Bridges. It is a Civil War–era film about young draft dodgers. The plot often strains credulity, but the landscape is unmistakably that of the central Flint Hills.

An excellent documentary film of the Flint Hills in general, *The Flint Hills of Kansas* (Kaw Valley Films, 1988), was made by Jim Whitefield, while Dave Kendall and Laura Mead's Prairie Hollow Productions has released two full-length films about the Flint Hills: *A Flint Hills Love Story: The Tallgrass Prairie National Preserve* and *Prairie Women: Engaging Women of the Flint Hills.*

In 1989 I was at a professional conference and talking to Nancy Koupal, who lives in Pierre and edits the journal of the South Dakota Historical Society. She happened to mention a movie production company that had been filming up there that summer. Film companies do strange, and expensive, things that often amuse and bemuse us ordinary mortals, and Nancy was telling me how that summer they had painted autumn colors on green tree leaves, then blew them all off when they needed to change from fall to winter. When she said something about seeing Kevin Costner in a local café, I realized that she was talking about *Dances with Wolves*, a film I had had a tenuous connection with a couple of years earlier.

That was when I was contacted by Jerry Jones of the Kansas Film Commission (merged in 1996 with the Kansas Arts Commission to form the Kansas Creative Arts Industries Commission) to see if I could take him and independent California film producer Jim Wilson on a drive through the Flint Hills to scout possible sites for that very Kevin Costner movie. For the setting Wilson needed a big stretch of native prairie with no traces of civilization—no electric lines visible, no fences, no roads, no houses, no croplands, and not many trees. He needed a flat meadow area large enough for a village of fifty or more lodges, with a large bluff rising behind it and a sizable stream of water running alongside. All this preferably within a few miles of a city with enough motels and restaurants to handle the horde of actors, extras, technicians, and assorted hangers-on that constitute a film crew.

Over the next two days we drove through four counties and found several possibilities, the best one along the upper Verdigris River in southern Chase County that was really good except for two things: the flow of water was not strong and might disappear during a dry spell, and the only route in was over some twenty-five miles of gravel road. People who are used to paved streets or the sandy roads of the High Plains really can't appreciate the severity of Flint Hills gravel, but the fact that early on our first day a flint rock knocked a hole in one of Jerry's tires, along with the accessibility to a large bison herd near Custer, undoubtedly influenced Wilson's decision to film in South Dakota.

It was fun to learn something of how the film industry works, and Jim Wilson completely negated all my stereotypes of the Hollywood producer: he was young, outgoing, unegotistical, and fully aware that real people lived between New York and Los Angeles. In fact, he kept me so busy with questions about me and my family and the history of the Flint Hills that my inquiring mind never got around to asking about the latest Hollywood gossip.

I did learn, though, that writing screenplays is no quick and easy way to wealth and glory. Wilson said that only 1 percent of the twenty-five thousand complete scripts that are filed with the Screen Writers Guild each year ever get made into movies, and of those 250 only about twenty-five make money. With those odds I think I'll stick to writing about the Flint Hills.

High Culture in the Flint Hills

As a folklorist and as a native of the place, I am deeply drawn to the folk culture of the Flint Hills with its roots planted deeply in the cattle industry. But, especially in the past few years, high culture in the form of music, literature, photography, and painting has found a muse in this calm and quiet landscape.

Music

For years I have hoped to chance upon a Flint Hills folk song, a piece of old-time, homemade music inspired by and reflecting the distinctive culture of the tallgrass prairie. Oh, I've heard plenty of folk music *in* the Flint Hills, from fiddle tunes to old cowboy songs. My father and uncle used to sing "Bury Me Out on the Prairie," a mournful song about a young cowboy who goes bad and is killed by a posse. He knows he is not worthy of being laid to rest back in his hometown, asking only that his grave be covered with rocks to keep the coyotes at bay. It was a favorite of theirs but not of my mother and aunt, probably because of the first verse, which goes like this:

> Oh, I've got no use for the women; a true one can seldom be found.
> They'll stick by a man for his money; when he's broke they'll turn him down.
> They're all alike at the bottom, selfish and grasping for all.
> They'll stick by a man when he's winning, and laugh in his face at his fall.

If there is a genuine folk song that originated in the Flint Hills, I've not yet heard it, although a tenuous case might be made for "The Cowboy's Lament." In 1876 Frank Maynard adapted an old Irish ballad to the cowboy way of life and called it "The Dying Cowboy." I don't think it qualifies, however, because even though Maynard's permanent address was in Towanda on the western edge of the region, he never cowboyed in the Flint Hills. He wrote the song while wintering cattle south of Medicine Lodge in the Gypsum Hills, and set it in Dodge City. Texas cowboys heard it in Wichita, moved it to the Mexican border, and today we know it as "The Streets of Laredo." In 2010 I edited Maynard's memoirs (*Cowboy's Lament: A Life on the Open Range*, Texas Tech University Press) in which he tells his story.

There may be no folk songs set here, but there are contemporary songs being written about the Flint Hills by musicians such as Barbara Anderson of Burns and Annie Wilson of Elmdale. Annie, in fact, was named Flint Hills Balladeer in 2013, nine years after she helped put together the Tallgrass Express String Band. The band has released several CDs featuring Annie's songs of the Flint Hills, of which she has written more than forty. Two of my favorites are "Clean Curve of Hill against Sky" and "Last Stand of the Tallgrass Prairie," songs that go deep into the soul of the Flint Hills—and carry listeners there too. She also has humorous songs such as "Dung Beetle Bill" and "Runaway Nell," an autobiographical tune about riding her horse home at a much faster pace than she had intended.

Another Flint Hills indigenous music group is Weda Skirts, a five-member, all-female acoustic group (guitar, mandolin, bass, fiddle, djembe drum/tambourine) that plays a variety of music. Included in their repertoire are original songs about Chase County and the Flint Hills.

So there is plenty of good music *about* the Flint Hills, just not a folk song that originated and is set in the region.

What no one would have anticipated, at least until 2006 and the first Symphony in the Flint Hills, was that the Flint Hills would become closely associated with classical music. In early June from 2006 on, the Kansas City Symphony has played an annual concert in some Flint Hills pasture, remote from a paved road or any of the villages that sparsely dot the hills. The exceptions were the summer of 2019 when the severe winds of a thunderstorm blew through that year's site near Bazaar the night before the concert and wrecked several of the tents, forcing the first cancellation. The second occurred the summer of 2020 in response to the COVID-19 pandemic.

A few years earlier at a site south of Clements, rainy weather and flooding had threatened the event, but although rain that day fell all around only a few miles away, it held off at the concert site itself until after the event was over, and the show went on. After-concert activities were cut short, however, and attendees were hurried away from an impending storm. Next morning a dead, lightning-struck steer was found about a hundred yards from the orchestra tent.

But I'm getting ahead of myself. The genesis of the Symphony in the Flint Hills was the 1994 birthday party Jane Koger threw for herself on her

Homestead Ranch east of Matfield Green. Jane arranged for an all-woman orchestra to play classical music out in the middle of a pasture and spread the word about her Symphony on the Prairie. Some three thousand people showed up. Many of the city people attending had never set foot in a bluestem pasture before, and many of the country people had never heard a symphony orchestra before. It was quite an experience for both groups.

Two years later Ann Birney and Joyce Thierer put together, also on Jane's ranch, a smaller version they called Brass on the Bluestem. In 2004 Phil and Kathy Miller of Matfield Green met in Council Grove with Joyce and Ann and several others interested in reviving a prairie concert. The result was the first Symphony in the Flint Hills, held in early June 2006, in the Windmill pasture of the Tallgrass Prairie National Preserve and featuring the Kansas City Symphony.

How the organizers ever pulled it off, considering the magnitude and the complexity involved, is mind-boggling. My wife, Cathy, volunteered to help out, and she was assigned, among other duties, to find barrels for trash receptacles and get them painted green and also to arrange for the many Porta-Potties needed to handle a crowd that they hoped would (and did) number several thousand people.

The price of admission was thirty-one dollars (it's now around ninety-five), and the locals scoffed at the idea that anyone would pay that much. But as spring progressed, so did the enterprise, and so did ticket sales. People who had earlier scorned the whole idea now began to scramble for tickets. Josh was asked to bring in his 1884 chuck wagon that had once accompanied a trail drive from Texas to Nebraska, and he also arranged for cowboys to serve as mounted ushers along the trail from the Spring Hill Ranch buildings to the event site a mile west. I helped with that, and also moderated recollections of several men and women who had lived and worked on the Z Bar before it became part of the National Park system.

The music was excellent, the crowd appreciative, and as the sun went down the orchestra played "Home on the Range" while the crowd all stood and sang along to the Kansas state song, a tradition that has been maintained every year since.

That next year Cathy was appointed to the board of directors, and we learned just how mind-boggling and complicated it really is to pull off this once-a-year event. Ticket sales cover only about a third of the cost, so sponsors and patrons are essential. People begin arriving at the concert site shortly after noon, but the music doesn't start until around 6:00 p.m. To provide distraction before then, there are flower walks, wagon rides, an astronomy tent, food and beverage tents, souvenir and art tents, a musical instrument "petting zoo" for children, and a patron tent for those who pay extra to help fund the event.

Josh serving dinner from the chuck wagon that went from Texas to the Platte River in Nebraska in 1884. (Photo by Gary Sneed)

Josh and Gwen catered the patron tent for several years. Most important, each year since 2007 four tents have been dedicated to education with speakers and panels presenting information on historical, cultural, biological, ecological, and artistic topics. Cathy was education chair for all six of her years on the board, and she worked hard, and successfully, at developing those education tents.

In 2008, during Cathy's term as board chair, the Symphony was held south of Council Grove in Morris County. One of her duties was to officially welcome the crowd and to introduce Governor Kathleen Sebelius before the concert began. It was a bit nerve-racking for her to speak in front of approximately seven thousand people (five thousand ticket holders, the rest the many volunteers without whom the event would collapse economically), but her voice didn't falter and her trepidation didn't show.

That year also started an annual tradition when a group of local cowboys drove a couple of hundred yearlings from south to north just west of the orchestra tent, to the great delight of the crowd. Those of us with knowledge of cattle work noticed that at one point the steers nearly got away from their handlers, but they held them together. Afterward I heard some amusing comments from those without knowledge of cattle work, such as, "I wonder how many times they had to practice moving those cattle?" and even, "Were those real cattle?" During the tenth anniversary concert, again held at the Tallgrass Prairie National Preserve, longhorn steers, rather than local pasture cattle, were imported for the drive.

The mission statement of the Symphony in the Flint Hills is to "heighten appreciation and knowledge of the Flint Hills tallgrass prairie," and there is no doubt in my mind that the event has succeeded in doing just that. People from urban areas such as Kansas City and Wichita have relished being able to walk among the wildflowers and grasses, while Flint Hills residents have learned elements of local history and ecology they hadn't known before. Visitors to the event have come from many states and foreign countries, some from as far away as Australia. Beginning in 2010, journalism students from Wichita State University have each year researched and produced a magazine, *Flint Hills Media Project*. The November 2018 issue of the *Smithsonian* had an article about the Symphony in the Flint Hills, and the Flint Hills in general, titled "American Rhapsody" (pp. 20–25, 94), which succeeded spectacularly in introducing a wide public to the tallgrass prairie: the estimated monthly readership for *Smithsonian* is over seven million.

Literature

In my opinion the best literature about the Flint Hills is nonfiction, and the best of that is William Least Heat-Moon's *PrairyErth*. This six-hundred-plus-page opus is subtitled "A Deep Map," and it is indeed a thorough contemplation of Chase County in the heart of the Flint Hills. Heat-Moon's first and best-known book, *Blue Highways*, is the story of his travels across America on back roads, but for his second book he concentrated on one of the smallest, poorest, and least populated of the 105 counties in Kansas.

One day when Cathy was reading *Blue Highways* she handed it to me, and when I saw the author's picture on the dust jacket I said, "I know that guy!" But not as Heat-Moon. Bill Trogdon was in graduate school at the University of Missouri when I was, and although I don't think I'd actually talked to him, we were in one class together. When I learned that he was working on a Flint Hills book, I got in touch, and he visited us several times during his eight or so years of research here. I was at the time collecting interviews with longtime Flint Hills residents for *Flint Hills Cowboys* (University Press of Kansas, 2006), and he sometimes went along with me.

One particular occasion stands out. Bill had accompanied me to the Bazaar schoolhouse (not used as a school for years, but as a place for community gatherings) for some sort of ranching meeting. Also in attendance was Pat Sauble, who had been outspokenly scornful (as were many Chase Countians) about this outsider who thought he could write a book about them. Part of the meeting was a field trip to a ranch south of Bazaar, for which attendees carpooled. Bill and I happened into a car in which Pat was also a passenger. Now Bill has a way of listening (essential to a good writer) that encourages people, even those who might be antagonistic, to open up to him. A few quiet questions from Bill and before we had gone two or three miles, Pat and Bill were deeply engaged in conversation, and Pat was telling him stories that found their way into *PrairyErth*.

Rolla Clymer, late editor of the *El Dorado Times*, was celebrated for his editorials lauding the Flint Hills with titles such as "April's Fledge of Grass," "Glory of the Hills," and "Majesty of the Hills." Back in the 1950s, when many of these editorial-page essays appeared, I thought the prose on the purple side, but as I read them now as an adult, I find myself nodding in agreement in his praise of the bluestem and what he liked to term the Big Beef Steer. And those *were* the days of big steers, two-year-olds that came in from Texas at forty-five to a railroad stock car, and left at twenty-five to the car on their way to the Kansas City stockyards.

For some half a century Zula Bennington Greene wrote a popular column of personal musings for the *Topeka Daily Capital* under the title "Peggy of the Flint Hills." Many of her musings were about the Flint Hills, including a 1946 piece in which she suggests that the fledgling United Nations should be headquartered in the Flint Hills because their serene presence would make world peace seem an attainable end.

An excellent collection of essays about Oklahoma's Osage Hills, the southern tip of the Flint Hills, is Gary Lantz's 2017 book, *Heart Stays Country: Meditations from the Southern Flint Hills*, but with a focus more on nature than on ranching culture.

Some good memoirs of life in the Flint Hills were written by Samuel Evan Boys, *My Boyhood in the Flint Hills of Kansas, 1873–1893*; Adaline Sorace, *Addie of the Flint Hills: A Prairie Child during the Depression (1915–1935)*, and John A. Edwards, *In the Western Tongue.*

It seems that most of the novels with a Flint Hills setting are of the formula or genre type. Some in the young adult category are Irene Bennett Brown's *Answer Me, Answer Me* and *Miss Royal's Mules*, Charles Hammer's *Me, the Beef, and the Bum*, Dorothy Bremer Francis's *The Flint Hills Foal*, and Jerri Garretson's *The Secret of Whispering Springs.* As far as I know, only one mystery novel is set in the Flint Hills, Nancy Pickard's *Bum Steer.*

One might think Westerns would be a natural for the Flint Hills, but not so. Don Coldsmith did set *The Sacred Hills*, a title in his popular Spanish Bit series, in the Flint Hills, but that's about it, as far as I know. I was excited a few years ago when I ran across a novel titled *The Flint Hills*, but disappointed when I read it. The book was a run-of-the-mill oater set in the generic West with no real sense of place, certainly not of the Kansas Flint Hills. The author (I don't recall his name) was apparently English with a knowledge of the American West that seemed to have been acquired from reading other generic Westerns.

If writers of Westerns have not been drawn to the Flint Hills as settings for their fiction, romance writers, by contrast, seem to have glommed onto them. Authors include Cassandra Austin (*The Hero of the Flint Hills* and *Flint Hills Bride*) and Janice Graham (*Firebird, Safe Harbor*, and *Sarah's Window* [in which the heroine starts out as a waitress in the Cassoday Café]). Then there is romance novelist and aficionado Tessa Layne, who likes her romance fiction "filthy and romantic . . . the smuttier the better." (I'm relying on her website here, not having read any of her novels.) Layne has written a whole series of bodice rippers (actually her book covers, as depicted on Amazon, are of bare-chested hunks wearing cowboy hats, not females in various stages of décolletage) under the umbrella title of *Cowboys of the Flint Hills.* The first, *Prairie Heat: Cowboys of the Flint Hills*, was published in 2016. There followed *Prairie Passion, Prairie Desire, Prairie Storm, Prairie Fire, Prairie Devil, Prairie Fever, Prairie Rapture, Prairie Redemption*, and, finally, *Prairie Bliss* in 2019. Ten books in three years. I suppose I should quit being a snob and read one just to see if and how accurately she (or any of the other romance writers) depicts the Flint Hills.

Poets, both the serious and cowboy variety, have been much more aware than fiction writers of the powerful feelings that can be inspired by the Flint Hills—the serenity, the openness, the sky, the beauty, and, particularly for the latter genre, the cattle and horses. Several years ago I edited *Prairie Poetry*, an anthology of Kansas cowboy and cowgirl verse, with the Flint Hills well represented by both poets and poems. Among Flint Hills cowboy poets who have published collections of their work are Tom McBeth, Jerry Wright, John Markley, and Elva Schouten.

Two of the best native-born Flint Hills poets are Steven Hind of Madison and Annie Wilson of Elmdale, while H. C. Palmer is a convert. I'm going to give, with their permission, an example here of a poem by each that particularly speaks to me. First, "Last Ridge of Hills," from Annie:

From a hilltop our eyes can gaze far out beyond
To the long layered weave of the land
'Til they rise to the high slender seam of the earth
And rest on that last ridge of hills

A thin distant ribbon of storm-colored blue
At the edge of the Earth's gentle curve
A dream-like horizon inviting us in
To rest in that last ridge of hills

Like an ancient pueblo the skyline lies low
In the tiers of long flat plateaus
Just one or two hilltops point up to the sky
Watching over that last ridge of hills

It's the last remnant wave of the vast inland sea
A reminder of when time began
Now forever it breaks and recedes in the sky
To rest in that last ridge of hills

Here is Steven's "Waking in the Flint Hills":

Piercing the peace of a morning moon,
an oil well bows its head and squeaks
up a dipper of crude. In the far darkness
a diesel fumbles gears to make the grade
as two crows by the roadway caw about
breakfast on the asphalt, and the native
grasses whisper under another assault
by the grazers. A Brangus ruminates
behind a scrim of sumac. A quavering
column of coyote song rises to the sky:
"This is a good day to cry!" they might
be singing. A poet in his tent joins in,
reciting his sword words over the world.

And finally, H. C.'s brief but evocative "After Driving Cattle in the Flint Hills":

for Dale Remsberg
Tallgrass tangled in stirrups.
Cowhands leaning on long shadows.
After all these years,
I am still in love.

As far as I'm aware, only one serious drama has been written about the Flint Hills, James Steerman's *Native Stone*, which is set in contemporary Chase County and won first prize at the Arrow Rock (Missouri) Lyceum competition in 1987. The author, a faculty member at Vassar, as a youth spent considerable time on Sam Stauffer's (his grandfather's) ranch in the western part of the county.

Photography and Painting

On one of his visits to our house Bill Trogdon was accompanied by conservation photographer Bob Lindholm. Lindholm commented on the difficulty photographers had with the Flint Hills because of their lack of physical contrast. This would have been in the mid-1980s, but obviously since then many serious photographic artists have found the key to capturing the beauty of the Flint Hills. One of the first was Terry Evans, whose photographs of the people and area around Matfield Green have received national recognition. Following is a partial list (in alphabetical order) of serious photographers who have featured the Flint Hills in their work (much of which, by the way, can be viewed online): Patricia DuBose Duncan, Mark Feiden, Teresa Groves, Bruce Hogle, Dave Leiker, John Morrison, James Nedresky, Edward Robison III, Kevin Sink, Crystal Socha, Casey Wilson, and Don Wolfe.

Pasture-burning season draws photographers, both professional and amateur, like flies to honey (or bees to flowers or, to use a more apt metaphor, moths to a flame), and the results are spectacular. I don't know if my former ESU colleague Larry Schwarm was the first to pursue the flames seriously, but he was certainly one of the pioneers, beginning his quest for fire in 1991. In 2002 his submission, one of five hundred, for the inaugural Honickman First Book Prize in Photography at the Duke University Center for Documentary Studies won first place and resulted in the book *On Fire.*

Jim Richardson's Flint Hills photographs have undoubtedly been seen by more people than those of any other photographer. That's because Jim is a *National Geographic* staff photographer, and the magazine has an international monthly circulation of nine million. After several attempts Jim convinced the editors that the Flint Hills deserved an article. After all, he says, in the spring the two greenest places on earth are Ireland and the Flint Hills. The article, written by Verlyn Klinkenborg and titled "Splendor of the Grass," was published in the April 2007 issue on pages 120–41. It featured a map and eleven color photographs, including close-ups of flowers, a panorama of the rolling hills, a prairie fire, sparring prairie chicken cocks, and a spectacular shot of the Milky Way. I asked him how many photographs he had taken for this piece, and he told me something over eight thousand. And if he'd been using digital instead of film, he said, he'd have taken a few thousand more.

Cassoday native Laurence Coffelt, Artist of the Flint Hills, in his Emporia studio.

As with photographers, oil and watercolor painters have also discovered the Flint Hills. The most famous artist to have lived in the Flint Hills area was Frederic Remington, who as a young man operated a sheep ranch near Whitewater. Although he made a few sketches of the ranch buildings, unfortunately the Flint Hills themselves were too subtle to catch his eye. The most critically acclaimed artist native to the area was Gladys Nelson Smith, but she, like Remington, did not paint the Flint Hills.

Two of the better-known painters who did incorporate the Hills into their art early on were Frederic James and Robert Sudlow, the latter spending a fair amount of time on the Wayne Rogler ranch near Matfield Green. Sudlow was a proponent of plein air painting, no matter what the weather, and much of his Flint Hills work was accomplished outside.

The late Laurence Coffelt, a native of Cassoday with a studio in Emporia, termed himself "The Artist of the Flint Hills," although the landscape in most of his paintings was of sagebrush, not bluestem.

Judy Mackey, who died in February 2019, was among the best and probably the best-known of the contemporary artists who paint Flint Hills scenes. She and her husband Ken (also an artist, in wood and leather) lived near Saffordville with a gallery in downtown Cottonwood Falls. Judy, like Phil Epp, is especially good at depicting the Flint Hills sky, its colors and its clouds. Montana might call itself Big Sky Country, but the Flint Hills sky is no less grand.

Each year the Symphony in the Flint Hills sponsors a juried art competition. Louise Carlin is responsible for the competition, and in response to a query gave me the following information:

> In 2007 and 2008 we invited twelve artists to submit one piece of work and one was selected as that winning poster for that year. All the entries were made into notecards for resale and all the paintings were sold at silent auction during the event. Many other artists requested information about having their work considered, so from 2009 to the present we have opened the program and titled it "Flint Hills Prairie Art." Each October a Call for Entry is posted on our website for any artist to submit up to two paintings, with a theme of what inspires them thematically or geographically about the Flint Hills. A different juror each year selects a winning painting. Prints of that painting are limited to 100, which are signed and numbered by the artist and sold for $125 each.
>
> In 2009 about fifty entries were submitted, which has grown to 140 in 2019. Of these about fifty are placed at silent auction at the concert. The artist receives half of the bid price, the SFH the other half. Because of the cancellation this year [2019], the artwork was auctioned online, as it was in 2014 when the Art and Retail tent was damaged by wind.

This competition has led to an increased interest in the Flint Hills among artists both from the region and beyond.

William Allen White once opined that painters had difficulty in capturing the majesty of the Flint Hills because "you can't paint silence." Art scholar Henry Adams believes, however, that artists have overcome that hurdle, in the process creating what he termed, in the June 2016 issue of *American Art Review* ("Painters of the Flint Hills," pp. 92–97, 111–12), a Flint Hills school of painting, along the lines of, but different from, the Hudson River school of the mid-nineteenth century. Noting the influence of James and Sudlow and acknowledging Judy Mackey as the "grand dame of Flint Hills painters," Adams also notes the work of Louis Copt, Lisa Grossman, Mark Flickinger, and others.

Two of the best art museums in the Flint Hills are the Coutts Museum of Art in El Dorado and the Marianna Kistler Beach Museum of Art, which opened in 1996 on the campus of Kansas State University in Manhattan. The Beach collection has grown from 1,500 pieces to some 10,000, while the Coutts houses around 2,000. Although nearly all genres of art are represented at the Beach, some pieces going well back into previous centuries, the focus is on art of the region. Visitors number around thirty thousand a year. The Coutts was established in 1970 by Warren Hall Coutts II as a memorial to his son. The collection includes work by Renoir, Thomas Hart Benton, Degas, and Picasso, as well as an extensive collection of Prairie Print Makers and sculptures by Frederic Remington and Charles M. Russell.

Despite its length, there is much more about arts and letters inspired by the Flint Hills than this chapter contains. To see more, check the annotated bibliography of the Flint Hills, "Life and Lore of the Tallgrass Prairie," with sections on Memoirs, Literature from and about the Flint Hills, and Art and Artists in the Flint Hills, published by the Center for Great Plains Studies at Emporia State University in the two-volume *Heritage of the Great Plains* (2016).

Dirt

Dirt. Like beauty, dirt is in the eye of the beholder. At least that's how I see it. What seems clean to one person can seem a total mess to someone else—just ask any husband who's been coerced into washing the dishes or any wife shanghaied into helping clean out the garage.

I don't know why, but I got to thinking about dirt the other day and the way the word is used. You'd think that out here in the Flint Hills, where we are surrounded by dirt and make our living from it (either directly or indirectly), there might be several positive attributes to the word, but I can only think of a couple. One is "pay dirt," which implies a reward after much hard digging and delving, sweating and swinking through ordinary dirty dirt. Dirt, in fact, is one of the terms applied to the dross that results from mining. Another is the term "honest dirt," which you get on your hands, along with honest sweat on your brow, by diligent toil in pursuit of an honorable goal.

But consider the many negative implications of the word: excrement and filth (its original meaning back in medieval times), worthless, unclean and repulsive, foul and sordid. If something falls to dirt, it comes to naught. If you throw dirt, you sling slander (normally called mudslinging, a term we are all too familiar with at election time). If you eat dirt, you allow yourself to be intentionally degraded—or, in the parlance of Western movie gunfights, you get shot and killed.

Dirt is usually a put-down word, as when Hamlet called the pretentious Osric, a court fop with large inherited estates, "spacious in the possession of dirt." This coming from a man who has just been in the cemetery handling the dirt-covered skull of alas poor Yorick and scuffling with Laertes in the dirt of Ophelia's grave. I daresay Osric's hands were cleaner than Hamlet's. But then Hamlet had washed his hands in dirty water (to borrow from Stonewall Jackson's song and mix a little country music with Shakespeare) when he undertook revenge for his father's murder. That was after he got the dirt on his uncle, who had done the dirty deed. No doubt about it, Claudius was a dirty dog, a real dirtbag who should have kept his dirty linen hidden away. All in all, a dirty business.

Dust, on the other hand, tends to be a pleasanter word. "Excuse my dust" has a far more positive connotation than "Excuse my dirt." "The Dust Bowl" has a nicer ring that "The Dirt Bowl," although the era is often referred to as "The Dirty Thirties." A British dustbin somehow seems downright elegant compared to an American garbage pail, although both are receptacles designed to hold rubbish and trash, that is, dirt.

City dwellers, I'm sure, think of farming and ranching as dirty occupations, and there's no doubt that a shower is not a bad idea after a day spent hauling hay, working calves, or combining wheat, but I feel more grimy, in a way, after a day behind a desk in an air-conditioned building than I do after a hot July day in the open on horseback. (I won't comment on odor because I personally prefer the smell of horse sweat to cologne.) I guess it's the difference between pollution and honest dirt. I still remember, as a kid, coming home on Saturday evening after a day of "trading" in El Dorado. Dad always had to wash the (invisible to my eyes) city dirt off his hands before he could go out to the barn to chore.

Dirt, it seems to me, is an inoculant. A little honest dirt on your hands protects you from at least a couple of the seven deadly sins—sloth and pride. Physically, it might do even more good than those ubiquitous hand sanitizers. Cleanliness might help ward off or wash off germs, but a little dirt will help you build up immunity to them. I've seen plenty of dirt-covered kids running around town, but the only ones I've ever noticed in the doctor's waiting room have been clean.

I vividly recall seeing the barmaid's small children playing on the dirty shag carpet of the Hitching Post in Matfield Green a few years ago, before, unfortunately, it went out of business. It was springtime and the cowboys were walking in and out with their muddy five-buckles on, while the kids, who ranged in age from toddler to maybe second or third grade, were disputing the contents of a spilled bag of popcorn with a sharp-toothed hound pup. As the baby slobbered it into her mouth with the pup tugging on her sleeve, the eldest, trying to clean up the mess, was picking popcorn off the floor by the handful and shoving it back into the bag. My first thought was, My god, those kids are never going to survive to adolescence. But after watching awhile I reconsidered: Nope, they're probably going to live to be a hundred. Mithridates, he died old.

Folk Signs

One of the nursery rhymes I remember from my childhood is about the little girl with the little curl right in the middle of her forehead: when she was good, she was very, very good, but when she was bad she was horrid. Another old rhyme was about horses: one white hoof, buy him; two white hooves, try him; three white hooves, let him go; four white hooves, feed him to the crows. Both verses seem to be about appearance, the first related to temperament and the second to physical capability. And both reflect a kind of folk wisdom manifested in external signs.

A folk sign generally concerns itself with the mundane, the things that ordinary people have to cope with in everyday life—such as the moodiness of a young daughter or the soundness of your mount. Or the weather. Here in the Flint Hills, where a balmy early December so warm (temperatures in the seventies) that roses and irises will actually bloom (as occurred in our yard in 1998) can overnight turn into winter (temperatures in the teens), weather is a major factor in our lives. Financial success for farmers and ranchers depends on the weather, particularly rainfall. In pioneer times, before automobiles with heaters, setting out on a journey in a wagon or on horseback without heeding weather signs might prove uncomfortable, maybe even fatal. I'm reminded of a poem, "Charlotte, the Frozen Girl," my father used to recite to my sister and me when we were riding pastures. It's about a vain young girl who doesn't dress warmly and freezes to death while traveling in a sleigh to a dance with her beau. "I'm getting warmer now," are her last words.

Anyway, the earliest weather sign I remember learning, from Dad Hoy, was that a sundog—that bright prismlike reflection that occurs in the clouds off to one or both sides of the sun—meant a change in the weather. So if things have been miserable, a sundog meant that good weather was on its way. Or, conversely, if we'd been having nice weather, then get ready for a bad spell. I've always noticed sundogs since then, and, you know, Dad Hoy seems to have been right; we usually do get a noticeable change within a couple of days. Of course, here in Kansas it's pretty safe, no matter what the current weather, to figure that we're about due for a change.

As to white hooves on horses, a white hoof is softer than a dark one, so a stocking-legged sorrel with a big white blaze in his face might look pretty in a parade, but out on a ranch where he's being used hard every day he's likely to go lame pretty quick unless you keep him shod. Many people do keep shoes on their using horses nowadays, but back in earlier times they sometimes didn't. Thus the advisory rhyme.

What about the curl in the forehead? Mood swings in little girls (and boys as well) are part of growing up, but in horses a swirl (or whorl) is a definite sign of temperament. If that whorl comes right between the eyes, you've got a smart, even-tempered, easily trained horse. The higher the whorl, the more high-strung the horse. If the whorl falls below the line between the eyes, then your horse is definitely slow-witted. Although this folk sign has been around a long time, Josh and I first heard it in the spring of 1998 and immediately checked it out. Sure enough, our better cow horses had whorls closest to the line between their eyes, our most flighty horses had high whorls, and our most aggravating ones had low whorls.

How scientifically accurate is this folk sign? A year or two after first learning of it, I heard animal behavior expert Temple Grandin give a talk about cattle, which have whorls similar to those of horses. She had conducted an experiment in which independent observers rated cattle from one to four on their excitability. Then she checked whorls. Calm cattle had center whorls; wilder cattle had high ones.

How in the world, she was asked by one skeptic in the audience, could forehead whorls have an effect on bovine or equine temperament? The answer, she said, was genetic and embryonic. It seems that the cells making up the brain and the forehead start out together in the embryo before they begin their specialization into distinct parts of the animal. Thus the level of calmness of the mature animal's brain is marked externally. And thus are folk signs sometimes confirmed by science.

Flint Hills Rock Signs

Many Flint Hills towns have their names spelled out on a nearby hillside using big chunks of limestone rock as the medium. The first one I remember seeing was north and east of Matfield Green as we would drive to the Strong City rodeo on K-13 (now K-177) in early June, and the second was at Strong City. In the early 2000s I was teaching a folklore class at Emporia State University, and one of the students, Andrea Wilcox, wrote her research paper on these Flint Hills rock signs. Andrea did a thorough and excellent job of field and library research, and this chapter is based on her paper, for which she received an A.

The earliest of these signs was not for a town but for Southwestern College at Winfield in the southern Flint Hills. In 1912 a large S (for Southwestern) was laid out on a hill north of campus. It was sixty feet wide and ninety feet tall. Some years later the sign was moved to the northeast to a hill that was visible from the football stadium and a C (for College) added.

In the northern Flint Hills, also at a college town and at roughly the same time period, students in the Civil Engineering Society piled up loose stones on Bluemont Hill in the shape of the letter K. Dissatisfied with the stones, in 1921 the society moved its efforts to Prospect Hill and made a foot-deep, eighty-foot-tall, sixty-foot-wide K from concrete, reinforced with wire netting. Total cost of the project (not counting labor, which was volunteer) was $350. Nine years later a concrete S was added, at an additional $500. When Kansas State Agricultural College became Kansas State University, there was talk of adding a U to the sign. But the cost (estimated at $10,000 in the early 1960s), in addition to a large gully that had washed out next to the S, ended the idea.

In 1927 the Manhattan Kiwanis Club also used concrete to spell out the name of the town on Bluemont Hill. The letters are sixteen feet wide and thirty feet tall. Today maintenance of the sign is shared by both the Kiwanis and the city of Manhattan. Back in 1996 after the K-State football team lost to

Nebraska, some Cornhusker fans slipped up the hill and covered the N with red paint.

An aside: Back in probably the late 1970s or early '80s, a time when K-State's football team was notoriously inept, some ESU colleagues and I were returning from a meeting in South Dakota. It was a Saturday and K-State had gotten whomped at home by Nebraska, then a national powerhouse. As we approached the Kansas border we began to meet car after car filled with Cornhusker fans returning home after the game (where they had far outnumbered beleaguered KSU fans). As we got into Kansas, the traffic got even worse, almost bumper to bumper. As we drove through Waterville, or perhaps it was Blue Rapids, we saw a boy, maybe ten years old, holding a large hand-lettered cardboard sign: "GO HOME CORNCOBS."

Back to rock signs. One could argue that the two hillside signs in Manhattan belong to a different category because they are made of concrete, not limestone rocks, as are all the others. These other signs are found, in alphabetical order, at Bazaar, Cedar Point, Cedar Vale, Clements, Elmdale, Florence, J (near Junction City), Matfield Green, Strong City, and Winfield. Most of them seem to have been erected in the 1920s and 1930s.

The S for Southwestern College in Winfield, as noted earlier, was apparently the first, while the sign spelling BAZAAR on Roniger Hill southwest of that town was the last. It wasn't until 1993 that Bazaar-area residents decided to follow the lead of the other five towns in Chase County with rock signs and put up their own on Roniger Hill. (It's rumored, but not certain, that there had been a rock town sign there years before, but maybe people are confusing that with the cone-shaped pile of rocks on top of the hill erected by the two bachelor Roniger brothers to honor the Indians whose arrowheads and other stone implements the brothers collected in the Southfork River valley. These artifacts, and other historical items, are on display in the Roniger Memorial Museum in Cottonwood Falls.)

Berthabelle Peterson, the Bazaar correspondent for the *Chase County Leader-News*, called for volunteers from the community to meet at Tom Heathman's on May 2. That effort was delayed by rain, but on May 15 and 16 the sixteen-by-forty-foot-letters were put into place by a dozen or more volunteers, using rocks that Gary Peterson (Berthabelle's son) and Tom Heathman had hauled up the hill with tractors.

Clements, in Chase County, is a ghost town these days, Cedar Point nearly is, and Elmdale is dwindling, but all three towns still have their rock signs. The Clements sign was probably built in the later 1920s. Warren Peterson remembered seeing no sign when he first moved south of Clements in 1924 or 1925. After an absence of two years the Petersons returned to Clements, and the letters were in place then. Gayland Park believes that high school students built the sign in 1928 or 1929, which nearly squares with Peterson's memory. Carl Dawson, on the other hand, thought the idea came in 1935 from Mr. F. Smithers, the grade school principal, who wanted the sign to signify the school, not the town. Others also thought the sign was erected in the early to mid-1930s. (That is the problem with relying on people's memories—they differ.)

According to Bob Reese the sign was a project of students at Clements High School, both in building and maintaining. Mike Yoder thinks that part of freshman initiation was whitewashing the sign each year, although the entire high school helped clear grass and sumac from the stones. Freshman initiation occurs in the fall and Sneak Day in the spring, and that is when Bennie Holtsclaw remembers helping whitewash the sign when he attended Clements High in the mid-1950s.

Whatever the difference in memories, there is no doubt that the sign was placed on land owned by Oscar Deuhn; that land is now part of the Flying W Ranch. When Josh first acquired the land, the sign was almost totally obscured by brush. No school kids had been available to maintain the sign since the schools closed c. 1957. A couple of years ago the Chase County High FFA cleared and whitewashed the sign as a class project, so now each spring, before the grass grows too tall, CLEMENTS once again shows clearly.

The Cedar Point, Elmdale, and Matfield Green signs were also high school projects, the first two likely begun in the 1930s and Matfield in 1940, give or take a year on either side. As with Clements, students at Elmdale enjoyed a watermelon feed once the yearly maintenance was completed each fall. Elmdale High closed in 1967 and the sign became more and more obscured until a few years ago when people in the community gathered to clean and whitewash it, an event commemorated in a poem by Flint Hills balladeer Annie Wilson. Matfield citizens have whitewashed their sign every couple of years since the high school closed in the mid-1960s.

The two most unusual Flint Hills rock signs are in Chase County, but neither one has a connection with a specific town. One is reputed to be the "first stone sign ever to be assembled in Chase County, Kansas, near Clements," according to the caption on a photograph held by the Chase County Historical Society. It reads, in all capital letters: TALK HOME—BELL TELEPHONE. I have never seen this sign, and have not found anyone who knows the location.

The second sign I have seen in the spring after pasture burning. It's on the south side of the paved road between Cottonwood Falls and Elmdale, just west of the road leading into the Chase County Lake. This sign is of a political nature and was most likely erected during the 1932 election season. It reads: LANDON 4 GOV.

Jake Leg

Back in the late 1940s and early 1950s we would go into El Dorado, the Butler County seat, nearly every Saturday to "trade"—that is, to shop. On those trips we would occasionally see an old man dragging a stiff leg as he walked around town. "He's got the jake leg," Dad would say if my sister or I asked about the hobbling man. Jake leg, Dad told us when asked what that meant, was an affliction caused by drinking Jamaica ginger. Jamaica ginger, we learned as we asked even more questions, was some sort of bottled liquid, maybe a patent medicine or a kitchen flavoring, that had a high alcohol content, the sort of thing, along with bay rum, that men with a bad drinking habit would drink when they couldn't get bootleg whiskey.

Dad was not a teetotaler, but neither was he a drinker, and as I think back on the somewhat moralistic and disapproving tone of his voice when talking about jake leg, he was obviously taking the opportunity to warn us against some of the pitfalls of life. Certainly the men we saw dragging a leg tended to be unkempt and dirty-looking—down if not quite completely out. I once touched my tongue to the opening on a bottle of Dad's bay rum aftershave. I knew then that you'd have to be pretty darned desperate for alcohol to drink stuff like that, and I figured that Jamaica ginger probably tasted as bad if not worse.

From the mid-1950s until the early 2000s I had never again heard anyone use the term jake leg, and I somehow had it in my head that if it was not a taboo term, then it was at least a disreputable one. So I was a little surprised when, sometime in 2003, I heard a promo for a jake leg segment on *All Things Considered*, the afternoon news program on National Public Radio. It was an interesting and informative piece that told the origin and extent of the affliction. Jake leg was most common in the Midwest and South—cities such as Cincinnati, Kansas City, Dallas, and Jackson, Mississippi.

The first case was diagnosed in Oklahoma City on February 27, 1930. Most of the victims were poor men, some married, some not, but all semitransient, moving from city to city, living in cheap rooming houses, looking desperately for work in the Great Depression. Their desperation was also what drove many of them to cheap drink, seeking temporary relief from their plight. Also part of the broadcast were two or three clips from blues songs about "the jake," sung by the Allen Brothers ("Jake Walk Blues") and the Mississippi Sheiks ("Jake Leg Blues"), music that undoubtedly did as much good as any official governmental pronouncements in helping to warn potential users away from the drink.

Dad was right—the term did come from Jamaica ginger, a medicinal extract that required something like 85 percent alcohol in order to be dissolved. At first bootleggers cut this strong mixture with castor oil, which caused no problems, but then they began using a chemical called TOPC, which was also used in paint, glue, and shellac. It was TOPC that caused partial or, in most cases, total paralysis of the legs of as many as 1.2 million victims.

I don't ever recall seeing anyone since the late 1950s that walked like he had jake leg, but I suppose a few could have survived into the early 2000s. The NPR broadcast stated that most victims never walked again. The men we saw hobbling around El Dorado were lucky.

Cattle Guards

I had a friend in graduate school who told me that you should pick a very precise and limited topic, learn everything possible there is to know about it, and you would thus become the world's leading expert on that particular subject, which is what he had done with some obscure desert plant that exists on only a few hundred acres in some remote part of Arizona. He didn't say whether or not there would ever be any call for your expertise, and I don't think he really cared. About a decade later I did, however unintentionally, follow his advice. Here's how that happened:

During the summer of 1977 I was teaching a three-week class on American folklore. On the first day, as per usual, I outlined the class, showed them the textbook, went over the topics to be covered, and gave the date of the final exam. But when I started to talk about the research paper, I was met with protests that three weeks just wasn't enough time for a research project. Nonsense, I said, I'll do one, too.

I had been thinking for a while about writing a material culture article on cattle guards for a folklore journal, so when class was over I went over to the library and started going through all the standard reference books (this was long before the days of Google). Nothing. I went back to the office and made phone calls to the Kansas Museum of History, the Agricultural Hall of Fame in Bonner Springs, the K-State Extension Service. Nothing. The only publication I was initially able to discover was a set of building plans from the Tennessee Agricultural Extension Service. So at the end of three weeks the students all turned in their research papers, but I had to give myself an Incomplete.

I'm assuming that readers know what a cattle guard is, but in case they don't, it's a grid of spaced iron bars or pipes placed over a pit in the roadway to let automobiles pass but stop cattle from straying from one pasture to another or onto the road, a kind of automatic gate for an automobile. Livestock, leery

Farrell and Josh cattle guarding with Jim in Greenwood County, 1981.

of the spaces between the bars, won't try to go over it. At least most livestock. It's pretty hard to deter a goat, but it generally works well with sheep, cattle, pigs, and horses. I was told recently, however, about a buffalo cow that repeatedly was getting out of a pasture and the owner just couldn't figure out how. The fence was in good shape and he had installed a cattle guard twice the width of a normal one, which is necessary if you want it to keep deer, elk, or bison from jumping over it. The mystery was solved when one day the owner happened to see his buffalo very carefully tiptoeing on the pipe bars in order to cross the cattle guard. A goat is one thing, but for an animal as large as a bison to maneuver across cattle guard bars is really unusual.

Anyway, although written sources on cattle guards were next to nonexistent, I had the advantage of age: without automobiles there was no need for cattle guards. There would not have been enough automobiles out in ranching country until at least the first decade of the twentieth century to be a problem, and in the late 1970s there would be plenty of men and women in their eighties and nineties who might well remember their first encounter with a cattle guard, which, in fact, turned out to be the case.

During the time of my investigation into cattle guards, I was also teaching the second part of the composition class required of freshmen, a class that focuses on research. In addition to the usual library resources, I also used

Left: A flat stone stile in Cornwall, 1982. Right: Jim demonstrating the pit depth of a Cornish flat stone stile, 1982.

examples from my own unconventional cattle guard research methods that involved, among other things, interviewing people out in the field (or pastures, to be more accurate), sending out letters of inquiry to newspapers, and devising a questionnaire that I distributed widely. I would also, sometimes accompanied by Farrell and Josh, go out cattle guarding, that is, driving around the countryside to photograph, measure, and otherwise document and describe the cattle guards we encountered. More than once a suspicious, sometimes belligerent rancher would roar up in his pickup, wanting to know what the hell I was doing with that tape measure and camera. When I told him I was writing a book about cattle guards, he would invariably laugh and then would often have an anecdote about them or give me a name of an old-timer who might be of help. No question about it, I was obsessed with cattle guards.

Five years later, after fieldwork that took me throughout the West, into Canada, and over to Cornwall (where Iron Age flat stone stiles, similar in concept to cattle guards with slabs of granite rather than iron bars placed across a pit, are still in use); after letters of inquiry to museums, historical societies, newspapers, and agricultural journals; after combing through patent records for both railroad and highway cattle guards; after interviews and correspondence with hundreds of people, my research project finally culminated in the publication of *The Cattle Guard: Its History and Lore* (University Press of Kansas, 1982). It sure wasn't a best seller (fewer than a thousand copies sold; out of print for decades), but, like my friend with his rare desert flowers, it does make me an expert on cattle guards, an expertise that was called upon even before the book was published.

Early in the spring semester of 1982 I got a phone call from a woman who said she was a secretary in a New Mexico law office. She said there would be a ticket to Albuquerque waiting for me at the Wichita airport and a room reserved for me at an airport motel. The firm had a lawsuit pending concerning cattle guards, and they needed an expert witness, she said. After running through a mental list of old college friends who might be capable of devising such an intricate practical joke, I decided to take a chance and drove to Wichita.

Sure enough, there was a ticket waiting and, once I had landed, a hotel room. Next morning a lawyer showed up, and we hopped in the company Cessna and flew to Alamogordo, then took a rental car to Tularosa and headed up U.S. Highway 54 (the same highway, incidentally, that runs through El Dorado, seat of my home county, Butler) to a spot a little way north of town to have a look at the cattle guard in question. Seems a motorist was suing a rancher and the state of New Mexico after having hit a cow that had eluded a cattle guard and ended up on the highway. The pit under the cattle guard was so filled in with gravel on both sides that a cow could easily walk across it. But who knows what its condition had been two years earlier when the accident had occurred?

I told the attorney, who was representing the state, that I really should be testifying for the other side. Don't worry about it, he said, adding that I could expect another trip to New Mexico in a couple of weeks when the trial began. Sure enough, two weeks later I had a call saying that a ticket was waiting for me in Wichita. But when I went to the airline desk to pick it up, I was told that the case had been settled out of court. I think what happened was that the state's attorney was using me, an "expert" and author of a forthcoming book on cattle guards, as a bluff to encourage the other side to settle out of court. And it worked.

One question I had asked the attorney on the flight back from Tularosa to Albuquerque was how he knew about my book, which wasn't due for release for a couple of months yet. It seems that a student in my composition class a couple of years earlier had married, moved to Albuquerque, and taken a job in his law office. She had overheard him pacing around in his office exclaiming, "I need an expert on cattle guards!"

"I know one," she said, and after about the third time she said it, he finally heard her. And that's when I got the call.

About twenty years later I had another occasion to utilize my cattle guard expertise, this in response to a request from another attorney in the Southwest. No cow, no car, no airline ticket involved in this case, but I did receive a fee. An attorney representing the state of Arizona called and asked a few questions about cattle guards, then wondered if I'd be willing to give an expert opinion. What was the situation, I asked, and what kind of opinion did he want? An opinion about the design of the cattle guard, he said. Sure, I replied, send me the information.

An accident had occurred on a cattle guard on the exit ramp of a four-lane highway. As is usual in such places where the road is wide, two or more grids are used to cover the width of the roadway, and, as is also usual, a small gap is left between each grid in order to allow for changes in the weather—metal expands in heat and contracts in cold. A bicyclist was suing the state after having wrecked his bicycle when exiting (or accessing—I wasn't told which) the highway. Apparently the bike's tire had hit the cattle guard in the crack between two grids (I wasn't given the specifics) and instead of roughly bouncing over the guard, the bike had flipped, flinging the hapless rider into the air and onto the grid. What his injuries were, I wasn't told, but I bet they were painful.

I didn't hear anything more for a while, then got another phone call asking for a mailing address. In a couple of days a set of plans arrived that detailed the construction of the particular cattle guard that had been used by the State of Arizona, along with a request that I evaluate the plans and give an opinion about the adequacy of the design and whether or not it was standard. During my research (which had occurred some quarter of a century earlier) I had seen, crossed, photographed, and measured dozens of similar cattle guards in many of the western states (although none in Arizona), and I could tell by the plans that it was a standard design, made from standard materials, and widely used throughout the region, which is what I wrote in my report back to the attorney.

Another couple of months passed with no further word, so I assumed that was the end of the matter. Then I received another letter telling me that the case had been settled and asking my fee. I had no idea what to charge for my half hour of looking over the documents and another half hour (the times are maximized) writing a letter giving my opinion. So I asked an attorney friend what expert witnesses charged. Anywhere, he said, from a couple of hundred dollars an hour to well over a thousand. "You would be in the two-hundred-dollar range," he said.

It's rather sad to be the world's leading expert on cattle guards and know that you're on the lowest rung of the expert-witness ladder. But it was two hundred dollars more than I had made on the book. I'd hate to try to make a living as an expert witness on cattle guards, but, at this rate, I can expect another cattle guard case to be dropped into my lap along about the year 2025.

Back in the summer of 2012 someone sent me an email purporting to show just how far out of touch with reality the Obama administration was. According to the email President Obama had received a report that Colorado had over a hundred thousand cattle guards. Because Colorado ranchers had protested proposed changes in grazing policy on public lands, Obama, in retaliation, ordered Secretary of the Interior Ken Salazar to immediately fire half of the cattle guards. At which point Vice President Joe Biden intervened and urged that the poor cattle guards who were losing their jobs be given six months of retraining.

Obviously, the email was meant to show the naivete of liberals, specifically President Obama, but what those who circulated the email apparently didn't know is that the same joke had previously been employed against that icon of conservativism, Ronald Reagan, who also wanted to fire half of the hundred thousand cattle guards in Colorado. So had Gerald Ford. And Jimmy Carter. Whether used by conservatives or liberals, this story has surfaced again and again, an illustration of the supposed stupidity of politicians. The first time I actually heard it was on September 8, 1978, when Paul Harvey reported it as fact (needless to say) on his radio broadcast.

As with all good folklore, it has variations. Sometimes it is Nancy Pelosi, not Joe Biden, who insists on the retraining of the cattle guards who are being fired. When the president was Bill Clinton, Colorado representative Pat Schroeder was the one who stepped in to ask for the retraining of her constituents. Also under Clinton, it was Bruce Babbitt who was instructed to fire the cattle guards. Some people were so ignorant of the facts that they still had Babbitt as the cabinet secretary Obama gave the order to.

It seems every president from Gerald Ford on—Carter, Reagan, Bush I, Clinton, Bush II, Obama—has been accused of firing cattle guards. So far, three years into his term, Trump doesn't seem to have fired any, but considering all the other turmoil going on in his administration, he probably just hasn't had time to get around to it yet. I wouldn't be surprised if this story didn't originate with William Howard Taft or Woodrow Wilson, about the time that Henry Ford's Model T was becoming ubiquitous and cattle guards were first appearing on roads.

Interestingly, on the internet it seems always to be Colorado where the hundred thousand cattle guards are located, but in the first printed version I saw of this urban (more rightly, rural) legend the state was New Mexico and there were only fifty thousand cattle guards. This appeared in the September

1979 issue of the *California Mining Journal*, and the New Mexico secretary for energy and minerals, Nick Franklin, had supposedly been contacted by federal officials in the Carter administration interested in saving money.

An alternate form of the joke caught up with George W. Bush, not as president but when he was running, unsuccessfully, for Congress in 1978. As a candidate, the younger Bush was traveling the Texas countryside, hunting votes. He stopped to ask a farmer for directions to the next town, and the farmer told him to turn right at the next cattle guard. "What color uniform will he have on?" the future president asked. This is a variant of the woman visiting Yellowstone National Park who was asking a ranger for directions to Old Faithful geyser. "Just follow this road to the first cattle guard," he told her, "and then turn left." She thanked him and then asked, "Will he be dressed like you?"

A Nebraska version defines a cattle guard as someone hired by the government to guard cattle from theft, one more expense to be paid for by taxes from city dudes. Or this comment from a Montanan: "We hope that bureaucrats don't pay too much attention to cattle guards or they'll want to put them in uniforms and the unions will want to organize them." Or this from Texas, where a city slicker is quoted as saying: "I thought a cattle guard was a deodorant for cows."

Maybe this whole thing got started during World War II in New Mexico (and this actually happened, so I am told), when Alice Bullock, an official in that state's Department of Education, requested from Washington six cattle guards for school bus routes. She was told that because of the war effort manpower was extremely limited. Therefore, she could have two cattle guards, but not six.

This rural legend has even made its way Down Under where Kevin Rudd, prime minister from 2007 to 2010, was the naive politician. When he read a report stating that there were over ten thousand cattle guards in New South Wales and Queensland, where sheep and cattle raisers had recently protested his proposed changes in grazing policies, Rudd immediately ordered half the cattle guards fired. At that point the minister for employment, Julia Gillard (who replaced Rudd as prime minister in 2010), asked that before any cattle guards were fired that they be given six months of retraining. The problem with this version is that cattle guards in Australia, as in Great Britain, are called cattle grids. Firing cattle grids just doesn't have the same resonance as firing cattle guards.

The earliest patent on a cattle guard was for the railroad variety, issued in 1837 to Thomas J. West of Whitehall, Virginia, just one year after the first reference to a cattle guard appeared in print. Back in 1996, after I had attended a meeting of the board of trustees for the American Folklife Center at the Library of

Congress, Cathy and I decided to drive down into Virginia. She had always wanted to see Monticello (as had I), and I also wanted to take a look at Whitehall, about a dozen miles northwest of Charlottesville, where Thomas Jefferson not only had his home but had also founded the University of Virginia.

Whitehall is surrounded by the tree-covered Blue Ridge Mountains, but not much is left of the town except a post office, a general store, a community center housed in an old schoolhouse, and a church. Most of the gravestones in the churchyard were from the twentieth century, so Thomas West's remains must lie in an older cemetery, one that we didn't find. Nor was there any sign of a railroad nearby, so I couldn't check to see if any trace of the cattle guard he designed might have survived for over a century and a half. Not likely in any case.

But I did make an unexpected cattle guard discovery at Monticello itself. Jefferson was possessed of one of the most inventive, independent, and complex minds in our culture, and a walk through his home is like visiting a shrine to the American notion of freedom. His garden, eighty feet wide and a thousand feet long, has been reconstructed to appear as it did in his own lifetime with many of the same plant varieties growing there. Four of the original 160 trees he had planted were still standing.

Among some archaeological projects under way during our visit was the excavation of Jefferson's version of an English haha, a type of nonfence fence that keeps large animals off the lawns of country estates without blocking the view from the manor house. Instead of a four-foot-deep, stone-lined, one-sided drop-off in the yard, however, Jefferson had a steep-sided, stone-faced ditch dug around his lawn, something like a dry moat six feet wide and four feet deep. Thus cattle, horses, and sheep could graze up to the edge of the ditch, but few if any would dare the leap onto the lawn itself.

When, after our visit, I phoned Peter Hatch, resident archaeologist at Monticello, to inquire about the haha, he told me that contemporary accounts noted that a series of split rails had been placed over the haha, giving the appearance of a section of "fallen board fence" spanning the moat. With the spaces between the rails it must have looked, he said, "something like a cattle guard." But, I responded and he agreed, these rails must have been placed there so people could walk over the ditch, not to keep livestock out of the yard since that was the purpose of the ditch itself.

Whatever the case, these rails over the haha would have looked remarkably similar to the rails that Thomas West placed over a pit to create his railroad cattle guard, according to the drawing that accompanied his patent application. Jefferson died on the Fourth of July 1826, only eleven years before West's patent. There is no proof, but no reason not to think that West may have visited

An English haha, 1982.

Monticello, either before or after Jefferson's death. If so, then he most likely would have seen the rails placed over the haha. It is quite possible that West devised his invention after a visit to Monticello. If so, then should not Thomas Jefferson be given credit as the inspiration for, if not the ultimate inventor of, the cattle guard? I'd argue for that.

Two more things about cattle guards: as far as I know I've only been plagiarized twice, and one of those times occurred in an article published in *Texas Monthly*. For example, from the book: "I have been able to document their use in every state of the union except the small, urbanized eastern states of Rhode Island and Massachusetts." From the article: "Cattle guards are found in every state of the union except the small eastern states of Rhode Island and Massachusetts." It was obvious throughout the article that the author had, without attribution, gotten his information, and often his words, from my cattle guard book. In a letter to the editor in the next issue of the magazine, a reader from one of those states wrote to say that they did indeed have cattle guards there. In response to which the plagiarizer finally acknowledged his source, but only to pass the blame for that omission on to me: "That's what Jim Hoy said in his book" was the essence of his response. Let me say here that I was more amused than offended. It was actually rather nice to have written something someone thought worthy of stealing.

Finally, back in 2006 Cathy and I took a horseback holiday to Los Potreros Estancia in Cordoba Province, Argentina. Every day we rode morning and afternoon through low mountains that were reminiscent of the Flint Hills, only with sparkling silica rather than flint rock under our horse's hooves. As we rode, we occasionally saw a cattle guard, and I would always hold back to take photographs. After I had done this a few times, our guide that day, the fiancée of one of the two brothers (fourth-generation Scots) who owned the estancia asked me what I was doing, and I told her I had written a book about cattle guards. She had the typical amused response, but expressed in a polite chuckle rather than the guffaw I often got in the States.

She also obviously mentioned the episode to her fiancé, because the next morning at breakfast (all our meals were taken communally with the proprietors and the other guests) the owner greeted me with words that revealed his earlier skepticism: "Well, you actually *did* write a book about cattle grids, didn't you? I looked it up on Amazon UK, and it's selling for 96 pounds sterling!"

Postscript

Thanks to a NEH–Mellon Foundation grant, the University Press of Kansas will be digitizing and thus making available several currently out-of-print books, including *The Cattle Guard: Its History and Lore.*

RIDING BACK:
CONCLUSION

Summer a Horseback

It's mid-August of 1994, the temperature in the nineties, and it hasn't rained for a month. The dog days of summer, some call them, but as far as I'm concerned summer has ended. It's over. Time for the semester to start again. Back to the old college grind, the routine of classes and grading papers and faculty meetings and wearing a necktie.

Oh, there are worse jobs. I could be stuck on an assembly line somewhere, drudging from eight to five, or worse, I might even own the factory and have to spend twenty-four hours a day worrying about inflation, recession, health care mandates, taxes, white-collar crime, OSHA inspections, rising interest rates, and meeting a payroll. No, college teaching is a job that suits me just fine. I enjoy both the give and take in an air-conditioned classroom and the opportunity to research and write about the history and culture of the Great Plains and the Flint Hills.

Still, even though I have a great job, I hate to see this summer come to an end, I guess because I've had the opportunity to spend more of it horseback than I have had for several years. Part of that time on horseback was actually spent teaching—the Center for Great Plains Studies offers, in conjunction with the Flint Hills Overland Wagon Train, a weekend class studying the flora, fauna, history, and folklore of the Flint Hills while camping out overnight in a pasture east of Matfield Green. Tom Eddy does the science, and I do the culture.

But the real fun this summer was reverting to my younger days by helping my son ride pastures, work calves, and ship cattle. Josh spent the last year or so working on an 83,000-acre ranch in Colorado, coming back late last winter to work on a ranch in Chase County. This summer he moved to live at the home place near Cassoday to daywork on area ranches. We even went together on a few head of steers, getting them bought (as usual) just before the market broke last spring.

Ranchers and cattlemen have to fret about things like that, but the joy of cowboying is letting the cattle owner do the worrying while you do the fun stuff—break colts, doctor for foot rot, ride pastures, rope strays. And all of it in the middle of a Flint Hills pasture on a bright summer day.

Looking for strays can be frustrating. We spent most of one hot day in late June riding miles of pasture looking for a couple of heifers before we finally found them. But even that tiring day had its pleasures—deer running through the timber, a badger waddling into his hole, red-tailed hawks soaring, and turkey vultures circling in a clear, windless sky. Once, when we had separated to check two different bunches of steers in Section 17, I noticed Josh running his horse a quarter of a mile away, rope swinging. I never did see the coyote (which was saved by the fence), but I knew what Josh was doing—just what I would have been doing at that age.

Best of all, I think, was helping Vestrings ship steers from the Watkins Flats, a pasture I hadn't been in for years, but one we used to go through many times each summer when we drove Frank Klasser's cattle from Greenwood County into the railroad pens at Cassoday.

Flint Hills sunsets are beautiful, but there is nothing that stirs my spirit more than sitting on a horse early in the morning in a green Flint Hills pasture, waiting to gather cattle, the stars slowly disappearing as the sky lightens until only the morning star remains, the dazzling colors of the clouds slowly transforming into white as the sun edges over the horizon.

Glossary

baloney bulls: older male bovines sold for meat, not for breeding
band shell: a bandstand concave in the rear to resonate sound outward
black baldy: cross between a Hereford and an Angus with a black body and a white face
boot: extra compensation received in a horse trade
break in two: when a horse suddenly begins to buck
build a loop: prepare to rope
canners and cutters: low-grade, older cows not producing good beef
chouse: to handle cattle roughly
cinched up: having tightened a saddle girth
corks: short ninety-degree extensions on each end of a horseshoe
CRP: conservation reserve program in which cultivated land is planted back to grass
dallying: wrapping the end of a lariat rope around the saddle horn after catching a steer
dewlap: fold of skin hanging down from the middle of a bovine's neck and chest
draw: a dry ditch in a pasture, created by erosion
feist dog: small but wiry and active canine
gant up: become gaunt
gooseneck: a type of livestock trailer
grass rope: lariat rope made of hemp fibers
graveled: lameness in horses caused by a small rock entering the bottom of the hoof
head stall: the part of a bridle made of leather straps that holds the bit
herd law: law that requires cattle owners to fence in their livestock
high pole gate: wire gate made of two tall posts wired at the top as a brace to keep a fence tight
hoolihan: type of lariat loop and throw used for catching horses
kaffir corn: a cultivated grain sorghum
KRS: an odiferous liquid medicine applied to an animal to kill screwworms

lights: the lungs and other offal remaining after an animal has been butchered
liquid halter: euphemism for a drug to calm a horse
milo: a small, drouth-resistant grain sorghum
muley: a cow without horns
nine in the tail: the tail carried straight up in the air of an excited bovine running away
piece bit: see snaffle
pot, potbelly: slang term for a three-deck, four-compartment cattle-hauling truck
power-take-off shaft: part of a tractor that powers separate machines such as mowers or augurs
remuda: a horse herd
right-of-way: the area on either side of a highway or railroad
rough-bellied sow: term for older female swine
sign of the moon: the belief that phases of the moon have an influence on different parts of the body, for both humans and animals
silk manila: high-quality grass rope
snaffle: a bridle bit made of two metal bars, fastened flexibly in the middle
soil bank pasture: government program in which cultivated land is planted back to native grass
son-of-a-gun stew: stew made of sweetbreads and other organs of a recently butchered bovine
springer: a cow heavy with calf, close to birthing
stocker cattle: young cattle not yet mature enough to butcher
stock rack: removable structure on a truck bed used to hold livestock
stump sucker: a horse that bites onto a piece of wood, such as a manger, and sucks in air
tame hay: cultivated hay (such as brome grass or alfalfa) as opposed to native grass hay
twitch: rope loop on the end of a handle twisted on a horse's upper lip to make it stand still
water gap: the section of fence where it crosses a stream, often washing out in high water
windbroke: horse that has been ridden so hard that its breathing is permanently damaged

Index